Customer Relationship Management in the Digital Age

Customer Relationship Management in the Digital Age charts the concepts, strategies, benefits and technologies of CRM in an evolving and increasingly digital business landscape.

It empowers readers with the skills to use CRM to forge enduring customer connections, optimize experiences and drive loyalty across diverse industries and markets. Building upon existing literature, this guide offers a holistic approach that bridges theory and practice, making complex CRM concepts accessible to a wide audience. It integrates the latest technological advances, market trends and customer-centric initiatives, providing a comprehensive view of CRM's role in an increasingly customer-driven era. Pedagogical features include case studies, practical strategies and real-world examples, as well as chapter summaries and discussion questions to guide the reader through the key learning points of each chapter.

This helpful book enables readers to navigate the complexities of CRM implementation and customer-centric approaches and tailor strategies for B2B and B2C markets. It is particularly suitable for advanced undergraduate and postgraduate students of CRM, Sales Management, Relationship Marketing and Customer Experience Management, as well as reflective practitioners.

Online instructor resources include a course manual, test bank and PowerPoint slides.

G. Shainesh, a Professor of Marketing at the Indian Institute of Management Bangalore (IIMB), India, has over three decades of research and teaching experience in India and abroad.

Jagdish N. Sheth, Charles H. Kellstadt Professor of Marketing, Goizueta Business School, Emory University, USA, is a renowned scholar and internationally recognized thought leader.

Varsha Jain, AGK Chair Professor of Marketing, is the co-chair of research and dissertation at the Mudra Institute of Communication (MICA), Ahmedabad, India.

CUSTOMER RELATIONSHIP MANAGEMENT IN THE DIGITAL AGE

G. Shainesh, Jagdish N. Sheth and Varsha Jain

Routledge
Taylor & Francis Group
LONDON AND NEW YORK

Designed cover image: dem10/Getty Images

First published 2025
by Routledge
4 Park Square, Milton Park, Abingdon, Oxon OX14 4RN

and by Routledge
605 Third Avenue, New York, NY 10158

Routledge is an imprint of the Taylor & Francis Group, an informa business

British Library Cataloguing-in-Publication Data
A catalogue record for this book is available from the British Library

ISBN: 978-1-032-85438-0 (hbk)
ISBN: 978-1-032-84456-5 (pbk)
ISBN: 978-1-003-51817-4 (ebk)

DOI: 10.4324/9781003518174

Typeset in Times New Roman
by KnowledgeWorks Global Ltd.

Access the Support Material: www.routledge.com/9781032844565

Contents

About the Authors

G. Shainesh, a Professor of Marketing at the Indian Institute of Management Bangalore (IIMB), India, has over three decades of research and teaching experience in India and abroad. His research and teaching focus on CRM, Digital Marketing Strategies and Service Innovations, and his online courses on those topics are offered on the edX and Swayam platforms. Shainesh has worked for several organizations in the public, non-profit and corporate sectors, including automotive, apparel, hi-tech, energy, pharma, telecom, software, engineering and service firms, both as an advisor and as a seminar leader. At IIMB, he leads the cross-functional research initiative on consumer insights. He serves the boards of the Academy of International Business – South Asia Chapter (AIB-SAC) and the International Sustainable Development Research Society (ISDRS).

Jagdish N. Sheth, Charles H. Kellstadt Professor of Marketing, Goizueta Business School, Emory University, USA, is a renowned scholar and internationally recognized thought leader. He has published more than 300 research papers and over 30 books on various disciplines and topics. His insights on global competition, customer behaviour, relationship marketing, strategic thinking, geopolitics and emerging markets are considered revolutionary. He is a recipient of the Padma Bhushan Award, India's highest civilian award for non-resident Indians, for his contributions to literature and education.

Varsha Jain, AGK Chair Professor of Marketing, is the co-chair of research and dissertation at the Mudra Institute of Communication (MICA), Ahmedabad, India. She serves as associate editor of four leading marketing journals and has authored over 140 publications, including multiple papers in leading journals, book chapters and case studies. She has received over 25 international awards and gold medals for her scholarly contributions. Her research and teaching focus on ABCD – advertising, branding, consumer behaviour and digital. Her co-authored books include *Consumer Behavior: A Digital Native*, *Purpose-Driven Branding* and *Qualitative Research Methods in the Digital Age*, among others.

PART I

The Concept of Customer Relationship Management

CHAPTER 1

CRM: The Strategic Imperatives

CHAPTER OVERVIEW

This chapter will help you understand:

1 The increasing importance of Customer Relationship Management (CRM) in marketing and information technology (IT)
2 Macro-environmental enablers driving interest and investment in CRM
3 The criticality of customer relationships for sustainable growth of businesses
4 Demand- and supply-side factors motivating firms to adopt CRM
5 Perspectives on CRM implementation experiences

Vignette

Shell and Uber joined forces to improve the well-being of Uber's partner drivers affected by the Covid-19 pandemic by enrolling them in Shell's Fleet Solutions programme so that drivers could access safe and hygienic places for refreshments while on the road. Launched initially in the four Indian states of Gujarat, Karnataka, Maharashtra and Tamil Nadu, this included a specially designed quick response (QR) code-based card usable across all 180 Shell outlets in those states. Membership offered discounts of 1.5–5%, cashback on purchases and other benefits to existing Uber drivers (Uber, n.d.). Drivers could potentially save up to US$18 per month. In January 2021, more than 20,000 Uber drivers registered for the deal, and by the end of the year 85,000 had signed up. The programme significantly boosted sales and profits for Shell from the very first year. Such a win-win partnership between Shell and Uber during a crisis highlights the potential of using relationship management principles to benefit all stakeholders.

DOI: 10.4324/9781003518174-2

OPENING CASE

The journey of online retailer Amazon underscores the key role of customer centricity in enabling its enduring success over the last three decades. Millions of customers engage with the company every day through its website, applications (apps) and stores. An unmatched selection of products, convenience, low prices, quick delivery and service, and a simple returns policy continue to attract customers worldwide. All this enabled the company to ride out the dotcom burst in 2000. The leadership's focus on offering customers compelling value right from the outset was reflected in the company's chart-topping score of 88 on the American Customer Satisfaction Index in 2002. Using technologies such as the recommendation engine facilitates purchase decisions by offering a personalised buying experience to customers (Ruiz, 2012). Dramatic improvements in customer self-service capabilities reduce costs and save time for customers while improving their overall experience.

Amazon Prime, the company's membership service, provides the foundation for fulfilling customer preferences by connecting the strands of its business model involving retailing, online ordering, fast delivery and physical stores. In 2022, the company generated $35.22 billion in revenue through subscription fees from its estimated 200 million Prime subscribers. A strong customer-first culture and a belief in the customer franchise being the company's most valuable asset has been instrumental in transforming the customer experience. At the same time, Amazon continues to disrupt multiple markets, from streaming to cloud services.

These brief outlines illustrate some of the approaches adopted by businesses to improve customer centricity and strengthen relationships.

INTRODUCTION

Customer Relationship Management (CRM) is a critical area of interest for business leaders, the media and academic researchers in a rapidly digitalising world characterised by attention deficit and fickle relationships. This chapter begins by identifying a few macro-level indicators that highlight the evolution and growth of CRM in marketing and information technology (IT).

Businesses facing new challenges arising from non-traditional competition, market maturity and misalignment between revenue and profits are seeking opportunities to strengthen relationships with existing customers to sustain and grow. Academic conferences, journal articles, special issues of scholarly publications and academic centres at prestigious universities reflect the growing interest in CRM. The rising implementation of CRM solutions, the entry of major software vendors and increasing business investment in customer-centric programmes all highlight the importance of CRM among business leaders. The following section will examine the critical macro-environmental factors driving global interest and enhanced investment in CRM. The emergence of the service sector and market economies, the global orientation of businesses and demographic changes due to the ageing population of economically advanced economies are some of the growth drivers for CRM. The third section will examine the issues confronting businesses in the 21st century. The fourth section will discuss the supply and demand factors that are likely to motivate more companies to adopt CRM in the future. Additionally, we identified rising customer expectations and cost-effective technology advancements as the primary drivers of CRM adoption. The fifth section will discuss experiences of CRM implementation. The chapter then concludes with a summary and discussion questions.

THE CRM EXPLOSION IN MARKETING AND INFORMATION TECHNOLOGY

CRM first began attracting the attention of academics and practitioners in marketing and information technology in the 1990s, when numerous research conferences focused on various aspects of evolving buyer–seller dynamics. For example, the Centre for Relationship Marketing at Emory University, USA, Scandinavian academics, the Industrial Marketing and Purchasing Group (IMP) and the annual International Colloquium in Relationship Marketing all organised conferences from 1993 onwards. The *Journal of the Academy of Marketing Science* (1995), the *Asia-Australia Marketing Journal* (1994 and 1997), *Industrial Marketing Management* (1997) and the *European Journal of Marketing* (1997) published special issues on relationship marketing (Payne, 2000). CRM was also the subject of a special section in the October 2005 issue of the *Journal of Marketing*. Journals devoted to relationship marketing (such as the *Journal of Relationship Marketing*) and forums and associations – such as the CRM Community and the Association for the Advancement of Relationship Marketing (AARM) and the American Marketing Association (AMA) Special Interest Group (SIG) on Relationship Marketing – have also contributed significantly to the advancement of relationship marketing's understanding and practice.

At the same time, businesses were experiencing rapid growth in adopting relationship orientation and implementing CRM solutions. These included financial services, retail, telecommunications, travel, hospitality and automobiles, and online businesses emerged as early adopters. Advances in information and communication technologies (ICT) enabled large businesses to recreate the personalised engagements earlier considered to be the domain of smaller businesses (Peppers & Rogers, 1999; Zineldin, 2000). Technology solutions were initially used to automate the sales process but later expanded to include automation of services and marketing as part of comprehensive CRM solutions. In the 1990s, the market was fragmented, with several firms claiming capabilities for automating customer-facing functions. Leading CRM product vendors included ACT, SalesLogix, Siebel Systems and Interact Commerce, among others. Several Enterprise Resource Planning (ERP) players, such as SAP, Oracle and PeopleSoft, then moved into the CRM market to capitalise on emerging opportunities. Software company Salesforce founded a market in 1999, offered a subscription model for sales force automation and focused on small and medium enterprises (SMEs) that would not consider investing in traditional CRM software due to the high upfront capital costs and long implementation cycle. The availability of CRM software at low cost through subscription-based pricing models started making it affordable even for startups and small businesses to adopt. CRM vendors have started tapping into the opportunities provided by small businesses through freemium pricing models. In 2023, CRM software generated $80 billion in revenue. Salesforce has emerged as the global market leader, with SAP, Oracle, Microsoft and Adobe being other significant players. The adoption of CRM by small businesses continues to drive market growth.

The following section will examine the factors that contributed to the growth of this phenomenon, which many have dubbed a 'new-old concept' (Berry, 1995; Grönroos, 1994; Sheth & Parvatiyar, 1995).

ENABLERS OF CRM GROWTH

The phenomenal growth in global interest and investments in CRM can be attributed to the macro-environmental factors shown in Figure 1.1.

The evolution of economies in advanced countries has seen significant transformation, especially in the 20th century. Initially rooted in agriculture and later transitioning into industrialisation, these nations started witnessing a shift towards services in the 1970s. This transition brought about a paramount need for customer orientation as the production and

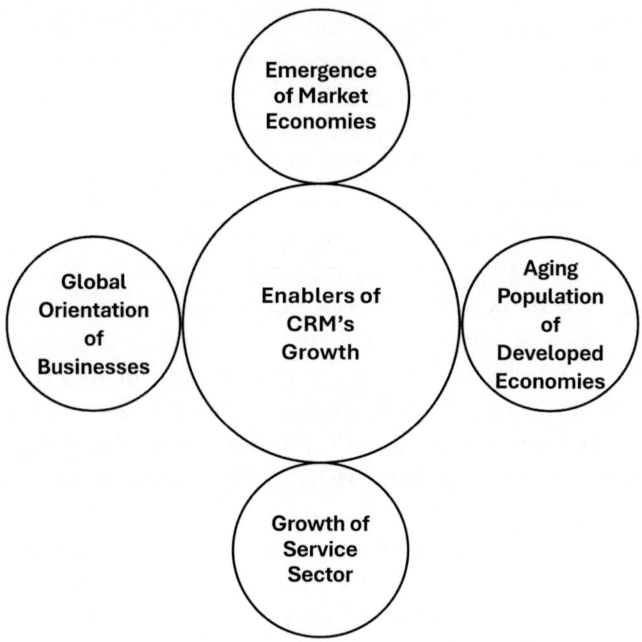

FIGURE 1.1 Factors Contributing to the Growth of CRM

consumption of services became inseparable. Unlike traditional physical goods marketing, customers today view the production process as an integral part of their service consumption experience, emphasising the critical role of customer-centricity (Grönroos, 1994).

Similarly, the emergence of the global market economy has resulted in a profound shift in economic paradigms. Granting greater power to the market than the controlled, government-regulated economies provides customers with more choice. Throughout the 1990s there was a notable acceleration in the deregulation of key industries such as banking, telecommunications, broadcasting and airlines, transferring decisions once controlled by the government to market-oriented firms operating in intensely competitive environments (Vietor, 1994). This shift towards a market-oriented economy necessitated a heightened focus on customers and increased the importance of CRM.

In today's interconnected world, businesses find themselves operating in an environment that knows no borders, creating a global orientation. This has given rise to international trading blocs and the liberalisation of markets and trade, fuelling robust economic growth. Simultaneously, it has made entry into foreign markets more accessible. To thrive in this global landscape, companies must adopt a stronger customer orientation, both to tap into opportunities in new markets and to defend their positions in their home markets. A global perspective has made customer-centricity an essential strategic component for success.

The demographic landscape in developed economies has witnessed a significant shift over the years. In 2000, 12.6% of the US population was 65 or older, reflecting a trend observed in most of Europe (Leeflang & van Raaij, 1995). By 2022, this share of US adults had risen to 17.3%, and in the European Union (EU) the share of this cohort increased from 16% to 21% during 2002–2022. The ageing population is a result of lower birth rates and increased life expectancy. While it brings opportunities in areas such as wellness, finance, safety and recreation, it also presents challenges as markets for products targeting younger demographics slow down (Sheth & Mittal, 2004). Marketers are now compelled to develop a deeper understanding of their existing customer base and adapt to their evolving needs. This has led to the rise in popularity of one-stop-shop solutions to cater to the diverse demands of an ageing consumer base.

CRITICALITY OF CUSTOMER RELATIONSHIPS

In recent years, businesses have been facing new challenges that have increased the criticality of customer relationships, as shown in Figure 1.2.

In the dynamic landscape of today's markets, non-traditional competition has emerged as a force reshaping industry. Startups such as Uber and Airbnb and new entrants like Reliance Jio in India continue to disrupt established markets. At the same time, substitute technologies such as smartphones have transformed traditional industries in areas ranging from cameras to music players. Suppliers are no longer confined to their original roles; they are becoming competitors through forward integration, and customers are stepping up competition through private labels and in-sourcing in business markets. Non-traditional competitors often enjoy the advantage of lower costs and higher margins by selectively targeting the most profitable customers of the incumbents. Consequently, incumbents are increasingly focusing on growing

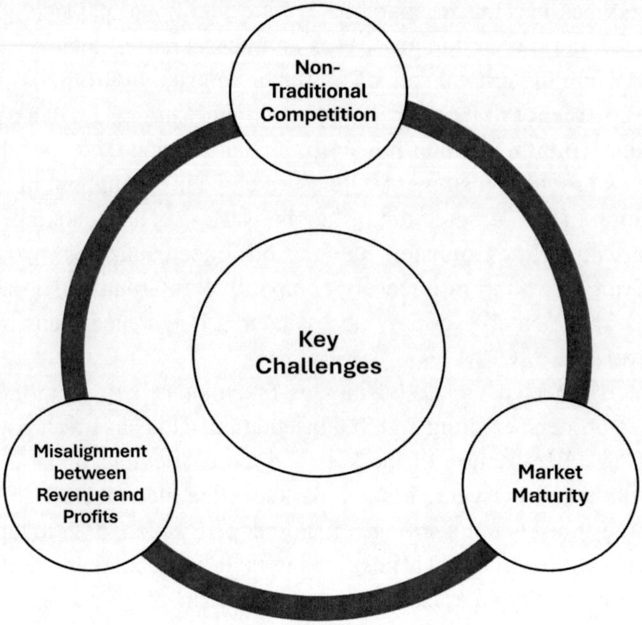

FIGURE 1.2 Criticality of Customer Relationships

their share of revenues by delivering superior service to existing customers and adopting a one-stop-shop approach to cater to ever-evolving customer needs.

In the aftermath of World War II, investments were made to boost capacities in several countries to meet pent-up demand. This collective effort resulted in a surplus of capacity across various industries in the advanced economies. Capacity creation remained a central theme, leading to significant growth in production in several sectors, including agriculture, commodities, aircraft, automobiles, appliances and other equipment. As companies started actively seeking market opportunities, firms from developed countries relied on business from domestic customers while expanding their international operations. However, the last three decades witnessed a significant shift in growth dynamics. New market opportunities started emerging from countries in Asia, Africa and South America, presenting promising avenues for growth. Success in these markets demands a deep understanding of unique customer needs, as well as the cultural, social, economic and regulatory factors that shape these markets. As markets mature, businesses are compelled to adopt a more customer-centric approach to retain their customer base in their home markets, recognising that customer loyalty is pivotal in maintaining competitiveness (Figure 1.3).

Customer subsidisation emerged as an issue of concern for many business leaders in the 1990s. In their efforts to attract customers and gain market share, companies had also built inefficiencies through customer subsidisation. While managers knew about subsidisation across products and markets, they had never considered subsidisation by customers. Companies started adopting activity-based costing (ABC) for analysing the cost of doing business with customers and comparing it to the revenue generated by them. Plotting customer revenue and profits will thus show the misalignment between revenue and profits (Figure 1.4).

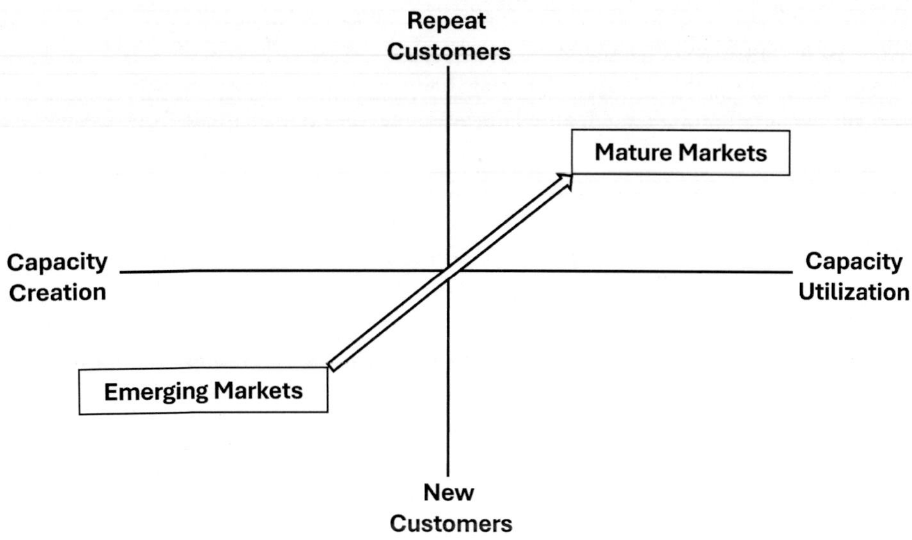

FIGURE 1.3 Market Maturity

Typically, the distribution of revenues is exponential, while costs are distributed in a more linear relationship with customer size. The revenue curve slopes down exponentially, and the cost curve slopes down gradually (Sheth & Sisodia 1999). Revenue is sharply skewed from the largest to the smallest customers, while costs tend to decline more gradually. In such cases, a small number of highly profitable customers subsidise a large number of non-profitable customers. These profitable customers are highly attractive targets for many of the non-traditional competitors who can exploit this distribution of revenues and costs to their advantage. In several industries (such as banking, airlines, telecommunications and

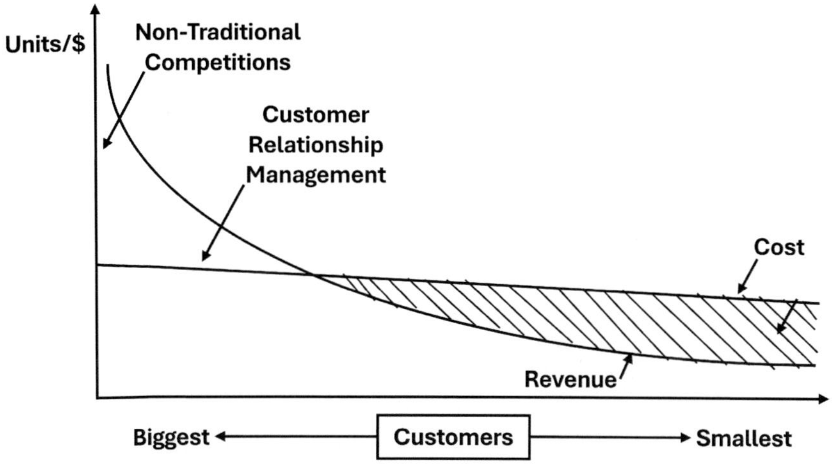

FIGURE 1.4 Revenue–Profit Misalignment

Adapted from Sheth and Sisodia (1999).

utilities) new entrants target heavy users and the most profitable customers, leaving the incumbent with unprofitable customers.

Data often shows that the biggest and the smallest customers are the least profitable. For example, in business markets, companies do not generate high margins from large accounts as these buyers often drive a bargain for lower prices. However in consumer markets, profit margins are higher in large accounts and among heavy users. For example, in August 1998, US telecom company AT&T announced that it was losing money on approximately 25 million of its 70 million residential customers (Sheth & Sisodia, 1999) – customers who never made long-distance calls and did not use value-added services. On an average, AT&T was spending $6 per month ($72 a year) on support and care for its customers.

Customer subsidisation is a problem created primarily by traditional accounting systems. Traditional accounting was usually organised around products, but sometimes around markets. When companies began to disaggregate revenues and costs at the customer or account level due to improved information and accounting systems, they discovered previously hidden customer subsidies. This also resulted in companies paying attention to their most profitable customers by adopting a relationship orientation.

WHY BUSINESSES ADOPT CRM

A combination of demand- and supply-led factors accelerated the adoption of CRM. On the demand side, rising customer expectations forced businesses to adopt CRM, while on the supply side, technological advances and declining costs of ICT reduced the barriers to the adoption of technology-led CRM initiatives.

Rising Customer Expectations

Customer expectations are rising due to greater prosperity in emerging nations, increased awareness due to the boom in media and growing customer diversity. The economic growth in emerging markets created a burgeoning middle class that is highly demanding and quality-conscious. Their transition from sellers' markets to buyers' markets and the growing purchasing power of the middle class makes these emerging markets attractive to businesses. In terms of purchasing power parity (PPP), the combined gross domestic product (GDP) of nine developing nations – China, India, Brazil, Mexico, Russia, Indonesia, Turkey, South Africa and Thailand – is larger than the combined GDP of Japan, Germany, France, the UK and Italy. The middle class includes a large mix of professionals with greater awareness and influence. This cohort can afford and is willing to pay for better-quality products and more personalised offerings.

Access to traditional mass media channels, including television, radio and newspapers, is being complemented by the rapidly growing reach of digital media. Greater consumer awareness due to easy media access is enabling consumers make more informed decisions. The number of TV households in the US increased from 102 million to 125 million between 2000 and 2024, while the percentage of the population using the internet rose from 43% to 97% in the same period. In the last two decades, households in China, India and Brazil have witnessed some of the fastest growth in TV penetration. The meteoric growth in access to the internet, mainly through mobile phones, has created better-informed populaces in all emerging markets. This rapid expansion of information has drastically raised consumer expectations and aspirations.

Customers prefer choices that are tailored to their needs and personalised in nature. Many mass-marketing practices fail with these customers who are increasingly diverse in lifestyle, age, income and ethnicity. Rising customer expectations necessitated the adoption of CRM to enable businesses to customise all aspects of their marketing mix to satisfy these customers. The good news for companies is that advances in affordable digital technologies enable them to meet these divergent needs of demanding customers.

Affordable Technological Advances

Advances in technology have made an impact on all stages of business, from production to final consumption, and are allowing marketers to offer unique solutions to individual customers. In the following we describe key technological advances in production, distribution, facilitation and consumption and their impact on marketing practices (Figure 1.5).

Production

Innovations such as computer-aided design and manufacturing (CAD-CAM), flexible manufacturing systems (FMS) and just-in-time operations (JIT) have enhanced quality while reducing costs. Early adopters gained a competitive edge and consumers benefited from mass customisation, receiving personalised products and services at prices comparable to mass-market offerings. Industry 4.0 technologies are now being used to optimise manufacturing operations with connected capabilities. Emerging digital tools such as the Industrial Internet of Things (IIoT), advanced robotics, additive manufacturing through 3D printing, the use of digital twins and augmented reality allow for the specialised production of unique and customised products. Consumers benefit from products tailored to their specific requirements through mass customisation at prices comparable to mass-marketed products.

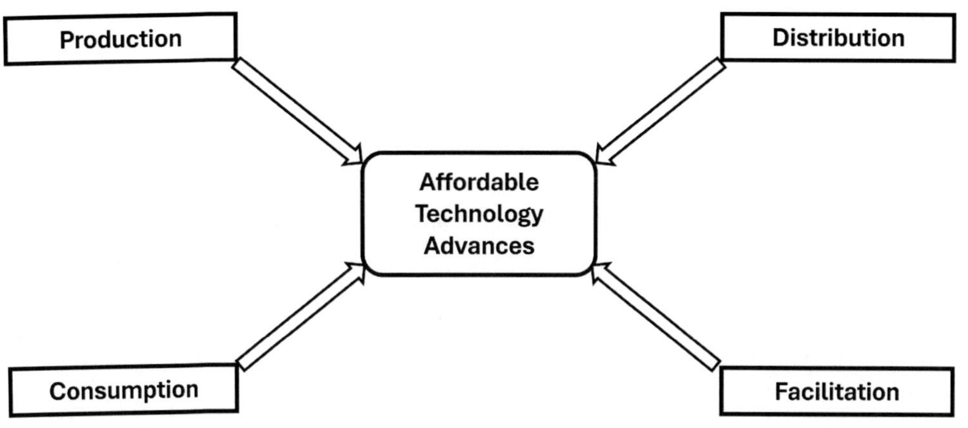

FIGURE 1.5 Affordable Technological Advances

Distribution

Computer-aided logistics (CAL), scanner technology and robotised warehouses have enhanced distribution capabilities by enabling faster replenishment with fewer stock-outs. Improvements in forecasting by leveraging big data through analytical tools such as artificial intelligence (AI), machine learning (ML) and cloud computing permit fine-tuned targeted approaches to customer engagement and close to real-time fulfilment. Distribution intermediaries and third-party logistics providers harness emerging technologies to deliver products at affordable prices and increase market coverage rapidly. Quick commerce (q-commerce) is also a rising trend, with startups such as Zepto, Blinkit and Swiggy Instamart in India catering to the culture of instant gratification and convenience among consumers, with 'order to delivery' cycles of less than 20 minutes. Leading players like Amazon and Walmart have thus been forced to invest in same-day and even one-hour delivery options.

Facilitation

The use of digital technologies to connect enterprises within and outside with suppliers and customers through e-business has resulted in major improvements in facilitating commercial and informational exchanges. Dramatic reductions in transaction costs have allowed even small businesses to aspire for global reach. Large businesses in airline, banking and financial sectors have leveraged digital technologies to offer services directly to their end customers – conveniently and at lower costs. In many industries, sellers as well as buyers have benefited from this process of 'disintermediation' – i.e. cutting down layers of intermediaries. While traditional intermediation process inefficiencies have been reduced through disintermediation, a new class of intermediaries (e.g. Tripadvisor and Policybazaar) has emerged to facilitate transactions between sellers and buyers. Customers are changing their shopping habits, accessing, evaluating and purchasing products and services with ease online and over mobile applications.

Consumption

Breakthroughs in consumption followed the development of affordable personal identities (e.g. individual logins) that helped personalise the consumption experience. Sellers can mine consumer transaction, purchase and usage data to offer personalised products. This empowerment allows consumers to be co-producers and provide input to co-create offerings. For example, Dell allowed buyers to configure the computer of their choice by co-opting them as co-producers before assembly. Similarly, Indian company MakeMyTrip enables customers to create their own holiday package combining travel, stay, tours and activities. Digital technologies, overcoming geographical and temporal constraints, are thus enabling personalised consumption. Businesses are driven to provide access to their products from any location, meeting customers' desires for instant gratification. Banks have also discovered that they save on costs as customers shift from time- and place-restricted channels such as branches and automated teller machines (ATMs) to internet and mobile applications.

These advances in digital technologies benefit both businesses and consumers, with online shopping witnessing significant growth. Retailers have adapted their supply chains to allow last-minute orders, simplifying e-commerce for customers and businesses. In emerging markets like India, customers are increasingly adopting digital channels for transactions, encouraging businesses to invest in cost-effective technology. New technology – including video and conference calls, instant messaging and cloud computing – enhances business processes, productivity and communication. Cloud computing, in particular, reduces upfront capital costs, enhances scalability and increases customer responsiveness. Social media platforms such as WhatsApp, LinkedIn, X (formerly Twitter) and Instagram enable businesses to connect with customers effectively and gather real-time insights.

In conclusion, digital channels and data-driven strategies have become essential in connecting with customers. Data plays a crucial role in building customer relationships, as exemplified by Verizon Wireless's customer-driven strategy, which focused on enhancing the customer experience through data analysis and personalised interactions across various media channels. By embracing technology and leveraging data, companies can improve customer engagement and drive business growth.

IMPLEMENTING CRM

Businesses can now maintain one-to-one relationships with their most valuable customers through advancements in information technology, data warehousing and data mining. Numerous organisations embarked on CRM initiatives in anticipation of the enormous potential for benefit. Benefits included lower customer retention costs and increased profits due to lower defection rates (Reichheld & Sasser, 1990). However, CRM may be an expensive option for businesses that have historically relied on mass marketing. As mentioned previously, the improving performance and decreasing costs of technology make CRM adoption attractive. Despite numerous technological options, organisations face multiple obstacles in identifying and implementing technology-intensive CRM solutions. These include leadership commitment, customer orientation, change management, developing customer-centric processes, integrating with legacy systems, identifying and establishing performance metrics, and evaluating return on investment (Adolf et al., 1997; Goff et al., 1998; Ernst & Young, 1999; Sisodia & Wolfe, 2000). Poor technology choices and ill-conceived implementation plans have derailed many customer relationship projects. The failure rate for CRM projects has been estimated to be high (Davids, 1999). The lure of early-mover advantages prompt many firms to invest heavily in technology, statistical tools, databases and restructuring, which increases the risk of these firms biting off more than they can chew (Adolf et al., 1997). Unfortunately many of these challenges persist despite so many implementation experiences.

CRM aims to connect multiple people, processes and technologies within a business that have previously existed in isolation in large enterprises (Ernst & Young, 1999). In the context of banking, Adolf et al. (1997) argued that:

> CRM cannot be simply grafted onto the multi-product, multi-organisation of most banks. The huge amount of information available to these banks, coupled with the wide array of products and services they sell, can make implementing CRM a complicated and time-consuming task entailing broad institutional change.

Day (2000, p. 24) identified three elements of market-related capability that a firm has to master to foster and maintain relationships with its most valuable customers on a durable basis for competitive advantage:

> First, a relationship orientation must pervade the mindset, values, and norms of the organization. Second, the firm must keep deepening its knowledge of these customers and putting it to work throughout the organization. Third, the key processes must be internally integrated and externally aligned with the corresponding processes of the firm's customers.

A process-oriented strategic approach driven by top management will be critical to successful CRM initiatives as this approach will connect the operational, informational and organisational components of CRM (Parvatiyar & Sheth, 2000; Pisharodi et al., 2003). The process approach enables a more precise delineation of the challenges associated with the formation, governance, performance evaluation and evolution of customer relationships. Similarly, segmenting relationship strategy into operational, informational and organisational components enables managers to comprehend, identify, quantify and manage the impact of each element on overall relationship effectiveness. Companies that have taken a holistic approach see improved results, while those that have not are battling technology for the sake of technology. Profitable customer relationships are critical drivers of success and require a holistic strategy and process to be successful.

SUMMARY

This introductory chapter presented an overview of the strategic aspects of Customer Relationship Management. In it we highlighted the pervasiveness of CRM in marketing and IT and underscored the critical enablers of CRM's rapid growth. We examined the macro-environmental factors that contribute to global interest and investment in CRM. We also identified a few challenges faced by businesses in the 21st century that may exacerbate the importance of customer relationships. Rising customer expectations and affordable technological advancements were identified as future drivers of CRM adoption. Finally, we discussed our perspectives on CRM technology implementation.

Industry Best Practices

Customer Relationship Management strategies are crucial to growing businesses, improving customer satisfaction and staying ahead of the competition. These strategies differ greatly across industries because of different customer needs, market conditions and technology use. A simpler breakdown is as follows:

What Makes CRM Work Well in Different Industries?

- Customisation and Personalisation: Understand and cater to what your customers want using data analytics. This makes customers more engaged and loyal.

- Technology Integration: Use the latest technology, like AI, for better predictions, automated services, and personalised marketing, improving customer experience and efficiency.
- Regulatory Compliance: Following legal rules builds trust and transparency in industries like healthcare and finance.

Common CRM Challenges and How to Solve Them

- Data Silos: Problems with disconnected data can make understanding customers harder.
  - Solution: Use integrated CRM systems to gather all customer information in one place.
- Changing Consumer Behaviour: Customers' needs and expectations can change quickly.
  - Solution: Keep up with market research and feedback to adapt CRM strategies accordingly.
- Data Privacy and Security: Customers are wary of data breaches and privacy issues.
  - Solution: Invest in strong security and clear data policies to build trust.

Adapting CRM to Market Requirements

- Emerging Markets: Focus on educating customers about your brand. CRM should help with customer education and support.
- Growth Markets: Stand out by offering personalised experiences and value-added services. Use CRM data for upselling and finding new opportunities.
- Mature Markets: Focus on retaining customers and increasing lifetime value with loyalty programmes, excellent support and feedback mechanisms. Use CRM to focus efforts on the most profitable customer segments and reduce churn.

In summary, managing customer relationships requires a deep understanding of the changing needs of customers, tackling common issues effectively and using market insights to engage with customers and grow.

CLOSING CASE

In 2024 Coca-Cola deployed the Salesforce platform (Salesforce.com) to manage its sales and service efforts with retailers and other business customers. The company managed multiple collaborations and unprecedented connectivity while scaling up different parts of its business with custom-built apps on the platform. These apps, connected across several departments, provide relevant information instantly to the team for quick resolution and tapping into sales opportunities. The sales team extensively uses this application while they are in the field. For example they can extract information about the bottling plant using apps connected through the Sales Cloud, which enables the company to serve its customers collaboratively as a single team. Cross-functional integration helps employees solve customer issues quickly as prompt customer connection and management are enabled by connecting all the dots instantly. For example, if delivery is inappropriate, the customer, the sales representative and the distribution team will know about it instantly and can work together to resolve the issue.

The technical call centre and repair team started working effectively. The Service Cloud provides instant access to a customer's history and pending service issues, as well as obtaining work orders and dispatch technicians through the mobile service app. The app then plans an appropriate route to complete all the service requests. Repair teams can easily track technicians' jobs through the Service Cloud, and customers receive alerts on the status of their repairs. Such coordinated efforts improved productivity by 30% (Binns, 2021).

The custom mobile apps in the Sales Cloud help make relevant and appropriate customer-oriented real-time decisions. The retailers can manage their inventory and use personalised promotions based on this information. In addition, connected apps help them resolve issues instantly.

CRM has offered several benefits to Coca-Cola's stakeholders, including internal departments such as sales and associated services, providing rapid information to better serve customers.

DISCUSSION QUESTIONS

1 What has been the impact of technological advances on CRM?
2 What is the impact of non-traditional competition on incumbent businesses? How is CRM helping them retain their customers?
3 What are the enablers for CRM? Are there any challenges?
4 How do effective CRM strategies facilitate the sales and marketing activities of companies?
5 How are benefits derived from effective CRM?
6 What is the impact of the emerging service and digital economy on the customer orientation of businesses? What role does CRM play in facilitating it?

REFERENCES

Adolf, R., Grant-Thompson, S., Harrington, W., & Singer, M. (1997). What leading banks are learning about big databases and marketing. *McKinsey Quarterly*, *3*, 187–193.

Berry, L.L. (1995). Relationship marketing of services: Growing interest, emerging perspectives, *Journal of the Academy of Marketing Science*, *23*(4), 236–245. https://doi.org/10.1177/009207039502300402.

Binns, R. (2021). How big brands do CRM: Case studies. Retrieved November 20, 2021, from https://www.expertmarket.co.uk/crm-systems/customer-relationship-management-case-studies.

Davids, M. (1999). How to avoid the 10 biggest mistakes in CRM. *Journal of Business Strategy*, *20*(6), 22–22.

Day, G.S. (2000). Managing market relationships. *Journal of the Academy of Marketing Science*, *28*(1), 24–30. https://doi.org/10.1177/0092070300281003.

Ernst & Young (1999). *Special report: Technology in financial services.*

Goff, J., Harding, D., Shah, R., & Singer, M., (1998). A new way to reach small businesses. *McKinsey Quarterly*, *3*, 172–176.

Grönroos, C. (1994). From marketing mix to relationship marketing. *Management Decision*, *32*(2), 4–20. doi:10.1108/00251749410054774.

Leeflang, P.S., & van Raaij, W.F. (1995). The changing consumer in the European Union: A 'meta-analysis'. *International Journal of Research in Marketing*, *12*(5), 373–387. doi:10.1016/0167-8116(95)00031-3.

Parvatiyar, A., & Sheth, J.N. (2000). The domain and conceptual foundations of relationship marketing. In J.N. Sheth & A. Parvatiyar (Eds.), *Handbook of relationship marketing* (pp. 3–38). SAGE.

Payne, A. (2000). Relationship marketing: The UK perspective. In J.N. Sheth & A. Parvatiyar (Eds.), *Handbook of relationship marketing* (pp. 39–68). SAGE.

Peppers, D., & Rogers, M. (1999). *Enterprise one-to-one: Tools for competing in the interactive age.* Currency/Doubleday.

Pisharodi, R.M., Angur, M.G., & Shainesh, G. (2003). Relationship strategy, effectiveness, and responsiveness in services marketing. *Journal of Relationship Marketing*, *2*(1–2), 3–22. https://doi.org/10.1300/J366v02n01_02.

Ramesh, S. (2025). Relationship Marketing Know How To Use It In Your Business!. Value Leaf Blogs. Retrived from https://www.valueleaf.com/blog/relationship-marketing/

Reichheld, F.F., & Sasser, W.E. (1990). Zero defections: Quality comes to services. *Harvard Business Review*, *68*(5), 105–111.

Ruiz, J. (2012). Relationship marketing: My Amazon CRM experience. Retrieved November 19, 2021, from https://www.business2community.com/marketing/relationship-marketing-my-amazon-crm-experience-0350111#5hYhFG2M2gmjUwJJ.97.

Salesforce (2024). Coca Cola: The formula for global success. Retrieved May 21, 2024, from https://www.salesforce.com/in/customer-success-stories/coca-cola/.

Sheth, J.N., & Mittal, B. (2004). *Customer behaviour: A managerial perspective*. Mason, OH: Thomson/South-Western.

Sheth, J.N., & Parvatiyar, A. (1995). The evolution of relationship marketing. *International Business Review*, *4*(4), 397–418, https://doi.org/10.1016/0969-5931(95)00018-6.

Sheth, J.N., & Sisodia, R.S. (1999). Revisiting marketing's lawlike generalizations. *Journal of the Academy of Marketing Science*, *27*(1), 71–87, doi:10.1177/0092070399271006.

Sisodia, R.S., & Wolfe, D.B. (2000). Information technology: Its role in building, maintaining and enhancing relationships. In J.N. Sheth & A. Parvatiyar (Eds.), *Handbook on relationship marketing* (pp. 525–563). SAGE.

Uber. (n.d.). Driver rewards with Uber pro. Retrieved November 19, 2021, from https://www.uber.com/gh/en/drive/uber-pro/.

Vietor, R.H.K. (1994). *Contrived competition*. Cambridge, MA: Harvard University Press.

Zineldin, M. (2000). Beyond relationship marketing: Technological marketing. *Marketing Intelligence and Planning*, *18*(1), 9–23, https://doi.org/10.1108/02634500010308549.

CHAPTER 2

Conceptual Foundations of CRM

CHAPTER OVERVIEW

This chapter will help you understand:

1. The evolution of Customer Relationship Management (CRM) in light of the new technological advances, intensive competition, the increasing relevance of the service sector and the adoption of total quality management (TQM) programmes
2. The marketing and service benefits of CRM
3. Differences between transactional with relationship-based marketing
4. Perspectives of different schools of thoughts on CRM
5. Definitions of CRM

Vignette

Honda Australia created a customer engagement plan, 'Customers for Life', to integrate the data in the company's systems and develop comprehensive profiles that offer a 360° view of customers. Details about customers were previously distributed in individual department spreadsheets and databases, leading to the underutilisation of potentially valuable assets. These details were subsequently merged into a single cloud-hosted platform from Salesforce. The database was complemented by additional data on customers curated from Honda Australia Rider Training (HART) and Automobile Association (AA) memberships. After developing this comprehensive database, customer management was shifted from individual departments to a newly formed CRM unit. Honda has further integrated workflows into customer touchpoints, such as customer satisfaction surveys, to ensure quick follow-up and closure, especially for any negative feedback.

This systematic flow of communication to and from customers immediately reduced the time taken to resolve complaints, which in turn led to a significant decrease in complaints. As a result, Honda could now focus on developing

DOI: 10.4324/9781003518174-3

long-term relationships with more satisfied customers. CRM further helped ease the flow of communication between the organisation and its customers, leading to improved trust and brand loyalty. It has also opened new opportunities for Honda to deliver outstanding customer engagement through enhanced product and service experience.

OPENING CASE

Narayana Murthy and his founding team of six engineers set up technology company Infosys in 1981 with an investment of $250. In 2023, Infosys generated $18 billion in revenues by offering digital services, software solutions and consulting to global corporations. The founders adopted a customer-oriented, transparent and value-driven business model from inception. Customers were the most important stakeholders for them. Referrals and positive word-of-mouth about quality services and ethical business practices helped Infosys win the trust of potential clients too (Kotler et al., 2022).

As the company continued to develop expertise and expand its portfolio of offerings, the leaders reinforced the importance of every single customer in competitive business markets where a small set of customers generates a significant share of revenue. They emphasised working closely with each client to develop the core information technology (IT) service delivery capability and then start handling multiple projects to broaden and deepen the relationship.

Along with long-term and in-depth relationships, the company's clients also developed high levels of dependency on the firm. In most instances, Infosys has developed its business by growing its share of customers' IT spending. Clients appreciate Infosys's simple and transparent system, in addition to its high-quality and core delivery capabilities. The leadership has a razor-sharp focus on the well-being of clients' business interests. By the first decade of the 21st century, Infosys had evolved as a strategic partner of many global clients in the banking, financial services and insurance verticals. Infosys would become an important part of several clients' strategic decisions. The company adopted a strategic account management approach involving business leaders from within Infosys and the client to enhance the value of its relationship with its most important clients. More than 97% of its business is generated from the same set of clients, while 3% of its annual revenue originates from new clients. Transparency and integrity are the key ingredients behind Infosys's strong client relationship, as reinforced through the tagline 'Powered by Intellect, Driven by Values'.

The company has been a trailblazer, achieving remarkable milestones. Records include it being the first India-registered company to be listed on NASDAQ. Its employee stock options programme created some of India's first salaried millionaires. The company's people practices deliver excellent employee experiences, and employee satisfaction and productivity are directly linked to the success of its projects for clients. Infosys experienced rapid growth by augmenting its stakeholder relationships. The company generated revenues of $100 million in 1999, $1 billion in 2004 and $10 billion in 2017.

The management uses health indicators that revolve around touchpoints which impact the overall performance of each project. Continuous monitoring of ongoing projects on parameters such as time, budget and quality enables the teams to meet clients' requirements profitably. They also serve as an early warning system for the leadership to take corrective action, including deploying additional resources and expertise to support projects experiencing challenges. Customer satisfaction surveys keep track of the impact of the client relationship on the customer's business (Shainesh, 2018).

With its focus on building and maintaining long-term customer relationships, Infosys has been a torchbearer of India's knowledge power on the global stage. As a leading technology company, Infosys now enables over 1,800 clients in more than 56 countries to navigate digital transformation.

The outlines on Honda and Infosys underscore the importance of CRM in sustaining business performance. This chapter will explain the foundational concepts of CRM to help demonstrate the relationship management practices of successful firms.

THE EVOLUTION OF CRM

CRM has become increasingly popular in the business world and is being viewed as a solution to many of the challenges businesses face. Popularised by the business press and marketed by consultants and solution vendors, it means different things to different people. For some, CRM means one-to-one marketing, while for others it means a contact centre. Others refer to database marketing as CRM, and many classify digital solutions as CRM. While we leave the definition to the end of the chapter, we will try to trace the evolution of CRM.

Is CRM a new concept? No, it is not. Merchants and traders have been practising customer relationship for centuries. Their business was built on trust. They could customise the products and all aspects of delivery and payment to suit the requirements of their customers. They paid personal attention to their customers, knew details about their customers' tastes and preferences, and had a personal rapport with most of them. In many cases, the interactions transcended commercial transactions and involved social interactions. Even today, this kind

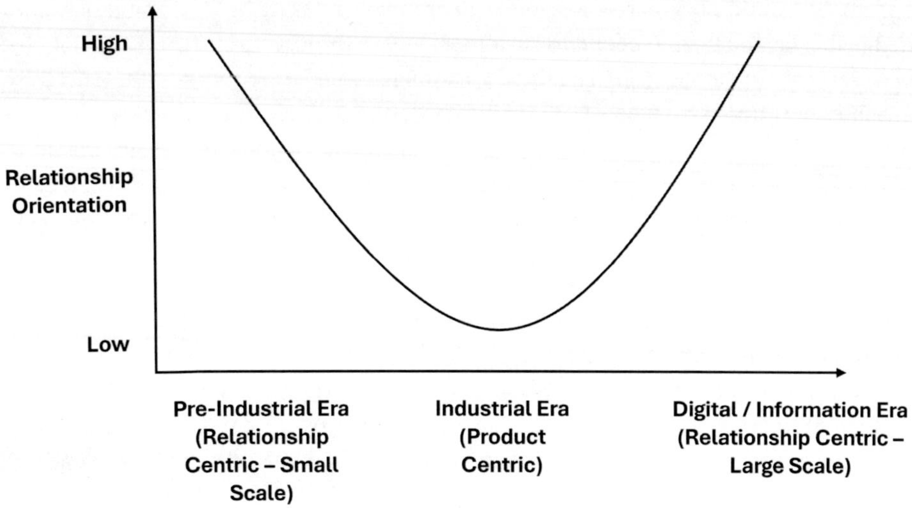

FIGURE 2.1 The Evolution of Relationship Orientation

Adapted from Sheth and Parvatiyar (1995b).

of relationship exists between customers and retailers, craftspeople and artisans – essentially in traditional, small markets classified as pre-industrial markets.

However the Industrial Revolution changed these relationship-oriented practices. Businesses adopted mass production, mass communication and mass distribution to achieve economies of scale. Manufacturers started focusing on manufacturing and efficient operations to cut costs. Intermediaries such as distributors, wholesalers and retailers took on the responsibilities of warehousing, transportation, distribution and selling to final customers. This resulted in greater efficiencies and lower costs for the manufacturers, but brought in many layers between them and the customers. The resulting gap reduced direct contact and had a negative impact on their relationships.

The Information Era has witnessed a re-emergence of relationship practices. Sheth and Parvatiyar (1995b) identified the following factors in this shift in orientation (Figure 2.1):

- Rapid advances in technology
- Intense competition in most markets
- The growing importance of the service sector, and
- Adoption of total quality management (TQM) programmes.

Let us look at each of these factors in more detail.

Rapid Advances in Technology

Advances in information, communication and production technologies have helped marketers move closer to their customers. Firms operating in diverse sectors ranging from packaged goods to services started using these technologies to get to know their customers, learn more about them and build stronger bonds through frequent interactions. Marketers could gain knowledge that helped them respond to customers' needs through manufacturing, delivery and customer service. Technology also enabled customers to undertake some of the responsibilities normally performed by marketers, such as ordering and services related to product use.

Although the emergence of CRM in recent times coincided with the growth in digital technologies, we must remember that technology is just an enabler. Technology enabled marketers to overcome several long-felt shortcomings of mass marketing. Some of these included:

- Inefficiencies of mass marketing: The 1990s witnessed some of the most radical business transformations, which resulted in cost reductions in almost all functional departments except marketing. Manufacturing and related operations costs were reduced through business process re-engineering; human resources (HR) costs were reduced through outsourcing, restructuring and layoffs; and financial costs were reduced through financial re-engineering. Still, marketing costs kept rising due to increased competition and product parity in virtually every industry.
- Lack of fast, effective and interactive modes of customer contact, feedback and information.
- Lack of consolidated information about customer interactions, purchase behaviour and future potential.

Technology helps ensure that consumers remember offerings and are provided with assistance in real time. In addition, technology has enabled firms to offer more value at lower costs, while also improving internal planning and logistics. For example, restaurant company Hard Rock Cafe used these technological advances to drive up sales by using techniques to transform online customers into regulars at its physical locations, thus improving the customer experience. Privy, Hard Rock's technology partner, provided hyper-local marketing platforms, developed specific and targeted coupons, and created unique campaigns for digital channels, such as Facebook ads and sponsored Twitter (now X) posts (VentureBeat, 2014). As a result, many customers who visited Hard Rock stores became fans on Facebook. With millions of followers on social media channels, the company developed an extensive database of loyal members. Analysis of the profile of franchise-specific customers helped develop a deep understanding of the customers to create customised and geo-targeted ads and campaigns. These campaigns in turn drove sales and boosted business performance by attracting more customers to the stores (Close, 2002).

Intense Competition

In competitive markets, especially those that were maturing and witnessing slow or no growth, marketers found it more profitable to focus on their existing customers. Studies have shown that it costs 6–8 times more to attract a new customer than to retain an existing customer (Gruen, 1997). Marketers have now started focusing on the lifetime value of customers. They are moving away from just trying to sell their products towards understanding customers' needs and wants, and then profitably satisfying them. This has led to the development of a firm-wide relationship approach, which creates opportunities to cross-sell products and services over the customer's lifetime.

Growing Importance of the Service Sector

The service sector contributes to over two-thirds of the gross domestic product (GDP) of most advanced economies, including over 50% of the economy in India. One of the characteristics of service industries is the direct interaction between the marketer and the buyer: the provider is usually directly involved in production and delivery. For example, professional service providers such as doctors or consultants are directly involved in the production as well as the delivery of their services. Similarly, the customers are directly involved in purchasing and consuming these services. These direct contacts create opportunities for better understanding and a better appreciation of needs, constraints and emotional bonding, all of which facilitate relationship building. Therefore, it should come as no surprise when one sees service firms pioneering many customer relationship initiatives. Firms operating in financial services, hospitality, telecom and the airline industry are the early adopters and extensive users of CRM practices.

Total Quality Management Programmes

The adoption of total quality management (TQM) programmes helped companies offer quality products and services to customers at the lowest prices. To enable this value proposition, organisations needed to work closely with their customers, intermediaries and suppliers, thus fostering close working relationships with members of the marketing system. Companies such as Intel, Xerox and Toyota formed partnering relationships with suppliers and customers to practise TQM. Similarly, leading players in the service sector (ranging from retailing, healthcare and hospitality to telecom) have adopted TQM to improve service quality and customer satisfaction (Yasin et al., 2004).

Other developments such as an increase in the number of demanding customers, increased fragmentation of markets and generally high levels of product quality forced businesses to seek sustainable competitive advantages. A competitive advantage is sustainable only when it is not easily replicated. One sustainable competitive advantage is the relationship a firm develops with its customers.

BENEFITS OF CRM

CRM offers several benefits to organisations, as outlined in this section.

Increasing Customer Profitability over Time

Studies show that a customer becomes more profitable over time because the initial cost to acquire a customer exceeds the gross margin for many businesses, while the customer retention costs are much lower (Reichheld, 1993). When an organisation retains a customer, it gets a larger share of the customer's wallet at higher profit – a 1% increase in sales to existing customers increases profits by 17%, while the same amount of sales to new customers increases profits by only 3%. This vast difference is explained by the fact that the cost of acquiring a customer is very high for most companies. As mentioned earlier, it costs 6–8 times more to sell to a new customer than to an existing one. Reichheld also highlighted that a company can boost its profits by 85% by increasing its annual customer retention by only 5%. Similarly, studies have shown that the probability of selling a product to a prospective customer is 15%, compared to 50% to an existing customer. Thus the time, effort and selling costs are much lower for an existing customer.

Customer Profitability Is Skewed

An analysis of revenue and profit contributions of the customer base of banks in the US, Europe and Australia showed the following:

- The top 20% of customers contribute 150% of the profits, the bottom 20% drain 50% of the profits and the remaining 60% just break even.

Indian organisations showed similar results:

- In a large public sector bank, the top 23% of customers contribute 77% of revenues, and the top 27% of customers of a leading cellular phone service provider contribute 75% of revenues.

The implications of such a skew in customer profitability and revenue contribution are startling for organisations that conventionally used to treat 'all customers as equal'. Competitors simply have to lure their most profitable customers to win in competitive markets. It also highlights the fact that companies must adopt different strategies for different customer groups:

- Programmes have to be developed to retain and build stronger bonds with 'gold standard' customers to prevent them being 'poached'.
- Activity-based costing analysis will have to be conducted to understand the true costs of serving different customer groups to identify ways to reduce the cost of serving the middle 'potentials' group of low- or zero-margin customers. In addition, opportunities for cross-selling and up-selling should be explored to increase these customers' profitability.
- Analysis of the bottom group helps identify those customers who can be shifted to the 'potentials' group. For the remainder, service costs can be reduced by encouraging them to use lower-cost electronic and digital channels. In extreme cases however, some customers will be encouraged to defect to competitors. Outsourcing loss-making customers to specialised low overhead agencies is an emerging trend.

Marketing Benefits of CRM

CRM will gradually reduce an organisation's dependence on periodic surveys to gather data. The collection of data related to buying and consumption behaviour will be an ongoing process. Transaction data is collected automatically, sometimes in real time, as in e-commerce

TABLE 2.1 Cost Calculation for 100,000 Mailshots

Particulars	Total in rupees (Rs)
Address database – Rs 500,000 Printing (mailer + envelope) – Rs 1,250,000 Handling and mailing – Rs 500,000	2,250,000
Hit rate, i.e. average response (~3%)	
Actual purchase (25% of respondents), i.e. 750 sales	
Direct marketing cost per sale	3000

transactions. This rich repository of customer information and knowledge updated through regular interactions and actual customer transactions and purchase behaviour will help marketers develop and market customer-centric products successfully.

Customised promotions based on customer preferences and purchase patterns will substantially reduce the wasteful expenditure of mass communications and even direct mailing. As customised promotions are more focused and based on deeper insights into existing customers, they have a greater chance of conversion to sales.

CEOs have always been pessimistic about the efficacy of mass advertising, as exemplified by a quote attributed to 19th-century US merchant John Wanamaker: "I know that half of my advertising budget is wasted, but I am not sure which half." Similarly, the top management carefully scrutinises the returns of promotional expenditure. A simple illustrative calculation in Table 2.1 indicates the massive potential for savings in a direct marketing exercise for an Indian organisation.

In this case, the margin per sale has to be substantially higher than Rs 3000 to justify the mailing exercise. This also highlights the potential for savings through low-cost media, improved targeting and higher conversion rates.

Using data mining, collaborative filtering and event-triggered offerings, a financial service provider with over a million customers can shortlist just four potential customers who are ripe for a sale, make a pitch via email, follow it up with direct contact and generate three sales. That is a conversion rate of 75%!

Service Benefits of CRM

Research findings across industries conducted as part of the Technical Assistance Research Programs (TARP, 1986) indicate that:

- Some 95% of customers do not bother to complain; they just take their business elsewhere.
- Most loyal customers take time to complain. This enables the product/service provider to improve and ensure mistakes do not recur.
- A typical dissatisfied customer will tell an average of 14 others about a bad experience with an organisation, but only six about a satisfying experience.
- Around 70% of customers who complain will do business with the company again if it resolves a service problem quickly.

Providers of products and services in competitive markets face tremendous opportunities and challenges. While the rewards for good performance help them remain competitive, the punishment for failure is fast and furious. Negative 'word of mouth' has a multiplier effect and deters lots of potential customers. On the other hand, satisfied and loyal customers can give feedback, which helps improve services/products. Some of these loyal customers may, in fact, turn into advocates for the firm.

While many researchers and consultants advocate for firms to focus on fostering customer loyalty, Reinartz and Kumar (2002) caution that, while customer loyalty is very important and enticing, the firm must ensure it does not seek to enhance customer loyalty as an end. Managers must be careful about addressing the important issue of customer profitability. The authors concluded that "no company should ever take for granted the idea that managing customers for loyalty is the same as managing them for profits". They also proposed a framework for the segmentation of customers on the dimensions of loyalty and profitability, which suggests that firms should implement loyalty strategies.

Firms are motivated to engage in relationship marketing due to the superior economics of customer retention and the competitive advantage of building better relationships. At the same time, it is important to understand the factors that motivate consumers to engage in relationship patronage. Relationship marketing represents ongoing cooperative market behaviour between marketers and consumers. The longevity of this relationship depends on the commitment made by the consumer to continue patronising a particular brand despite the availability of alternatives. In other words, the marketers' motivation to engage in relationship marketing is tempered by the consumers' motivation to reduce their choice set to be in a relationship with a firm. A relationship results in brand patronage over time. Consumers will not be inclined to such a loyalty unless they are motivated to reduce their choice set. Therefore, it is important to take the consumer perspective and understand their motivations to stay loyal.

Most consumers generally prefer patronising a brand, store or firm as long as they are satisfied with the offering. In addition to firm-related factors, consumers engage in relational market behaviour because they want to simplify their buying and consuming tasks, simplify information processing, reduce perceived risks and maintain cognitive consistency and a state of psychological comfort (Sheth & Parvatiyar, 1995a).

Consumers' and marketers' willingness and ability to engage in relational marketing will lead to greater marketing productivity unless consumers or marketers abuse interdependence and cooperation.

TRANSACTION VS. RELATIONSHIP ORIENTATION IN MARKETING

Conventional marketing was centred on exchanging goods and services to meet the customers' requirements while meeting the organisation's goals. Back in 1985, the American Marketing Association's (AMA) definition of marketing management emphasised this focus on exchanges and transactions: "Marketing management is the process of planning and executing the conception, pricing, promotion and distribution of goods, services, and ideas to create exchanges with target groups that satisfy the customer and organisational objectives."

FIGURE 2.2 Sample Exchange Map for Boeing and FedEx

Marketing's primary objective is to facilitate exchanges that benefit both the customer and the organisation. Generally, an exchange is a value-creating process that benefits both parties. Exchange is a process, not a one-time event. If two parties negotiate and work toward an agreement, they are engaged in an exchange. When an agreement is reached, a transaction occurs. As a result, transactions serve as the fundamental unit of exchange. A transaction is the exchange of goods and services between two parties. Most transactions are monetary, meaning money is a traded value. On the other hand, non-monetary transactions, such as barters, also result in a value exchange and are perhaps more prevalent in specific markets, such as rural agricultural markets. Marketing is defined as actions taken to elicit desired responses from a target group at its most fundamental level. The marketer can analyse and map the expectations of each party regarding what they will give and receive.

An exchange map showing the *want* list of participants can be displayed for Boeing, a leading aerospace firm, and FedEx, a leading courier and logistics partner for manufacturing firms (Figure 2.2).

A successful exchange is possible if both parties' desires are met. However, satisfied customers may defect to competitors' offerings in competitive markets. As a result, successful marketers strive to establish long-term, trusting, 'win-win' partnerships with highly prized customers and suppliers by shifting their focus away from transactional profit maximisation and working towards mutually beneficial relationships. While promising and delivering high-quality products, excellent service and reasonable prices results in satisfaction, the partnership is strengthened through financial, technological and social bonds. Relationship marketing reduces costs of transactions, effort and time by focusing on reusing transactions rather than negotiating them. The guiding principle is to establish positive relationships, and financially viable transactions will follow.

The AMA's updated 2024 definition of marketing has expanded the scope to include other stakeholders in addition to customers: "Marketing is the activity, set of institutions, and processes for creating, communicating, delivering, and exchanging offerings that have value for customers, clients, partners, and society at large."

Table 2.2 highlights the differences between traditional (transactional) and relationship marketing.

A relationship orientation is built around the idea of treating customers in an individualised way. The development of long-term, mutually beneficial relationships with customers is favoured in place of a short-term orientation on transactions.

TABLE 2.2 Transactional vs. Relationship Marketing

Transactional Marketing		Relationship Marketing
One-off Exchanges Brand Management	Focus	Ongoing Exchanges Customer Management
Short-term Focus	Time Perspective	Long-term Focus
Mass Communication	Primary Communication	Personal Communication
Isolated Market Research	Customer Feedback Mechanism	Ongoing Dialogue
Mass Markets or Market Segments	Market Size	Markets of One
Market Share	Criteria for Success	Mind Share (Share of Customers)
Profitability of Transactions and Brand Equity	Critical Metrics	Lifetime Value of Customer and Customer Equity

Adapted from Grönroos (1991).

In some situations however, a transactional orientation is more appropriate. The marketer focuses on single transactions, and profits are expected to follow from these transactions. Brand management and image development offer a long-term perspective for building loyalty with customers who remain a 'faceless' part of a larger market segment. Mass media is the primary means of communicating with these customers. Traditional market surveys are the primary means of understanding their requirements and getting their feedback. Markets tend to be large, and a stable or growing market share is one of the key criteria for success.

In many other marketing contexts, a relationship orientation, which focuses on the lifetime value of customers, is more profitable. Customer management is emphasised through personal communication and ongoing interactions with each customer. The key criterion for success is 'share of the customer' rather than market share. A relationship orientation is based on the concept of treating customers uniquely. The advancement of long-term productive relationships with chosen customers replaces a transactional focus on the short term.

Traditional market surveys are used to ascertain customer requirements and solicit their feedback. Markets are typically sizable, and maintaining or increasing market share is critical for success.

A relationship-based approach that prioritises customer lifetime value is more profitable in several marketing contexts. Personal communication and continual interaction with each customer also emphasise customer management. The critical success metric again is 'share of the customer' and not just market share.

As the attention shifts from acquisition towards retention and selection of customers in the current environment, the role of selling moves from a short-term and sales-oriented environment to one of 'partnering' and 'relationship'. These changes are evident in many organisations and companies through reward schemes such as the Tesco Clubcard and Sainsbury's Nectar card in the UK, whereby these supermarkets' customers earn points which can be redeemed for purchases or to obtain discounts. The retailers leverage the customers' perceptual and behavioural data to understand their individual buying patterns and behaviours. They then use this understanding to develop more customised and personalised offerings.

SCHOOLS OF THOUGHT ON CRM

The growing research interest in different facets of this concept supports the growth of the practice of relationship marketing. Researchers in various countries observed this shift in marketers' orientation towards customer relationship and started exploring the phenomenon. For example, Coote (1994) broadly classified the different approaches to CRM as: (1) the Anglo-Australian; (2) the Nordic; and (3) the North American.

The Anglo-Australian Approach

As shown in Figure 2.3, this approach integrated the contemporary theories of quality management, services marketing and customer relationship economics to explain the emergence of relationship marketing.

The Nordic Approach

The Nordic approach views relationship marketing as the confluence of interactive network theory, services marketing and customer relationship economics (Figure 2.4). The interactive network theory of industrial marketing views marketing as an interactive process in a context where relationship-building is a primary concern for marketers.

FIGURE 2.3 The Anglo-Australian Approach to Relationship Marketing

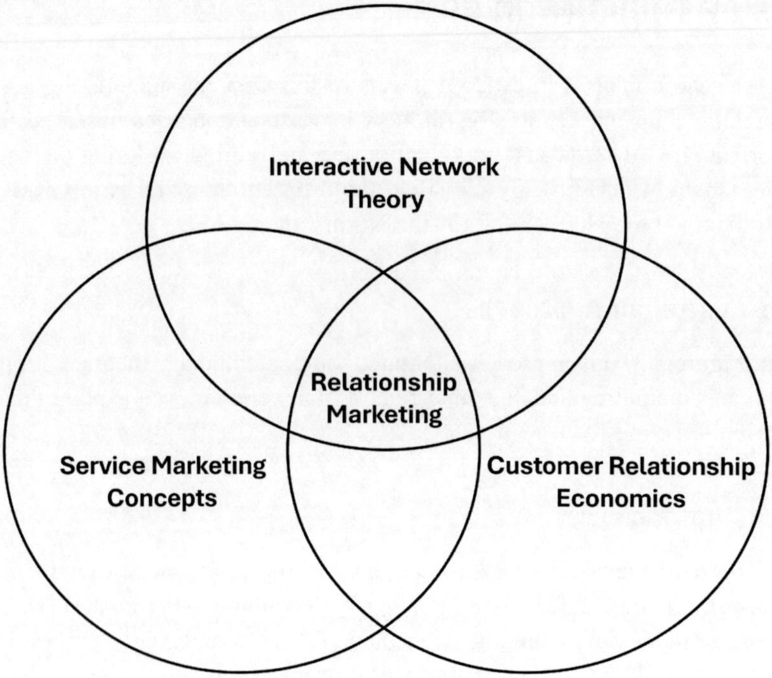

FIGURE 2.4 The Nordic Approach to Relationship Marketing

The North American Approach

In contrast to the first two approaches, the initial focus of North American scholars was on the relationship between the buyer and seller operating within the context of the organisational environment, which facilitated the buyer–seller relationship (Figure 2.5).

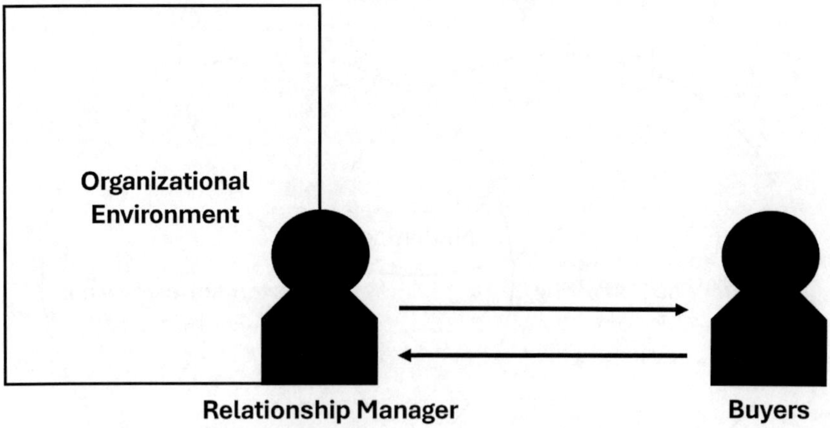

FIGURE 2.5 The North American Approach to Relationship Marketing

Adapted from Coote (1994).

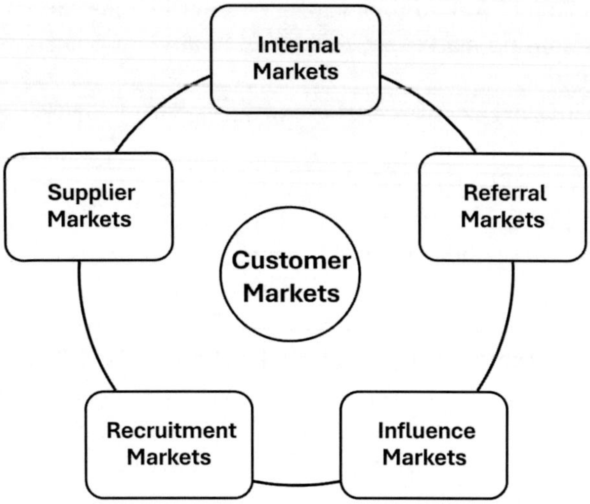

FIGURE 2.6 The Six Markets Framework

The Six Markets Framework

One of the broader approaches to CRM emerged from research conducted by academics at the Cranfield School of Management, UK (Payne, 2000). The broadened view of relationship marketing addresses six key market domains, not just the traditional customer market (Figure 2.6). It also advocated for a transition of marketing from a limited functional role to a cross-functional role and a shift towards marketing activities for customer retention in addition to conventional customer acquisition. Payne's six markets framework comprises:

1. Customer markets – existing and prospective customers, as well as intermediaries
2. Referral markets – existing customers who make recommendations to other prospects, and referral sources or 'recommenders', such as doctors who refer patients to a hospital or a consultant who recommends a specific IT solution
3. Influence markets – governments, consumer groups, business press and financial analysts who influence the company and the industry
4. Recruitment markets – institutions to attract the best talent to the organisation
5. Supplier markets – suppliers of raw materials, components, services, etc.
6. Internal markets – the organisation, including internal departments and staff.

DEFINING CUSTOMER RELATIONSHIP MANAGEMENT

The preceding discussions highlight the range of perspectives researchers adopt in understanding and explaining relationships. Similarly, in the marketing literature, the terms 'customer relationship management' and 'relationship marketing' have been used interchangeably to reflect various themes and perspectives. Some of these themes offer a narrow functional marketing perspective, while others offer a broad and somewhat paradigmatic perspective in approach and orientation. After a review of the extant literature, Harker (1999) identified 26 definitions of relationship marketing, reflecting the diverse academic and socio-political backgrounds of the scholars.

A narrow perspective of customer relationship management is database marketing, emphasising the promotional aspects of marketing linked to database efforts (Bickert, 1992). Another viewpoint is to consider CRM only as customer retention, where various post-marketing tactics are used for customer bonding or staying in touch after the sale is made (Vavra, 1992). A more popular approach with the application of information technology is to focus on individual or one-to-one relationships with customers that integrate database knowledge with a long-term customer retention and growth strategy (Peppers & Rogers, 1993). Jackson (1985) applied the individual account concept in industrial markets to suggest CRM to mean "Marketing oriented toward strong, lasting relationships with individual accounts" (p. 2). McKenna (1991) offered a more strategic view by putting the customer first and shifting the role of marketing from manipulating the customer (telling and selling) to genuine customer involvement (communicating and sharing knowledge).

Berry, in broader terms, also had a strategic viewpoint about CRM. He stressed that attracting new customers should be viewed only as an intermediate step in the marketing process. Developing closer relationships with these customers and turning them into loyal ones are equally important aspects of marketing. Thus, Berry (1995) defined relationship marketing as "attracting, maintaining, and – in multi-service organisations – enhancing customer relationships" (p. 236).

Focusing on the value of interactions in marketing and its consequent impact on customer relationships, a broader perspective espouses that customer relationships should be the dominant marketing paradigm. Grönroos (1990) stated that: "Marketing is to establish, maintain, and enhance relationships with customers and other partners, at a profit, so that the objectives of the parties involved are met. This is achieved by a mutual exchange and fulfilment of promises" (p. 5). The implication of this definition is that customer relationships is a firm's *raison d'être* and that marketing should be devoted to building and enhancing such relationships. Similarly, Morgan and Hunt (1994) suggested that relationship marketing "refers to all marketing activities directed toward establishing, developing, and maintaining successful relationships" (p. 22).

The core theme of all CRM and relationship marketing perspectives is their focus on cooperative and collaborative relationships between a firm and its customers and/or other marketing actors. Dwyer et al. (1987) characterised such cooperative relationships as being interdependent and long-term oriented rather than concerned with short-term discrete transactions. The long-term orientation is often emphasised because it is believed that marketing actors will not engage in opportunistic behaviour if they have a long-term orientation and that such relationships will be anchored on mutual gains and cooperation (Ganesan, 1994).

Another important facet of CRM is 'customer selectivity'. Studies have shown that all customers are not equally profitable (Storbacka, 2000). It is therefore recommended that the company must be selective in tailoring its strategies and marketing efforts by segmenting and selecting appropriate customers for its marketing programmes. In some cases, it could even lead to the 'outsourcing' of some customers so that a company can better utilise its resources on those customers it can serve better and create mutual value. However, the objective of a company is not to really prune its customer base but to identify appropriate programmes and methods that would be profitable and create value both for the firm and for its customers.

As defined by Parvatiyar and Sheth (2000): "Customer relationship management is a comprehensive strategy and process of acquiring, retaining and partnering with selective customers to create superior value for the company and the customer." As implied in this definition, CRM is meant to improve marketing productivity. Marketing productivity is improved by increasing marketing efficiency and by enhancing marketing effectiveness. CRM improves marketing efficiency through cooperative and collaborative processes by reducing transaction costs and overall development costs for the company. Marketing effectiveness is enhanced by seeking and achieving strategic marketing goals – e.g. entering new markets, developing new products or services, serving new or expanded needs of customers and redefining the competitive playing field (Parvatiyar & Sheth, 2000). Processes of CRM, including proactive customer business development and building partnering relationships with the most important customers, lead to the creation of superior mutual value.

To summarise, the various definitions of CRM address several frequently occurring issues, including the following:

- A process-oriented perspective that examines interactions over time
- An explicit emphasis on the cooperative and collaborative state of the relationship for mutual benefit in the long run
- That relationship performance metrics include enhanced value.

The goals of CRM are to:

- Build long-term and profitable relationships with chosen customers
- Get closer to those customers at every point of contact with them.

These can be achieved by establishing a learning relationship, as shown by the iterative process in Figure 2.7.

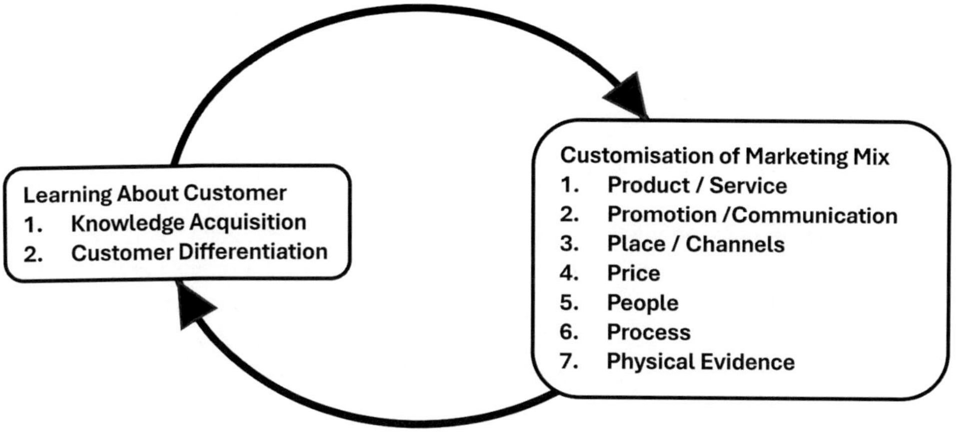

FIGURE 2.7 The Learning Relationship Process

CRM entails gathering information about customers and then tailoring the marketing mix. The term 'knowledge acquisition' refers to gaining customer insights by collecting data at each point of contact and converting it into insights that can meaningfully differentiate customers. This organisational learning is then used to create customised offerings and tailor all elements of the marketing mix. Communication and information technology allows this interactive process at very cost-effective prices to the mutual benefit of customers and the organisation.

Thus, CRM started to be institutionalised in the 1990s with real efforts to manage and build relationships with customers. CRM has evolved in organisations and is now digitally driven by technologies for cloud storage and computing, mobile, social and analytics. Digital engagement with customers and connectedness are evident as businesses transform CRM processes. These digital platforms enable companies to understand customer needs, views and perceptions instantly and at scale. This understanding is achieved by introducing multiple touchpoints, including chat, email, phone, retail, transaction, sales and marketing. In turn, these interactions – involving customers' use of media and channel, their expectations and their entire conversation journeys – can be used to enrich customer experiences through personalisation.

SUMMARY

We started this chapter by examining the evolution of CRM in light of new technological advances, followed by the pivotal role that competition plays in refining and creating new CRM strategies. We then evaluated the role of better production techniques, the service sector's growing importance and its impact on CRM. Further, we discussed the advantages of CRM, followed by elucidation of transactional and relationship-based marketing and the various 'schools of thought' on CRM. Finally, we reviewed some of the most commonly used definitions of CRM and adopted a comprehensive definition for our purposes.

Industry Best Practices

In today's fast-paced business world, mastering Customer Relationship Management (CRM) is key to achieving customer satisfaction and fostering growth. A smart way to stay competitive is by blending technology with CRM strategies, focusing on total quality management (TQM) and keeping pace with changes in customer behaviour and tech advancements. Some of these practices may involve the following:

- Blending technology with CRM and TQM
  - Tech in CRM: Using advanced technologies such as AI, the Internet of Things (IoT) and cloud computing can make customer service smoother, offer deep insights through data analysis and enable personalising customer experiences effectively.
  - TQM with CRM: TQM emphasises continual improvement across the business, aiming to surpass customer expectations. Integrating TQM into CRM makes customer feedback a cornerstone of product development and service improvement, boosting customer loyalty.

- Understanding and adapting to changing customer behaviour
  - Insights into behaviour: Analysing customer data with AI and data analytics helps uncover customer preferences, behaviours and issues. These insights enable businesses to tailor their CRM approaches to meet unique customer needs precisely.
  - Evolving CRM: Customer needs change over time, necessitating an adaptive CRM strategy. Staying agile and responsive to new customer trends ensures CRM strategies remain effective and relevant.
- Navigating technological changes
  - Keeping up with tech: Actively exploring and adopting emerging technologies enhances CRM by staying ahead of trends. This forward-thinking approach can lead to better customer engagement and more efficient operations.
  - Tech's influence on behaviour: New technologies can reshape how consumers expect to interact with brands. The growth of mobile commerce and social media, for example, requires CRM strategies to adjust and meet customers on their preferred platforms.

Leveraging evolving digital technologies enables businesses to better understand, respond to and anticipate customer needs and preferences. Adapting to their behavioural shifts is crucial for staying relevant and satisfying customers.

CLOSING CASE

People for the Ethical Treatment of Animals (PETA)

Many individuals now communicate with a limited number of characters, viz. 140 or 160 characters. Given this need for concise communication, it becomes imperative for organisations to grab customers' attention quickly. PETA's experience illustrates that organisations can successfully engage with customers by adopting cross-channel approaches based on a good understanding of changing user contexts and preferences. Animal rights non-profit organisation PETA was keen to promote its action alert campaigns. Conventionally, it used to send emails to its customer base. Unfortunately, these emails were not helping as most would get blocked and end up in spam folders.

The organisation then experimented with Short Message Service (SMS) for the action alert process by asking customers whether they would like to receive emails from PETA, with emails sent only to those customers who replied 'yes' through SMS. This permission-based approach thus provided PETA with engaged customers. Later, it offered donation and sign-up instances for customers, a campaign that received 20% higher conversion rates than the conventional practices; indeed, 43% of customers responded within two minutes of the action alert. Although customers were in different locations when they received the text messages, they reflected on the cause and responded quickly.

Critical learning was achieved through digital platforms as people are also connected. Mobile communication created value with potential for follow-up actions. This value made a strong connection between the organisation and its customers. Effective communication strategy was enabled by integrating the databases of email and mobile subscribers. Mass communication with these customers is now focused and hence more effective. The data collected through the response to communication was effectively used for more focused targeting.

DISCUSSION QUESTIONS

1 How is relationship-based marketing more beneficial for the company as compared to transactional approaches?
2 Discuss the role of 'competition' in compelling organisations to implement better CRM strategies.
3 Discuss the role and importance of CRM with regard to non-profit organisations.
4 Discuss the six types of market and the role of CRM in enhancing the capacity of these markets.
5 Explain the role of exchange logic in the market situation and in maximising customer satisfaction.
6 Discuss the importance of the service benefits of CRM and the role of technology in enhancing them.

REFERENCES

Bell, L., (2008). Hard Rock riffs on CRM strategy. DMN News Article. Retrieved from https://dmnews.com/hard-rock-riffs-on-crm-strategy/

Berry, L.L. (1995). Relationship marketing of services: Growing interest, emerging perspectives. *Journal of the Academy of Marketing Science*, *23*(4), 236–245. doi:10.1177/009207039502300402.

Bickert, J. (1992). The database revolution [Anon.]. *Target Marketing*, *15*(5), 14–18.

Close, W. (2002). CRM at Hard Rock Cafe: Improving customers' experiences. Retrieved April 17, 2017, from https://www.gartner.com/doc/360826/crm-hard-rock-cafe-improving.

Coote, L. (1994). Implementation of relationship marketing in an accounting practice. In J.N. Sheth & A. Parvatiyar (Eds.), *Relationship marketing: Theory, methods and applications*. Atlanta, GA: Emory University, Center for Relationship Marketing.

Dwyer, F.R., Schurr, P.H., & Oh, S. (1987). Developing buyer-seller relationships. *Journal of Marketing*, *51*(4), 11–27.

Ganesan, S. (1994). Determination of long-term orientation in buyer–seller relationships. *Journal of Marketing*, *58*(4), 1–19.

Grönroos, C. (1990). Relationship approach to marketing in service contexts: The marketing and organisational behavior interface. *Journal of Business Research*, *20*(1), 3–11, doi:10.1016/0148-2963(90)90037-e.

Grönroos, C. (1991). The marketing strategy continuum: Towards a marketing concept for the 1990s. *Management Decision*, *29*(1), doi:10.1108/00251749110139106.

Gruen, T.W. (1997). Relationship marketing: The route to marketing efficiency and effectiveness. *Business Horizons*, *40*(6), 32–38. doi:10.1016/s0007-6813(97)90065-3.

Harker, M.J. (1999). Relationship marketing defined? An examination of current relationship marketing definitions. *Marketing Intelligence & Planning*, *17*(1), 13–20. doi:10.1108/02634509910253768.

Jackson, B.B. (1985). *Winning and keeping industrial customers: The dynamics of customer relationships*. Washington, DC: Heath & Company.

Kotler, P., Keller, K.L., Chernev, A., Sheth, J.N., & Shainesh, G. (2022). *Marketing management (16th edn, Indian adaptation)*. New Delhi: Pearson India.

McKenna, R. (1991). *Relationship marketing: Successful strategies for the age of the customers*. Addison-Wesley.

Morgan, R.M., & Hunt, S.D. (1994). The commitment-trust theory of relationship marketing. *Journal of Marketing*, *58*(3), 20–38. doi:10.2307/1252308.

Parvatiyar, A., & Sheth, J.N. (2000). The domain and conceptual foundations of relationship marketing. In J.N. Sheth & A. Parvatiyar (Eds.), *Handbook of relationship marketing* (pp. 3–38). SAGE.

Payne, A. (2000). Relationship marketing: The UK perspective. In J.N. Sheth & A. Parvatiyar (Eds.), *Handbook of relationship marketing* (pp. 39–68). SAGE.

Peppers, D., & Rogers, M. (1993). *The one to one future: Building relationships one customer at a time*. Doubleday.

Reichheld, F.F. (1993). Loyalty-based management. *Harvard Business Review*, *71*(2), 64–73.

Reinartz, W., & Kumar, V. (2002). The mismanagement of customer loyalty. *Harvard Business Review*, *80*(7), 86–94, 125.

Shainesh, G. (2018). CRM: Interview with Kris Gopalakrishnan. Retrieved November 21, 2021, from https://iimbx.iimb.ac.in/catalog/customer-relationship-management/

Sheth, J.N., & Parvatiyar, A. (1995a). Relationship marketing in consumer markets: Antecedents and consequences. *Journal of the Academy of Marketing Science*, *23*(4), 255–271. https://doi.org/10.1177/009207039502300405.

Sheth, J.N., & Parvatiyar, A. (1995b). The evolution of relationship marketing. *International Business Review*, *4*(4), 397–418. https://doi.org/10.1016/0969-5931(95)00018-6.

Storbacka, K. (2000). Customer profitability: Analysis and design issues. In J.N. Sheth & A., Parvatiyar (Eds.), *Handbook of relationship marketing* (pp. 565–586). SAGE.

TARP. (1986). *Consumer complaint handling in America: An update study*. Washington, DC: United States Office of Consumer Affairs.

Vavra, T.G. (1992). *After-marketing: How to keep customers for life through relationship marketing*. Business One Irwin.

VentureBeat. (2014, July 19). The Hard Rock Cafe spotlights how it uses online marketing tech to drive growth. Retrieved November 19, 2021, from https://venturebeat.com/marketing/the-hard-rock-cafe-spotlights-how-it-uses-online-marketing-tech-to-drive-growth/.

Yasin, M.M., Alavi, J., Kunt, M., & Zimmerer, T.W. (2004). TQM practices in service organisations: An exploratory study into the implementation, outcome and effectiveness. *Managing Service Quality*, *14*(5), 377–389. doi:10.1108/09604520410557985.

CHAPTER 3

Building Customer Relationships

CHAPTER OVERVIEW

This chapter will help you understand:

1. Relationship building as a process and approaches to build strong customer relationships
2. The 'ladder of loyalty' to convert a prospect into a customer, and ultimately into a partner
3. Different types of bonds – financial, social, customised and structural – that help companies build strong and long-lasting relationships with customers
4. Zero customer defections and its impact on long-term profitability
5. A Customer Relationship Management (CRM) framework that examines the three stages of building and managing long-term customer relationships – initiation, development and maintenance.

Vignette

JetBlue, a US-based low-cost airline, is known for its courteous and supportive customer service and has won several J.D. Power customer service awards. JetBlue uses social media to connect with customers and solve their queries in real time to improve customer service. The business gained attention when, on 14 February 2007, a sudden failure of the reservation systems led to the cancellation of several hundred flights and left thousands of passengers stranded at a number of airports. This could have been a public relations disaster but JetBlue's CEO swiftly released an unscripted video on YouTube apologising for the inability to rectify the problem. In addition, the company announced its 'Customer Bill of Rights' with a statement listing all the measures it was taking to remedy the service interruptions. These steps enhanced positivity from the customers and boosted trust and loyalty. On another occasion, the social media team responded promptly to a tweet from a customer who had left his sunglasses at a check-in counter. They liaised with the local team to recover the sunglasses and return them to the customer before he boarded the flight.

DOI: 10.4324/9781003518174-4

These customer-friendly actions have enabled JetBlue to build a strong brand in the competitive airline industry. JetBlue has a considerable fan base on social media channels, with more than a million followers on YouTube and X (formerly Twitter) and over 500,000 on Facebook. This fan base also facilitates two-way communication to build long-term relationships.

OPENING CASE

Profitable customer relationships are frequently formed long before a sale occurs. Innovative businesses can also develop learning relationships with prospective customers through engagement. Consider luxury automobiles. Companies such as BMW are shifting away from purchasing lists and focusing more on cultivating those prospects who already know about the brand as they found that individuals interacting with the company before making a purchase are up to three times more likely to become buyers than those found through other channels.

Luxury car makers like BMW therefore now track the paths a consumer takes before he buys. Did he request a brochure or visit a dealer? Did he attend an event, such as one of the company's 'Ultimate Driving Experience' rallies? Did he build a car online at the virtual centre? BMW then parses the relevant data based on customer interactions and across touchpoints collected. Certain combinations of actions indicate a higher propensity to purchase; and, once identified, the marketing team allocates more resources to those prospects with a higher propensity score. If the timing is right, BMW takes the conversation forward with a series of personalised communications via email, direct mail and personal invitations to attend special events. Each interaction and conversation helps the company understand the customer's future requirements and preferences – a critical step toward converting prospects into customers.

After a prospect makes a purchase, the company continues to nurture the relationship. Dealership personnel receive training on customer-focused processes for 'handing over the keys each year'. Upon receipt of their vehicles, customers are presented with a welcome kit inviting them to delve deeper into the 'ownership experience' – an invitation to 'customise and manage' how they interact with BMW. This empowers the customer by limiting BMW's communications to the channel and frequency of contact the customer prefers. Buyers receive a customer satisfaction call two weeks after the purchase. New owners provide feedback on their dealership, delivery and purchasing experiences, which the company relays directly to the dealers. The dealer then responds to any grievances. This results in converting complaints into opportunities to listen to customers and quickly respond to their post-sale needs.

In sum, mapping and managing the customer journey enables the company to develop profitable relationships at every stage of the sales process, from prospect to repeat customer. The company discovered that individuals who spend time and are immersed in the BMW experience are significantly more likely to purchase than those who are left alone (Velázquez, 2024)

RELATIONSHIP BUILDING AS A PROCESS

Effective CRM is established on the basis of an iterative process of learning and customisation. Companies interact with their customers and learn about them – who they are, what they want, how much they buy and when they buy, and how much it costs to serve them. By analysing this data, companies can identify profitable and potentially profitable customers. This analysis would also show that many loyal customers contribute disproportionately to profitability. Therefore, it is imperative for companies to retain those customers. To do so, companies must learn to tailor their offerings to suit the needs and wants of these profitable customers by customising some aspect of the marketing mix of their offerings as each customer has specific needs and expectations from a company. The business should aim to treat each customer in a way that reinforces the trust that the customer has shown in the business. Based on cumulative learning from multiple interactions with the customer, the company's offerings can better match customer needs, which in turn should lead to greater perceived value for the customer and create a strong switching barrier. As a result, we observe an iterative learning process that aids in developing a relationship between a company and its customers. This process is also visible in relationship building with other stakeholders such as intermediaries and suppliers.

Peppers and Rogers (1993), proponents of one-to-one marketing, proposed the IDIC framework – identify, differentiate, interact and customise – to explain the four key steps to converting existing customers into loyal customers.

Identify

This step requires the company to locate and contact many customers directly and gain as much detail about them as possible – including names, addresses, phone numbers, account details (where relevant), habits, preferences, etc. – as this kind of information cannot be collected easily or through a one-time questionnaire-based activity. Although most organisations possess a great deal of customer data, it is typically dispersed across different databases in various departments. Several banks have therefore successfully integrated customer-related data into their core banking solutions by creating unique customer identity files that are linked to multiple product offerings used by customers. Every interaction with the customer through any channel should be seen as an opportunity to learn about them, and this knowledge must be used to serve them better.

Differentiate

Customers can be differentiated based on their needs and the value they represent. The value represented indicates the customer's worth to the company – the more valuable they are, the more the company should be interested in retaining them. Although the most straightforward measure of customer value is the revenue they contribute, this can become tricky if the cost to serve high-revenue customers is also high. Thus, the ideal measure of customer value is profit contribution, which in many cases is difficult to measure as the cost to serve customers is difficult to isolate due to the sharing of overheads and the use of common services.

Some customers need fairly standard products and services, while others have highly specialised needs. Customers with specialised needs create opportunities for customisation, which helps meet these needs and ties customers in for mutual benefit. Differentiation should help the company tailor its offerings to each customer to reflect the customer's values and needs.

Interact

The purpose of interaction is to learn more about customers, starting with the most valuable. These interactions can happen when the customer is making a purchase or using a service, or even when making a complaint. Interactions can be through formal surveys, telephone communication or self-service channels such as the internet, call centres or automated teller machines (ATMs) in banking services. They should add to the existing knowledge about customers, and should be done in a cost-effective manner by using the lower-cost electronic channels. The learning relationship becomes smarter with each interaction.

Customise

The last step in the IDIC framework is the most critical as it builds on all the learning about customers to offer them real value by tailoring some aspect of the service related to a product or even mass customisation of the product. When customisation is based on what the customer has indicated during interactions with the company/brand, it improves the company's ability to fit the product and service to this customer's exact needs. This helps the customer enjoy a high level of convenience, which a competitor cannot easily duplicate without the customer having to spend time and effort teaching the competitor the lessons already learned by the existing company.

Despite overlaps across the steps, the IDIC framework is helpful in understanding the process for building relationships with existing customers. It is equally important to know the stages through which a prospect becomes a customer and then a loyal customer. Not all customers necessarily progress through these four stages as there will be drop-offs at any stage.

Vodafone, a leading telecom player, employed this process to improve its operations and gain an edge over competitors. It implemented the initiatives outlined above and changed the way it operated to adapt to the market and build on its CRM activities. Seth Godin describes the complete process in his best-selling book *Permission Marketing* (1999, p. 43):

> There's a continuum that runs from strangers to friends to customers to loyal customers to former customers. One-to-one marketing is focused on turning customers into loyal

> customers, and on preventing them from becoming former customers. The big idea behind permission marketing is that this continuum begins before thc person spends the first dollar. It's silly to ask strangers to become customers without spending the time to teach them, to gain their trust, and to have a mutually beneficial dialogue instead of a narcissistic monologue.

The concept of the *loyalty ladder* will be used to examine the entire relationship-building process.

The Ladder of Loyalty

The loyalty ladder depicts the stages a prospect goes through to become a customer, a client and, eventually, a partner (Figure 3.1).

1 **Prospect:** A prospect is a person in the retail market or a firm in the business market that meets the conditions of the marketer's target definition. For example, a cellular service provider might segment the market and provide a unique offering to executives of large public sector banks.

2 **Customer:** When a prospect is attracted by the marketer's offering and purchases the product/service, she becomes a customer.

3 **Client:** A customer becomes a client when she purchases the product or service more than once. While a customer may make the initial purchase as a trial or test, a client is someone who makes a repeat purchase. The trial was likely a satisfactory experience for the client.

   In many buying situations, customers turn into clients due to the nature of the product or service. For example, the purchase of a durable product like a PC, TV or car may result

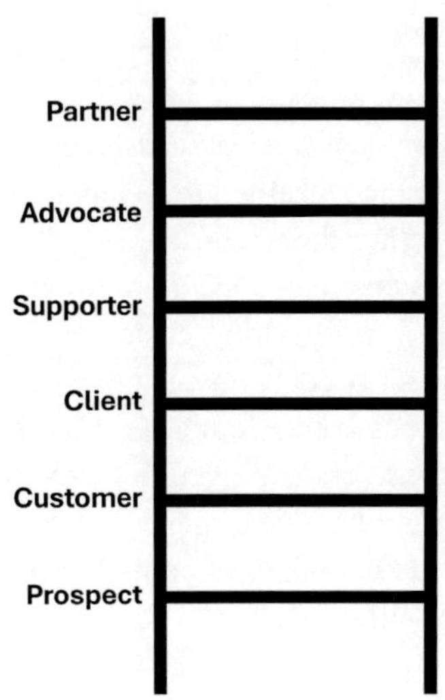

FIGURE 3.1 The Ladder of Loyalty

in the customer becoming a client of an associated service, such as maintenance. Some services – such as banking, insurance, clubs, mobile services, etc. – are 'membership' services, which makes it difficult (if not impossible) for customers to switch. Prospects may spend a lot of time and effort searching for information, making comparisons and selecting. Subsequently, once they open a bank account, take out an insurance policy, join a club or sign up for a mobile connection, they plan to continue using and patronising that company/service. Therefore, in these categories, the customer and the organisation are likely to have a longer relationship.

However, in many buying situations (such as hospitality, airlines or fast-moving consumer goods), customers can switch after a trial period – i.e. testing a product/service and then deciding to use a competitor's offering. The nature of the product or service does not automatically ensure repeat purchases. It is the customer's satisfaction with the trial that determines repurchase.

Customers can also become clients when organisations cross-sell multiple products to an existing customer. Financial services company Wells Fargo is a good example. On average this firm sells more than four of its services to each customer – that is, over twice the industry average. This has ensured that customers who use multiple services stay with the firm, thus generating higher profits.

However, the transition from customer to client is not guaranteed. For example, a customer who visits a department store and purchases a pair of trousers, some shoes and a shirt might never return.

4 **Supporter**: Satisfied customers become supporters when they spread positive word of mouth (WOM) about an offering. WOM is a potent source of information amplified in the digital age through social media. A client becomes a supporter when he is satisfied with the offering and recommends it to his friends, relatives and acquaintances. This positive WOM has a tremendous impact as it helps the company gain new customers. WOM has therefore been identified as the most influential source of information in converting prospects into customers. For example, hygiene product company Dettol successfully used this approach in China, resulting in increased brand awareness and sales.
5 **Advocate**: An advocate is a supporter who proactively works with a company to improve its products and services in addition to referrals that lead to sales. When developing new products, software companies regularly depend on feedback from the lead users of their clients during the Beta test phase. This is also the case in new product development situations in many industrial firms that install a prototype in a client's premises for use and feedback, which helps in improvements. In these situations, interaction between the customer and the company is on a much higher plane. There is a sharing of vital information, more comfort and high levels of trust and commitment between the parties. Advocates have a significant influence on other customers. Companies such as Apple, Microsoft and Sony have leveraged such advocates to promote their products.
6 **Partner**: Advocates become partners when they become actively involved in the company's decisions. Any relationship that attempts to develop customer value through partnering activities will likely create greater bonds between customers and marketers. In many cases, joint investments result in structural bonding. Examples include the kind of relationship that exists between Procter & Gamble (P&G), a leading consumer

goods marketer, and Walmart, the world's largest retailer. This relationship is characterised by genuine partnership. For example, Walmart shares scanner data from checkouts in its 4500+ stores with P&G, which shows the movement of products and the status of stocks in outlets, and thus helps the joint teams of P&G and Walmart executives plan replenishments. It also helps P&G plan its production, better manage its production runs and keep its inventories low as it receives actual sales data and no longer depends on sales forecasts. Overall, this reduces the costs for P&G. Walmart also gains as it does not have to keep inventories, gets faster replenishments, incurs lower costs and can pass savings on to customers, thus reinforcing its ethos of 'everyday low prices'.

Consider the relationship between Federal Express and IBM, where Federal Express stocks IBM's spare parts in its own warehouses and delivers them across the world on instructions from IBM's service personnel. The reliability and efficiency of FedEx's service and operations due to specialisation and particular processes make using the company cheaper and faster than the alternative of in-house processing by IBM.

The marketer's emphasis during the first two steps in the loyalty ladder – namely, prospects and customers – is customer attraction, while the emphasis in the subsequent steps is on developing and enhancing the relationships. Therefore, relationship marketing goes far beyond repeat purchases. Repeat purchases are only a precursor to relationships. Greater value is added through the involvement of customers, sharing of information and bonding between customers and marketers. The greater the enhancement of the relationship through bonding, the more committed customers will be to the relationship and, hence, the less likely they are to patronise competitors.

Let us now explore the concept of bonding.

BONDING FOR CUSTOMER RELATIONSHIPS

Berry and Parasuraman (1991, pp. 136–142) identified four levels of bond:

1 **Financial:** Volume and frequency rewards, bundles and cross-selling, and stable pricing
2 **Social:** Personal relationships, continuous relationships and social bond customers
3 **Customisation:** Customer intimacy, mass customisation and anticipation/innovation
4 **Structural:** Integrated information systems, joint investments, and shared processes and equipment.

Level 1 – Financial Bonds

Financial bonds tie-in customers in primarily through financial incentives – lower prices for higher purchase volumes or customers who have patronised the firm over time. Loyalty programmes such as frequent flyer schemes and reward programmes of hotels and credit cards are examples of financial bonding through volume and frequency rewards.

Bundling and cross-selling options are offered for software-as-a-service (SaaS) subscriptions, credit cards, and mobile and internet data services through which customers can buy other services from the same provider or someone else at a lower cost. Companies also offer the assurance of stable prices or lower price increases than those paid by new customers to retain their customers. Some retail chains, such as US consumer electronics company Best Buy, offer price guarantees where they match competitors' lowest price for any product.

One of the biggest disadvantages of financial bonds is that they can be easily imitated. They also attract many price-sensitive customers, who will switch to a cheaper option at the first opportunity as financial bonds are weak. In addition, when industry players resort to this type of bonding, it creates a negative spiral that depresses the industry's profitability.

Level 2 – Social Bonds

Marketers build social bonds with customers by viewing them as 'clients', not merely nameless faces. They find ways to keep in touch and interact with them to identify their changing needs and offer solutions. It is easy to visualise social bonds of the personal kind in the context of relationships between clients and professional service providers (doctors, tax consultants, accountants, etc.) and personal service providers (e.g. hairdressers, fitness coaches, babysitters). As information sharing and rapport building are necessary for providing such services, these interactions cement social, interpersonal bonds.

Social bonding opportunities also exist in business markets where account/relationship managers work very closely with the client's team, which helps build bonds that transcend commercial transactions. Continuous relationships are provided to customers when companies have stable, long-standing dealers who bring local market knowledge and maintain close relationships with customers. Social bonding often develops among customers instead of relationships between company and customer. This can happen in settings where customers interact with each other – e.g. in a club, gym, library, etc. It can also be facilitated by marketers such as the Harlel Davidson's Harley Owners Group (H.O.G.), the Saturn Performance Club and various clubs promoted by car maker Volkswagen. These clubs create opportunities to share common interests and participate in activities that bring customers together and help retain them through the social bonds they build among themselves. Social bonds are relatively more difficult to break and, hence, more enduring.

Level 3 – Customisation Bonds

Intimate knowledge of customers and their needs developed through learning relationships is beneficial in retaining valuable customers. Customer intimacy connotes that the customer actively shares information during interactions and contributes to the marketer's efforts to customise products, services or any other aspect of the marketing mix. Every member of the organisation uses each opportunity to interact with customers to learn new things about them and add to the organisational knowledge. For example, Marriott Hotels knows the likes, dislikes and special habits of its over 5 million customers. This information is shared across its hotels worldwide. If you have stayed at Marriott Chicago and are visiting Singapore with a reservation at the Marriott, the receptionist could surprise you with your favourite welcome drink. She might also give you your favourite room with a swimming pool view. This information comes from the data input by Marriott employees when you stayed in Chicago.

Mass customisation refers to using flexible processes and organisational structures to produce varied and often individually customised products and services at the price of standardised, mass-produced alternatives (Pine 1993). It does not mean providing customers with endless choices, but rather tailored products or services with little additional effort and cost using production and communication technologies. For example, at particular Levi's outlets, customers have the option of buying jeans made to their specifications by providing their own measurements instead of buying their preferred 501s with a standard 36-inch waist. These measurements are passed to the factory, which will make a customised pair of 501s for delivery within a week. Similarly, the National Industrial Bicycle Company, Japan could potentially assemble over 11 million varieties by leveraging its flexible manufacturing systems and delivering custom bicycles within two weeks. My CNN.com and myBBC.com are examples of online information services that help users personalise their specific requirements.

Lenskart is an online marketer of customised eyewear, including spectacles, sunglasses and contact lenses. It collects customer information by asking specific questions to understand their requirements. After uploading their prescription for glasses, customers can select the colour and style of frame by uploading an image of their face. Checking various combinations to suit their face helps finalise the choice and cost. The company then delivers the spectacles to the customer. Its 'no questions asked' returns policy gives customers the confidence to buy online.

The ability to customise, in combination with customer intimacy, can be used to anticipate customer needs and recommend innovative solutions to meet those needs. Anticipation brings an element of pleasant surprise – the WOW factor! It is like being offered a glass of cold water when you walk into an office on a hot summer afternoon. Amazon uses collaborative filtering techniques to anticipate customer needs. When a customer buys a book on one-to-one marketing, Amazon also provides them with information on similar books, such as Godin's *Permission Marketing*, bought by other customers who also bought the one-to-one marketing book. Amazon's collaborative filtering technique even uses the knowledge gained by the purchase behaviour of customers with similar profiles and requirements to anticipate the needs of a prospect who registers to use the service and, in the process, shares information.

Customisation bonds are also difficult to break as the customer would need to start from scratch and teach the new potential provider even if the provider has the ability to meet the customer's requirements. However, firms must be careful about trying to establish customisation bonds. For example, some customers are very clear about the products they need, and do not appreciate being prompted to make other purchases. It is therefore important to understand the psychological profile of the customer before providing customized offers.

Level 4 – Structural Bonds

The partnership between Walmart and Procter & Gamble, described earlier, is an example of structural bonding through integrated information systems, joint investments, and shared processes.

Financial services company American Express (Amex) bonds with customers through its debit, credit and charge cards and travel/tourist-related services (TRS), which take care of all the business travel and stay needs of executives of its corporate clients. TRS personnel, in many cases operating out of the client's premises, arrange visas, passports and bookings for airlines, taxis and hotels at special prices through arrangements with partner organisations, thus, providing a 'one-stop shop' and a hassle-free experience for the executives as well as the client organisations. All expenses are paid for through the Amex card when the executive travels; but the service does not stop here. Amex then consolidates travel and entertainment (T&E) expenses and presents them to the client organisation in the format that its accounting/financial system requires – for example with regard to executive, location or budgeted vs. actual expenses. Thus, by meeting the requirements of the executive, the personnel and administration department and the accounts department of the client organisation, Amex provides good service value and builds strong structural bonds with its customers.

Federal Express ties customers in with PowerShips – free computers at client sites to store addresses and shipping data, print mailing labels and help track packages. The client thus saves time and can keep track of daily shipping records.

Structural bonds are the strongest of the four types and, hence, the most difficult to break. As organisations move from Level 1 to Level 4, they will observe the following:

- The bonds become stronger. Structural bonds are stronger than customisation bonds, and customisation bonds are stronger than social bonds and financial bonds.
- As the bonds become stronger, customer loyalty increases and the opportunities and scope for reaping the benefits of relationship marketing increase.

In business-to-business contexts, we also see other kinds of bond, such as legal, planning and technical bonds.

ZERO CUSTOMER DEFECTIONS

We have discussed various types of bonds and their impact on customer loyalty. Businesses engage their customers at multiple levels to ensure they do not defect. In the 1980s, the quality movement emphasised 'zero defects'. Now, we are on our way to achieving 'zero defections' (Reichheld & Sasser, 1990; Reichheld, 1996). Concern about reducing and eliminating customer attrition emerged from studies that indicated the following:

- Customers are profitable over time. The longer they stay with an organisation, the more profitable they are likely to be.
- Across industries, profits can increase by 35–85% by increasing customer retention by only 5%.

Figure 3.2 indicates that the net present value (NPV) of profits from a customer is in the shape of an exponential curve – i.e. profits from a customer increase exponentially

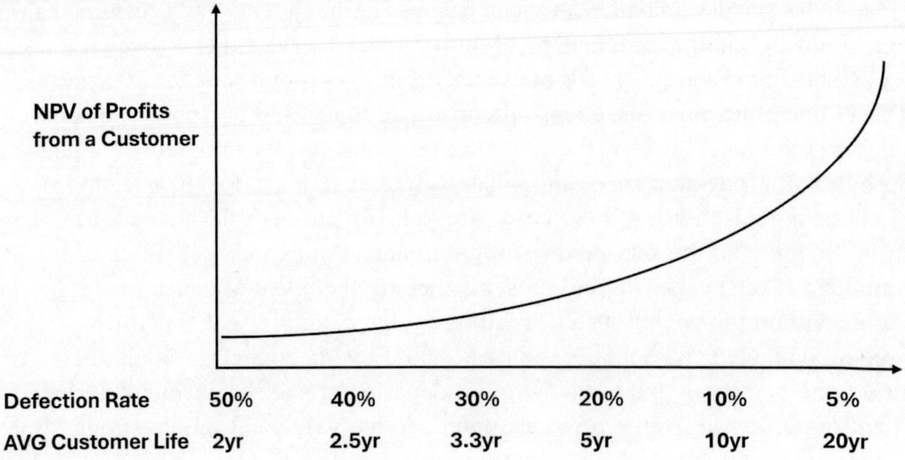

FIGURE 3.2 Customer Defection Curve

over time. If retention is important, it is essential to understand why customers leave and how defections can be reduced. Studies show that about 70% of the customers defect due to the perceived indifference of their current provider (Figure 3.3). Perceived indifference includes lack of proper response to queries about service, inefficient complaint handling, lack of courtesy, etc.

In service businesses where customers repeatedly come back and ensure a continuous stream of revenue – such as hospitality, retailing, telecom, finance, etc. – customer defection has significant implications on profitability. Unfortunately, this gets hidden because most organisations do not measure customer defection. This is also true for product markets which are commodified due to technological parity, such as with personal computers and durables like household appliances and consumer electronics. In such markets services attached to

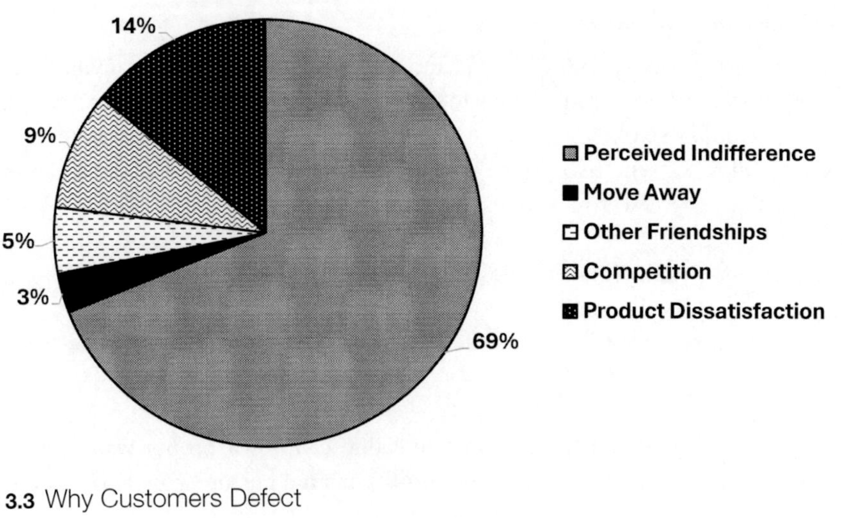

FIGURE 3.3 Why Customers Defect

the product (financing, after-sales service, etc.) emerge as major sources of differentiation. Superiority in services is sustainable as they are relatively more difficult to copy.

In 83% of cases, customers shift to competitive offerings on account of issues that are under control of the company. However, not all defections have the same impact on the company –attrition of valuable customers has a disproportionate impact. Customers who defect can be broadly categorised as doing so because of price, product, service, market, technological or organisational factors.

1 Price defectors are customers who switch to a competitor offering a cheaper price. In most cases, these customers are compulsive 'bargain hunters', so one may be better off without them. However, in some cases, customers do not see value in patronising their existing service provider as a competitor is offering a similar or better service at cheaper rates. It is also important to note that some firms inadvertently encourage this behaviour by providing special 'offers' to new customers only and not to existing customers. In such cases, an existing customer may feel neglected and cheated.
2 Product defectors are former customers who are dissatisfied with their existing product. This may be due to a bad experience with the product performance or the availability of better products.
3 Service defectors are former customers who are dissatisfied with the service. Findings from the Profit Impact of Market Strategy (PIMS) project indicate that: perceived good service providers could charge an average of 9–10% more for the same basic product or service; they grow twice as fast as their competitors; and perceived service leaders improve their market share at an average of 6% a year, whereas perceived poor service providers lose as much as 2% market share per year (Buzzell & Gale, 1987, pp. 6–17).

   Studies by the Technical Assistance for Research Programs (TARP, 1986) showed the following:

   - Around 96% of unhappy customers never bother to complain.
   - On average, each dissatisfied customer will tell 15 other people.
   - In contrast, each satisfied customer will tell no more than six other people.
   - Smart organisations never allow an irate customer to repeat their complaint to more than one employee in the company.
   - Some 71% of customers feel their complaint has been handled satisfactorily if they only need to deal with one individual, falling to 61% if more than one employee is involved in solving the problem.
   - If a customer complaint is handled well, 95% of customers will continue to do business with the organisation.

   These findings indicate that the impact of service dissatisfaction is normally very high, and that customers are given enough opportunity for organisations to retain them.
4 Market defectors have stopped patronising a product or service provider as they have shifted to another location, city, state or country. This group also includes users who no longer use/need the products/services – for example, kids outgrow toys or even the services of a paediatrician.
5 Technology defectors are those who switch to other, normally superior, technologies. Examples include customers shifting from fossil fuels to the use of electric or hybrid vehicles, or from a laptop to a tablet, etc.

6 Organisational defectors – individuals who belong to a group (organisation, club, association, etc.) – may shift to an alternate supplier/provider when their group switches, even though some of them may be satisfied with the existing service. This can happen in the case of an organisation switching to a new broadband service provider.

Every organisation, especially in the service industry, can plan a customer retention programme to reduce customer defection by following the process outlined below.

1 Measure customer retention – This is a valuable beginning. Start by looking at how many customers were lost in the previous year. In many cases it is difficult to identify which customers have defected as, typically, customers do not stop doing business altogether. For example, I have held an account with a local bank for over five years. A competing bank opens a branch in the neighbourhood and I open an account there. However it is unlikely that I will shift all my business to the new bank immediately. Like me, most customers defect slowly. They start by reducing their volume of business. At the end of the year my account may be still alive with the minimum balance, but I start doing all my business transactions with the new bank. So, one must be careful in defining customer retention – a dead account with a minimal balance must be treated as a lost customer. Once the quantum and percentage of customer attrition have been found, calculate the cost of these lost customers using the net present value (NPV) of future cash flows if these customers had stayed for the entire 'customer life'.
2 Interview former customers – This helps identify why customers defect. It is helpful to get a customer's view on the reasons behind their switch as these insights can help set up systems and procedures to eliminate the root causes of defection. Thus, an 'exit interview' with customers may help the organisation avoid having many ex-customers.
3 Analyse complaints and service data as these also help identify recurring themes with customers. Complaints are often due to systemic errors and would need a review of the service and complaint handling process. In several instances, the root cause analysis leads to a redesign of the service delivery process.
4 Identify switching barriers – This is the final task, and may include convenient operating hours, speed of transactions or tie-in through multiple offerings. For example, telecom service providers offer multiple benefits to subscribers to form groups, such as through friends and family rate plans and closed user groups. Such schemes help retain customers who sign up to benefit the group.

CRM FRAMEWORK

We will now tie up the above discussions with a framework that connects the various stages of relationship development to the psychological processes during each phase (Figure 3.4). Mookerjee and Shainesh (2000, pp. 31–32) indicate the following:

> In competitive markets, even satisfied customers switch or defect to competitive offers. As loyal customers are more profitable for any organisation, there is a need to

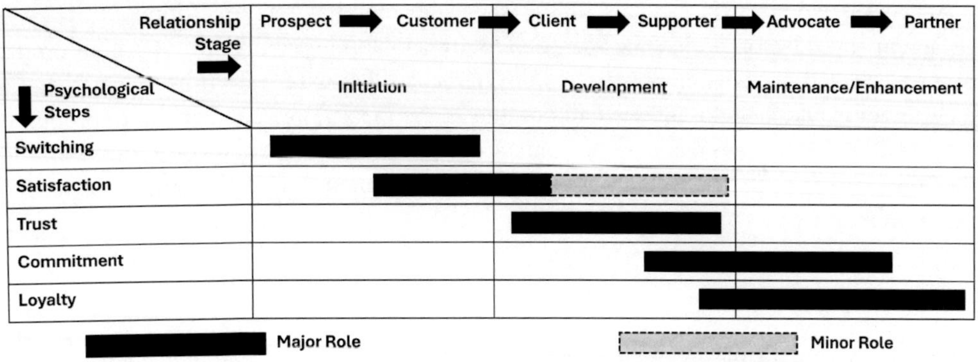

FIGURE 3.4 Psychological Steps across Relationship Stages

> identify better predictors of loyalty. Relationship strength indicators like trust, satisfaction, and commitment are better predictors of loyalty. By including these parameters in customer satisfaction surveys, managers can modify service delivery to focus on customer loyalty.

In some instances, relationships deteriorate to the point of dissolution. Our emphasis, however, is on the initial formative, development and maintenance or enhancement stages. You will notice that these stages also correspond to the loyalty ladder discussed previously. Let us now look at each of the psychological steps.

Switching

Switching is very common in the initial stages of a relationship process. A prospect attracted by a company's marketing programme may try out its product or service offering and become a customer. However, the initial interactions and experiences will determine whether or not the customer is willing to continue. In the health and fitness industry, for example, a club might provide a personal trainer when a customer signs up in order to encourage the customer to start using the service. Subsequently, the customer is signed up for an extended period. This prevents switching, at least in the short term.

Satisfaction

Satisfaction is a complex emotion that depends on the nature of the offer, expectations and usage situation. Customers are satisfied when a product or service's performance matches or exceeds their expectations. Hence, it is also important for marketers to manage customer expectations as setting a very high level of expectation is likely to lead to customer dissatisfaction for the same level of performance. Satisfied customers are more likely to continue their patronage. Therefore, satisfaction is an important intermediate step in the relationship-building process, and many of the satisfied customers will become clients.

Successful companies, such as online shoe and clothing retailer Zappos, go beyond satisfaction and develop a customer-centric culture as adopting a customer-first culture and customer-oriented systems empowers employees to go the extra mile. Firms that focus on the customer experience do not use call volume as the measure of contact centre productivity because such a system enables the contact centre executive to focus on issue resolution rather than productivity. Customers reward Zappos for their excellent experience through repeat purchases.

Trust

Satisfaction over multiple interactions leads to a stage where the customer begins to have faith in a company's offering and consistent performance. Satisfaction then leads to trust when certain more antecedent conditions are fulfilled, such as shared values and goals, dependence based on stable expectation/perception of performance and perceived switching costs. Trust is the willingness to rely on an exchange partner in whom one has confidence. It exists when a party has confidence in an exchange partner's reliability and integrity and when they share common goals and values. It is a consequence of interdependence due to a stable customer experience of expectations being exceeded and of the existing firm providing the best value, so that switching is not seen as a better option. Instead, helping the firm improve its performance by working together on mutual needs (sharing goals) seems a better option.

The concept of trust is common among marketers in the packaged goods industry, and trust is used to build brand loyalty. As Niall FitzGerald, former chairman of Unilever, stated in India's *Economic Times* of 24 October 2001:

> In order to function at all, human societies rely on the existence of trust. Good brands invite trust, earn trust, honor trust and reward trust. Good brands guard their reputations with their lives, and if by accident they transgress, they apologise with grace and true humility – quickly. Every change that we face in marketing today makes the establishment of trust and the maintenance of trust more necessary and more valuable, because for consumers the mounting complexities of choice will make the need for trust more urgent. It is a promising future for brands that live up to and deliver on these expectations.

Commitment

Commitment to a relationship is defined as an enduring desire to maintain a valued relationship. Therefore, commitment exists only when the relationship is considered important. It can be operationalised using two dimensions: (1) attitude towards mutual interaction; and (2) the formation of bonds, which may be legal, planning, knowledge, social, technical and structural.

Trust and commitment are key variables because they encourage marketers to work at the following:

- preserving relationship investments with partners/clients, and
- resisting short-term gains, which may be lesser than expected benefits of remaining in the relationship.

They also view potentially high-risk actions as acceptable since they expect that partners will not act opportunistically. Further, both key variables should be present for the existence of loyal behaviour patterns such as increasing purchases, referrals and sharing of information.

Loyalty

Loyalty is not simply repeat buying. Loyalty also includes future purchase intentions, price sensitivity, complaining and referral behaviour – viz. positive word of mouth. In terms of measurement of loyalty or loyalty-related behaviour, typical questions would concern:

- intentions regarding the next purchase,
- whether a change in supplier would be considered if the price is increased,
- the number and intensity of complaints,
- the tendency to talk about the supplier to other clients, and
- the desire to share positive experiences (word of mouth).

While the CRM framework is useful in understanding the progression of a relationship through seemingly discrete psychological steps, it must be kept in mind that not all buyer–seller relationships necessarily go through them sequentially. In some cases clients may exhibit a lot of loyalty-related behaviour when they are satisfied with the seller's performance over multiple interactions.

Following examination of the various concepts, approaches and methods of building customer relationships, we should now understand how managers try to implement them.

CLOSING CASE

Titan Company's 'Tanishq' is one of India's most successful jewellery brands. The company's initial foray into the fragmented market for gold items in the early 1990s, with contemporary designs, did not meet with much success. Customers traditionally bought gold artefacts as a store of value (investment) and preferred to buy 22-carat items from family jewellers, so Tanishq's 18-carat offerings were perceived as being of low quality. In the late 1990s, Tanishq created a powerful image of trust with its 'Karatmeter' campaign, which invited customers to bring their old jewellery to the company's stores to get its purity tested for free. Many customers were disappointed when they found that their old jewellery, purchased from family jewellers, was of lower quality than the promised 22 carats. Tanishq then offered an attractive 'Impure to Pure' scheme for gold items, whereby customers could bring in jewellery that was higher than 19 but lower than 22 carats and exchange it for Tanishq's 22-carat jewellery by just paying manufacturing fees.

In addition to winning the trust of millions of customers, Tanishq soon emerged as a strong alternative to traditional jewellers, with its better-quality products, aesthetic designs and outstanding retailing experience. The company adopted an exclusive customer-centric programme, the 'Tanishq Way of Life', which involved each store employee focusing on customers and providing them with an outstanding experience, from entering to exiting the store (Shainesh, 2017). They concentrated on making the store experience memorable and distinctive through activities such as greeting customers, understanding their requirements, demonstrating the products, closing the deal and billing. The training programme for store employees is fine-tuned by incorporating customer feedback. Research was conducted to understand customers' in-store expectations and experiences. These insights helped the company learn that customers wished to be received with a smile and cheerfulness in the stores, whether or not they made a purchase. These initiatives enabled the brand to consistently deliver an outstanding in-store experience even though most Tanishq outlets are run by franchisees. The company also leverages a digital experience platform to strengthen its relationships with over 10 million customers enrolled in 'Encircle' – Titan's unified loyalty scheme (Kotler, et al. 2022).

SUMMARY

In this chapter we viewed relationship building as a process because every relationship has a time dimension. Relationships are built over time, and companies can build learning relationships with valuable customers so that every interaction becomes an opportunity to make the company smarter and better at serving the customer.

The 'ladder of loyalty' helped us understand the stages of converting a prospect into a partner. Different types of bonds were explored to help companies build relationships of varying strength and durability. The concept of 'zero customer defections' helped us understand a parameter that is not usually captured by a company's financial statements but has a significant impact on its long-term profitability. Finally, we tied up the discussions with a CRM framework that links the psychological steps with the relationship progression.

In today's competitive market, businesses must excel in building and maintaining profitable customer relationships. A successful strategy includes a deep understanding of customers' needs and goals, continually innovating products, focusing on effective communication and creating rewarding loyalty schemes.

Industry Best Practices

Understanding Customers' Goals and Needs

- **Gaining Insight:** Use data analytics and feedback to understand your clients' needs and expectations in depth. This is about knowing not just what they need now but predicting what they will need in the future.

- **Delivering Value:** Aim to provide maximum value with your products or services by aligning them closely with what your clients are looking for, possibly through customisation or innovative pricing models.

Product Innovation

- **Ongoing Improvement and Innovation:** Stay ahead of the curve by continually improving your offerings and being open to exploring new ideas and technologies to meet changing customer needs.
- **Aligning with Consumer Needs:** Make sure that any new product development is in tune with what your clients currently need and might need down the line. Regular engagement with your client base is crucial for gathering insights that inform innovation.

Effective Communication

- **Clear Communication Strategy:** Develop a strategy that guarantees timely and consistent communication across all platforms to deliver the right message, to the right audience, at the right time. Measuring the impact will be required to make necessary adjustments.
- **Consistent Brand Messaging**: Ensure your brand's messaging is consistent across all communications, from marketing to customer service, to build reliability and trust in your brand.

Rewarding Loyalty

- **Loyalty Programmes:** Create loyalty schemes that offer real, tangible benefits to your loyal customers, from discounts to early access to new products.
- **Relationship-Oriented Culture:** Foster a sense of community around your brand by appreciating customers' engagement and feedback, not just their purchases. This helps build emotional connections and encourages loyalty.

By implementing these best practices, businesses can foster lasting relationships with their customers, thus enhancing retention. Understanding client needs ensures relevance; product innovation keeps the company competitive; effective communication sets the stage for a strong brand presence; and a focus on loyalty maximises customer lifetime value. Together, these strategies provide a solid foundation for sustainable growth.

DISCUSSION QUESTIONS

1. What are the different steps and processes required to develop and maintain relationships with customers?
2. What factors can lead to customers defecting to competitors?
3. What steps should a company take to prevent customer defection?
4. How will you use your understanding of the different psychological stages to strengthen relationships with customers of a retail chain?

REFERENCES

Berry, L.L., & Parasuraman, A. (1991). *Marketing services*. New York: Free Press.

Buzzell, R.D., & Gale, B.T. (1987). *The PIMS principles: Linking strategy to performance*. New York: Free Press.

Godin, S. (1999). *Permission marketing: Turning strangers into friends and friends into customers*. Simon & Schuster.

Kotler, P., Keller, K.L., Chernev, A., Sheth, J.N., & Shainesh, G. (2022). *Marketing management (16th edn, Indian adaptation)*. New Delhi: Pearson India.

Mookerjee, A., & Shainesh, G. (2000). Developing measures for the service quality and relationship strength determinants of customer loyalty. In M. Raghavachari & K.V. Ramani (Eds.), *Delivering service quality: Managerial challenges for the 21st century* (pp. 29–35). New Delhi: Macmillan India.

Peppers, D., & Rogers, M. (1993). *The one-to-one future: Building relationships one customer at a time*. Doubleday.

Reichheld, F.F. (1996, March–April). Learning from customer defections. *Harvard Business Review*, 56–69, https://hbr.org/1996/03/learning-from-customer-defections.

Reichheld, F.F., & Sasser, W.E. (1990). Zero defections: Quality comes to services. *Harvard Business Review*, *68*(5), 105–111.

Shainesh, G. (2017). Tanishq: CRM Interviews on edX, https://bit.ly/3zv8SEH.

TARP. (1986). *Consumer complaint handling in America: An update study*. Washington, DC: United States Office of Consumer Affairs.

Velázquez, A. (2024). BMW customer journey: Car buying journey innovation & evolution. Retrieved July 22, 2024, from https://www.questionpro.com/blog/bmw-customer-journey/.

CHAPTER 4

Economics of Customer Relationship Management

CHAPTER OVERVIEW

This chapter will help you understand:

1. The differences between market share and the share of customers, and the approaches adopted by organisations to enhance consumer centricity
2. The importance of the lifetime value of customers – comparing customer profitability with the company's cost to serve (CTS), lifetime value analysis helps identify a customer's current and potential value
3. The importance of applying activity-based costing (ABC) for a company's customer relationship management (CRM) programmes to manage customers for profits and to develop a deeper understanding of customer value.

Vignette

Carrefour Taiwan was the leading hypermarket chain in 2018, with 126 stores operational in all major cities of the island state. The company offered consumers an omnichannel experience with supermarkets and e-commerce. Almost 85% of Taiwanese households were enrolled in the company's loyalty programme. The CRM team had two key objectives: (1) to encourage current members to shop more; and (2) to attract new members to the loyalty programme. Carrefour Taiwan selected the marketplace model to expand its product offerings without investing in additional stock or logistics while offering its customers endless aisles. Relying on third-party sellers allowed the company to extend its range by offering an expanded choice in categories such as electronics, appliances and white goods that are easier to sell online. The marketplace model allowed the business to remain competitive while enlarging its range by relying on specialised and selected vendors who offered competitive prices and high service quality.

The new platform, with an accessible digital onboarding experience and wider choice, provided quick and more convenient access to Carrefour Taiwan's

DOI: 10.4324/9781003518174-5

vast customer base. The digital marketplace kept current customers happy while encouraging new customers to join the loyalty scheme by offering products and services they wanted. The CRM team focused on personalised communications programmes after assessing its customers' present status and potential. This enabled them to invest in resources based on the expected returns from each customer and segment while lowering the cost of serving them.

OPENING CASE

Asian Paints – Beautiful Homes

Asian Paints, India's largest paint company, has been diversifying its offerings by shifting from 'share of surface' to 'share of space'. The company launched its home décor business in 2013 with modular kitchens, kitchen components and wardrobe solutions. Later, it expanded the product portfolio to include taps, showers and sensor-based products, including bathroom accessories. This enabled the company to broaden its focus from the four walls to the space in between the walls of a home. The company's 'Beautiful Home Stores' carry entire ranges – including kitchen, bath and sanitaryware, lighting, tiles, flooring, fabrics, wallpaper, bedding, rugs, furnishings, furniture, doors and windows – that offer a one-stop solution for customers' home décor needs. Customers use 3D visualisation services to build 3D models of their space by uploading photographs of their rooms and trying out different combinations and customisation options before purchasing.

The company expanded its home painting service in 2021 to offer a convenient, personalised and hassle-free interior design service. Professional execution helps customers create their dream home. The company launched beautifulhomes.com, a content and design editorial microsite on its digital properties, to gain insights by being part of customers' décor-related conversations. Its community of over a million subscribers and followers enable the company to engage directly with them. The decorating service, offered under the company's brand name, is provided by its dealers and executed by contractors. Customers receive a personalised and bespoke interior that meets their requirements and is within their budget and timespan. A professional team manages the entire interior design journey by offering a single point of contact, thus simplifying the process for customers. A Customer Experience Specialist representing the company and based out of the dealer's store oversees the entire project and liaises with all the relevant vendors to ensure a smooth and stress-free experience. The process involves four key stakeholders – the dealer, the decorating contractor/team, the specialist and the company management (which hires, trains and supervises the specialist to manage the service) – to ensure an enjoyable customer experience. This distributed service intervention is creating sustainable business impact and is rapidly being scaled up.

THE EVOLUTION OF MARKETING CONCEPTS

Carrefour Taiwan and Asian Paints underscore the benefits of focusing on customers. However, customer centricity is a relatively recent phenomenon. Marketing practices have evolved dramatically in the last century, with mass marketing coming into vogue in the United States and Europe after the Second World War. As a result of wartime shortages, mass production coupled with mass distribution and communication created a mass consumption society, and the focus of marketing activities was on promoting, pricing and distributing products for the mass market. The emphasis was on products rather than markets, leading companies to adopt organisational forms focused on products. We term this phase *product-centric marketing*. The primary focus was on the production capacity of the company, its product distinctiveness and/or superiority and sales force capability. The prevailing assumptions for advantage were linked to greater production capacities, lower costs, the development of technologically superior products and superior selling skills to attract customers. Some marketing concepts that evolved during this phase include unique selling proposition or point (USP) and brand image.

As more firms entered the market, the resulting increase in product variety rendered mass-market techniques less effective. Gradually, firms started paying more attention to markets rather than products. This shift in the marketing discipline occurred primarily in the late 1950s when the marketing concept was first recognised.

With an increasing emphasis on markets, segmentation was a logical approach. Segmentation suggested a rational and more precise adjustment of products and marketing efforts to match customer requirements. Several demand schedules were now explicitly recognised, whereas only one was recognised before. The shift from a product orientation to a marketing concept led to many changes in marketing thought and practice (Figure 4.1). The concept of market orientation suggested that organisations should focus on the markets they serve. In practice, firms organised around markets and segments – that is, they created segment-based organisations. For example, US telecom giant AT&T divided its marketing department into groups dedicated to household and business markets, with subsequent subdivisions within each market, while technology multinational IBM organised itself into vertical industry-based groups. With increased competition, marketers started defining smaller and smaller segments, including niche segments. One manifestation of this phenomenon was a proliferation of brands and channels. This phase, categorised as *segment-centric marketing*, emphasised gaining competitive advantage through segmentation, targeting and positioning. The concept and practice of positioning emerged during the 1970s to explain how consumers

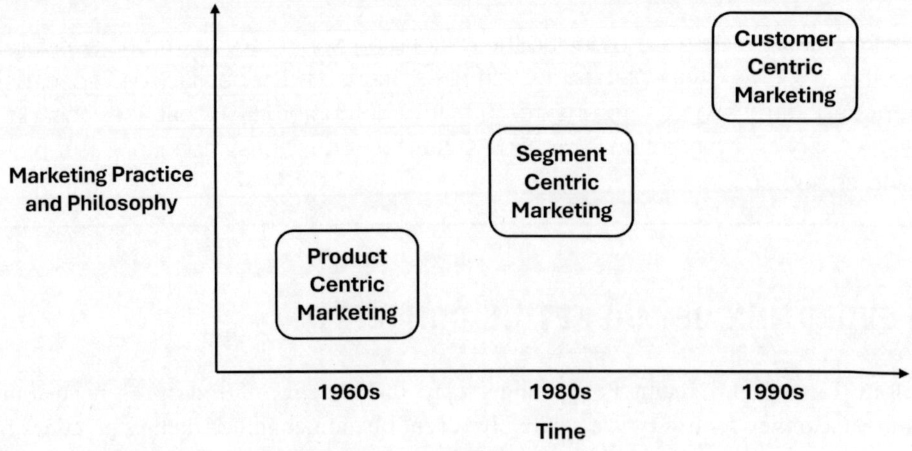

FIGURE 4.1 The Evolution of Marketing Practices, 1960s–1990s

perceived competing brands in their 'mind space', and recommended strategies to win this 'war in the minds'.

The third phase, which emerged in the 1980s, puts the customer at the centre of all organisational activities. *Customer-centric marketing* emphasises understanding and satisfying the needs, wants and resources of individual consumers and customers rather than those of mass markets or market segments (Sheth et al., 2000). In customer-centric marketing, marketers assess each customer individually to determine whether to serve that customer directly or via a third party. Customer-centric marketers also determine whether to create an offering that customises the product and/or some other element(s) of the marketing mix or to standardise the offering. These actions are guided by analysis that seeks to maximise marketing productivity, encompassing both efficiency and effectiveness.

MARKET SHARE VS. SHARE OF CUSTOMERS

Efficiency entails cost–benefit analysis and seeks to maximise the output-to-input ratio of the marketing function for individual customers. Effectiveness entails the enhancement of customer loyalty and 'share of customers'. Customer-centric marketing aims to maximise marketing productivity at the customer level. It focuses on customers' needs, wants and resources as the starting point of the planning process, in contrast to the product-centric approach, which takes the product as the starting point. The customer is visible within such organisations in all key management and operational processes:

- Customer management becomes everyone's priority.
- Customer-centric measures become part of every employee's performance appraisal, and customer feedback is reviewed at the top management level.
- Key result areas (KRAs) include customer flow, customer acquisition costs, lifetime value, customer satisfaction, customer retention and customer share.

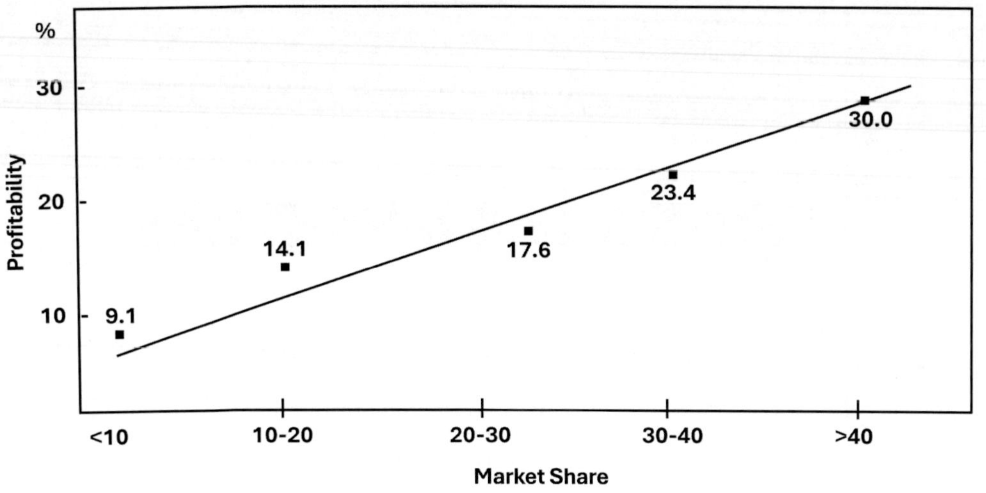

FIGURE 4.2 Profitability vs. Market Share

Adapted from PIMS (Buzzell & Gale, 1987).

Managers have always believed in the dictum that increasing market share improves profitability. A share point increase in many markets is worth tens of millions of dollars. For example, in the US market, a gain of one share point in the soft drinks market is worth $120 million. Studies by the Profit Impact of Market Strategy (PIMS) project across a wide range of industries in over 2600 business units revealed that a company's profitability, measured as pre-tax return on investment (ROI), rises with the *relative market share* of its served market. The PIMS study showed that businesses with market shares of over 40% earn an average ROI of 30%, or three times that of those with market shares under 10%. On average, a 10% difference in market share is accompanied by a difference of about 5% in pre-tax ROI (Figure 4.2).

Other studies have identified low-share businesses that enjoyed pre-tax ROI of 20% or more, specifically in the industrial components or supplies sector. Most industries have a V-shaped relationship between market share and profitability. Typically, we see one or a handful of highly profitable large firms, several profitable small and focused firms, and several medium-size firms with lower profitability.

In all these cases, market share has always been a measure of organisational performance. A market share orientation can be represented by the two dimensions of 'needs satisfied' and 'customers reached' (Figure 4.3). Companies with this orientation will satisfy limited needs through their products and services but try to reach a large segment of potential customers. For example, Amazon started as an online bookstore, with founder Jeff Bezos aiming to make it the world's largest bookstore. To achieve its goal, the company focused on convenience and low prices, and provided a huge selection of books to its customers.

In contrast, a company that adopts a customer share orientation will try to meet all the category-related needs of its customers. This might require the company to embark on new businesses in which it is currently not operating. Consider again the example of Amazon,

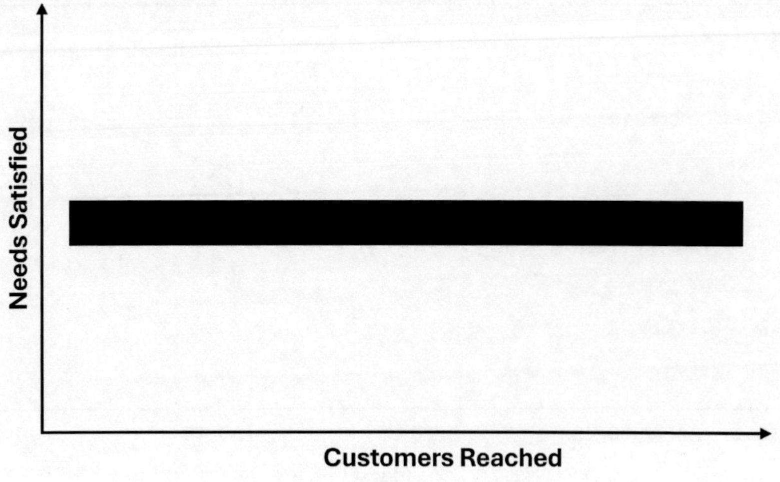

FIGURE 4.3 Customer Needs Satisfied vs. Customers Reached

which realised that a significant portion of its customer base had other similar needs that could easily be fulfilled through its delivery model. The company therefore started selling new products such as games, toys, clothing, electronics and appliances. Similarly, Maruti Suzuki, India's largest car manufacturer (with annual sales of almost 2 million vehicles), meets its customers' personal transport needs.

A typical manufacturer will be categorised as a 'product company' when its products contribute a significant share of its revenues and profits. Maruti Suzuki had a very strong product focus in its first two decades. A typical purchaser of Maruti's small car in India incurs various significant expenses over the car's estimated seven-year lifespan, as shown in Table 4.1. Expenses

TABLE 4.1 Typical Customer Expenses Related to Car Purchase/Ownership

Item and Expense (Rs lakh, 100,000)	0	1	2	3	4	5	6	7
Purchase	5.00							
Interest*			0.87					
Fuel**				3.8				
Servicing and Spares					1.75			
Comprehensive Insurance						0.40		
Total	Rs 11.82 lakh							

Shading indicates the time (in years) over which the expense is incurred. For example, purchase expense is incurred at the outset (Year 0), while fuel expense is spread over the entire ownership period (i.e. seven years).

*Based on a loan of Rs 4 lakh (80% financing) at an interest rate of 8% with repayment spread over five years.

**Assuming an average daily run of 30 kilometres, fuel efficiency of 20km per litre and a constant price of Rs 100/litre.

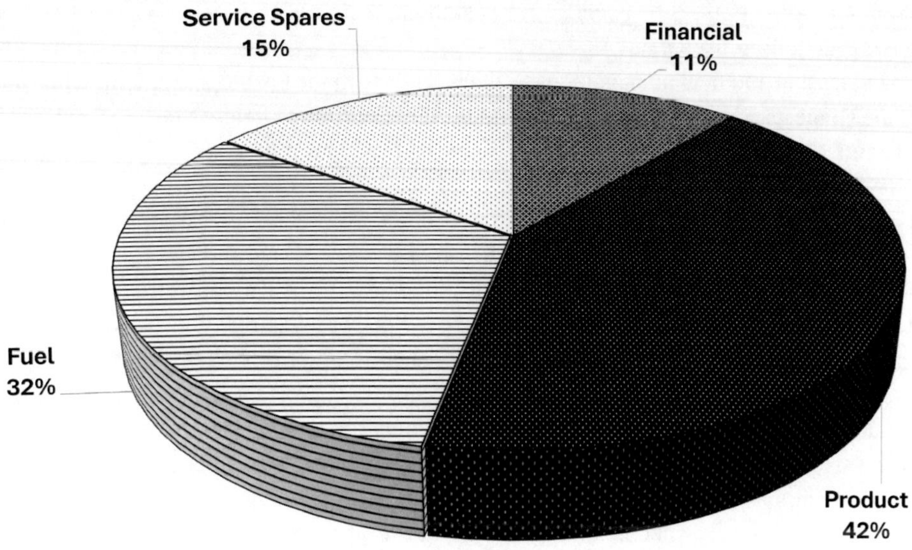

FIGURE 4.4 Share of Customer Expenses Related to Car Purchase/Ownership

can be grouped as relating to: product – the purchase price of the car; financial services – such as loans and insurance; servicing and spares; and fuel (Figure 4.4).

As the pie chart indicates (Figure 4.4), when the company concentrated on expanding its market share through vehicle sales, it targeted only 42% of each customer's expenses. Additionally, attracting customers is costly because the industry is very competitive. When Maruti started focusing on increasing its share of each customer's expenses it did so by:

- Offering car loans through its network of dealers at the point of sale (POS)
- Expanding its service and spares network
- Offering comprehensive options for motor insurance.

It then targeted a possibility of 68% for all expenditure incurred by the customer over seven years. As a result, its share of customers could potentially improve from 42% to 68%. In addition, these services offer the opportunity of higher margins. Therefore, the shift from a single purchase-centred transaction at the start of the sale and the focus on services open new opportunities for numerous interactions over several years.

The 'share of customer' focus on the long-term needs of car buyers and owners requires companies to expand into new business areas to tap into available opportunities. Some of the initiatives of Maruti Suzuki included:

- Partnering with banks and other financial institutions to offer competitive financing options to customers
- Entry into the auto insurance business through partnerships
- Increased focus on the service and spare parts business
- Purchase and sale of pre-owned cars through Maruti True Value Exclusive outlets to

offer additional options, especially for customers wanting a hassle-free experience while buying or selling used cars

- 'N2N' leasing and fleet management services targeted at the business segment, which, as the name suggests, cater to all the end-to-end needs of corporate fleets. Maruti Suzuki was the first automobile manufacturer to offer bespoke leasing solutions to corporate clients.

The company thereby aimed to increase its revenue from services to approximately 50% within a decade by increasing its share of customers.

In parallel, Maruti undertook several initiatives to improve its customer experience by integrating the data from marketing, sales and service that was residing in silos within the company and its dealerships and service centres. Data integration helped Maruti create multiple customised and effective sales, marketing and service-oriented channels and boosted collaborative efforts within these customer-facing departments.

Analysis helped identify potential areas for strengthening customer relationships, creating relevant campaigns and boosting Maruti's share of customer revenue. Access to 24/7 services, a user-friendly mechanism for complaints and the use of digital technologies to understand customer preferences enabled the provision of personalised solutions and products, such as adding accessories of choice. Other initiatives – such as express bays for faster car servicing, regular camps for check-ups, doorstep service for mobile support, driving schools, and pick-up and drop delivery for women car owners – helped the company maintain its leadership position.

LIFETIME VALUE OF CUSTOMERS

The lifetime value calculation looks at customers from the point of view of their profit contribution to a firm (Figure 4.5) over time. This concept is useful when a company plans to build long-term relationships with chosen customers.

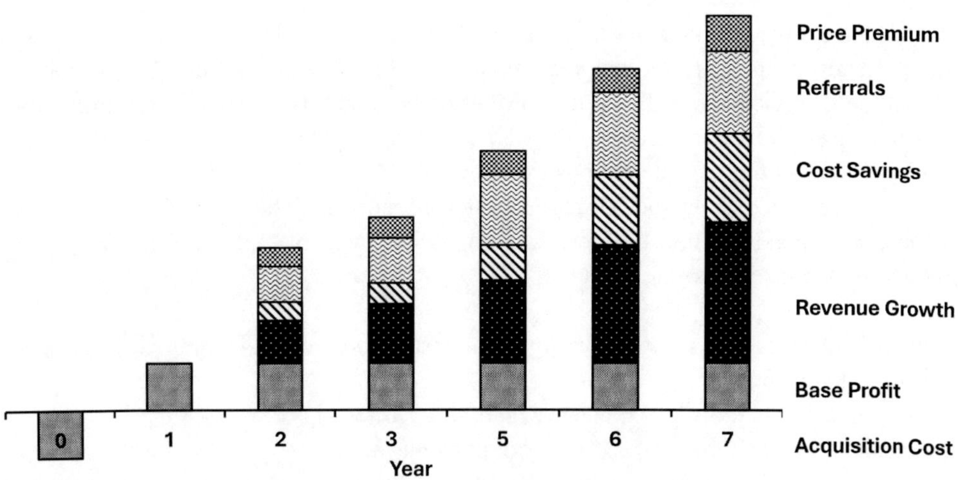

FIGURE 4.5 Lifetime Value of Customers - Profit Drivers

So what is the financial value of long-term relationships? The lifetime value of a customer depends on:

- The length of the 'lifetime' or the duration of the customer's relationship with the firm.
- Average profit generated per relevant period over the lifetime (yearly in most cases)
- Profits from sales of additional products and services over time,
- Profits from referrals given by the customer over time, and Price premium generated by loyal customers.

Lifetime value represents the net present value generated by a customer through out her relationship with a firm.

How do companies benefit by focusing on the lifetime value of customers? Over time, existing customers increase their purchases to generate additional profits. Also the costs of interactions reduce over time due to customers getting familiar with usage, habit formation, learning, confidence in using lower cost self service technologies (SSTs) and digital channels. In addition, many of these satisfied customers recommend products and services to other prospects, thus providing free advertising through word of mouth. There is also the potential for price premiums from long-standing customers as they do not switch easily even when slightly cheaper alternatives are available. Let us try to apply this concept to mobile services.

Acquisition Cost

The acquisition cost of a new cellular service customer averages between \$250 and \$300 in the US market, but the churn rate is about 30%. The cost involved in retaining an existing customer is much less. However, most cellular service providers are focused on customer acquisition rather than improving customer retention. For most organisations it takes about six months of use by newly acquired customers to recoup their acquisition costs.

Base Profit

Once the customer starts using the mobile phone service, she starts contributing to the firm's revenues and even profits after the recovery of acquisition costs. Moreover, the customer may sign up for value-added services, such as data plans and subscriptions during the iniial purchase itself. The customer could also use more than the allotted quota or data allowance, further contributing to the firm's revenues and profits.

Profits from Revenue Growth

The relative cost increase for providing data services beyond the allotted quota is marginal, so any additional revenue from incremental data usage boosts the bottomline. Similarly, several other services including streaming, bill payment and subscriptions offered by mobile phone companies generate higher margins and improve customer stickiness. Therefore, once a customer has been acquired, firms try to persuade them to use as many services as possible. sometimes by providing certain services for free for a limited time period.

Cost Savings

As customers become familiar with the services, their requirements by way of customer support decline, which helps the company save costs. Further, most firms encourage customers to sign up for e-bills and to pay via web services or mobile applications. This further reduces the cost of doing business with customers.

Referrals

When customers are satisfied with service offerings over some time, they are more inclined to recommend the service to others. This positive word of mouth is the most influential medium to convert prospects into customers – at virtually no cost to the company. To encourage this behaviour, many mobile service providers also provide incentives including free calls and additional data packs. Thus, families are likely to sign up with the same service provider to benefit from offers such as 'Friends and Family' or 'Closed User Groups'.

Price Premiums

Loyal customers continue their patronage even when competitors with lower-priced offerings enter the market. Some firms overcome low-priced competitors by providing better services and expanding their product portfolio.

Firms are leveraging digital capabilities to understand customer requirements and enhance value while offering a brand promise that aligns with the changing demands of competitive markets. Businesses are undertaking programmes for digital transformations that improve the customer experience throughout the entire journey, involving communications, products and services.

Table 4.2 shows the sample revenue and profit stream of a customer at 'The Resort', a weekend getaway hotel located on the outskirts of a metropolitan city in India. The last row, labelled net present value (NPV), is the lifetime value of the customer.

Customer lifetime value is a futuristic metric that helps estimate the total value of profits from a customer. It is also helpful in identifying the potential of prospects as customers may often have low current profit potential. For example, when a bank provides a credit card to students pursuing professional courses such as engineering, medicine or business administration, those students may not be very profitable in the initial years while they are studying. If the bank can retain them after graduation, they will become profitable as most of them move into high-paying careers.

Managers intuitively love the concept of lifetime value, but face problems when they try to apply the concept. Lifetime value is a powerful tool for identifying and managing customers by focusing on their profit potential. Profit calculations require revenues as well as cost details. While it is easy to identify revenues accrued from each customer, allocating all the costs to each customer is difficult. Why?

The reason has to do with indirect costs, also referred to as overheads. Although it is not difficult to determine the amount of labour and materials that go into any product or service, it is hard to allocate costs that are spread among many products or services. These indirect costs include everything from electricity, rent and insurance to the wages of supervisors overseeing many workers in a factory. Traditional accounting techniques allocate costs to products based on attributes of a single unit. Typical attributes include the number of direct labour hours required to manufacture a unit, purchase costs of merchandise resold or number of days

TABLE 4.2 Sample Customer Lifetime Value

	Year 0	Year 1	Year 2	Year 3	Year 4	Year 5
Revenue (Rs)[a]		12,000	13,200	14,520	15,972	17,569
Costs[b]	2000	9600	10,560	11,616	12,778	14,055
Customer Lifetime Value						
Profit	–2000	2400	2640	2904	3194	3514
Profit from increased spending on stay	–	–	800	960	1152	1382
Profit from other services[c]	–	–	1000	1200	1440	1728
Profit from reduced overhead allocation[d]	–	–	1320	1452	1597	1757
Profit from referrals[e]	–	–	1980	2178	2396	2635
Total Profit	–2000	2400	7740	8694	9779	11,017
Present Value	(2000)	2087	5853	5716	5591	5477
Net Present Value	22,725					

a. Revenue is assumed to increase by 10% every year.
b. Costs increase by 8% every year; Rs 2000 is the cost of acquisition in Year 0.
c. Other services include a restaurant, travel desk, gym, etc.
d. Declines at 10% with respect to revenue to reflect lower customer relationship costs associated with both customer and supplier learning effects.
e. Estimates are based on assumptions about the importance of referrals to new customers – i.e. the frequency with which satisfied customers refer new customers and the lifetime value calculations for new customers.

occupied. Allocations therefore vary directly with the volume of units produced, the cost of merchandise sold or days occupied by the customer. However these allocation formulas do not produce reasonable approximations of indirect costs. We face similar problems in identifying the cost of serving a customer. Therefore, many organisations now use activity-based costing (ABC) to determine the costs to serve a customer and identify customer profitability.

ACTIVITY-BASED COSTING FOR CRM

Accurate and relevant cost information is critical to any organisation that hopes to improve its competitive position. For decades, managers operated under the assumption that their cost information reflected the costs of their products and services when, in reality, it did nothing of the kind. While hiding their shortcomings behind a cloak of precision, over-generalised cost systems were misleading decision makers. This resulted in decisions that were inconsistent with their organisations' needs and goals.

Activity-based costing emerged as a concept that can be used to correct the shortcomings in the over-generalised cost systems of the past (Kaplan & Anderson, 2007). It is a means of creating a system that ultimately directs an organisation's costs towards the products and services that require those costs to be incurred. In other words:

> *ABC is a budgeting and analysis process that evaluates overheads and operating expenses by linking costs to customers, services, products and orders.*

It allows managers to assess which products, services or customers are profitable or losing money. It measures the cost and performance of activities, resources and cost objects. Resources are assigned to activities, and then activities are assigned to cost objects based on their use. Thus, ABC is a process for calculating true costs.

First, it takes traditional functional costs and allocates them to all the activities undertaken by the company based on the usage of those activities. This means measuring the volume and amount of time required for activities carried out by people and equipment. In the second stage of the process the cost of each activity is then allocated to any number of 'cost objects' based on the amount of activity each uses or consumes. A cost object is typically a product or a service, a customer or a distribution channel, and calculations can be carried out for each category so that firms can see product, customer and channel costs.

The basic distinctions between traditional cost accounting and ABC are therefore as follows:

- Traditional cost-accounting techniques allocate costs to products based on the attributes of a single unit.
- Typical attributes include the number of direct labour hours required to manufacture a unit, the purchase cost of merchandise resold or the number of days occupied.
- Allocations therefore vary directly with the volume of units produced, cost of merchandise sold or days occupied by the customer.
- In contrast, ABC systems focus on activities required to produce each product or provide each service based on a product's or a service's consumption of the activities.

Using ABC, overhead costs are traced to products and services by identifying the resources and activities and their costs and quantities to produce output. A unit of output (a driver) is used to calculate the cost of each activity. Cost is traced to the product or service by determining how many units of output each activity consumed during any given period of time.

ABC applies not only to manufacturing organisations but also to service organisations such as financial institutions, medical care providers and government units. In fact, some banking organisations have been applying the concept for years under a different name – 'unit costing'. Unit costing calculates the cost of banking services by determining the cost and consumption of each unit of output of functions required to deliver a service.

Now, let us consider how ABC can be applied to assess customer profitability. Shapiro et al. (1987) classified business customers as high vs. low cost to serve (CTS) in the manufacturing sector. Managers easily identify customers who exhibit some or all of the high cost-to-serve characteristics. It is not a disadvantage to have high cost-to-serve customers if the company can obtain high margins from them. Similarly, you should not consider yourself lucky if you have low cost-to-serve customers as some of these customers demand low prices when they realise that their behaviour results in low costs to their suppliers. Table 4.3 assists in categorising high- and low-cost customers.

Figure 4.6 gives an example of customer classification using ABC shown as a matrix:

- Cost to serve includes order-related costs and the specific customer-sustaining marketing, technical, selling and administrative expenses associated with serving each customer, which can be measured using an ABC customer costing model of those expenses.

TABLE 4.3 Customer Classification

High Cost-to-Serve Customers	Low Cost-to-Serve Customers
Order custom products	Order standard products
Small order quantities	High order quantities
Unpredictable order arrivals	Predictable order arrivals
Customised delivery	Standard delivery
Change delivery requirements	No change in delivery requirements
Manual processing	Electronic processing
Large pre-sales and post-sales approach	Little to no pre-sales and post-sales support
Require company to hold inventory	Replenish as produced
Pay slowly (high account receivables)	Pay on time (low account receivables)

- Net margin equals net price, after all sales discounts and allowances, minus manufacturing costs (again measured using an ABC product costing model).

Profitable customers fall into different quadrants, with the best ones obviously in the upper left-hand quadrant. Profitability depends on whether and how much the net product margins recover the customer-specific costs. While such customers are a rarity, if present they should

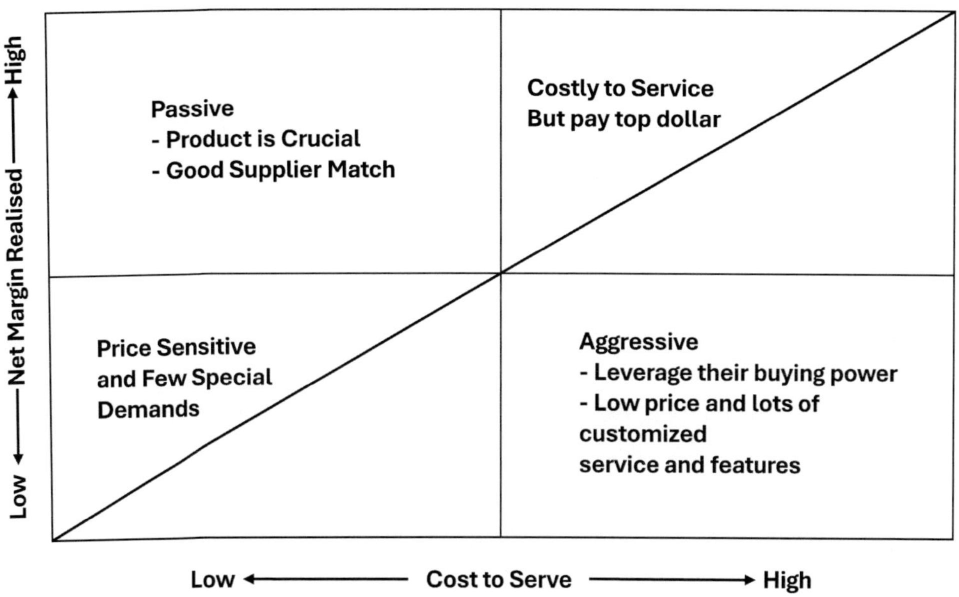

FIGURE 4.6 Customer Classification Using Activity-Based Costing

Adapted from Shapiro et al. (1987).

be cherished and protected as they are the prime targets for competitors. Therefore, they should be retained through bonding strategies.

Customers who are price sensitive but have few special demands help reduce CTS. Additionally, many of them are willing to work with suppliers to improve the overall system, which helps reduce costs. High-cost/high-margin customers are also profitable as they are more than covering their expenses. These customers value unique functionality, features and extensive support and service, and they pay for them.

The most challenging customers are those categorised as low margin and high cost to serve. These include:

- Convertibles: Some customers can be made profitable by identifying internal processes that may be costly and inefficient, leading to high CTS, by negotiating improved ordering and delivery relationships, reducing discounts and establishing menu-based pricing for special services and features.
- New customers: These may not be profitable initially but have profitable potential over time. Therefore, they need to be monitored carefully based on lifetime value potential.
- Strategic customers, who bring prestige and repute or help the supplier learn and improve internal processes. For example, software service providers work with very demanding clients despite low billing rates as these customers help build reputation, open doors with prospects and sometimes create opportunities to learn.

Understanding the various elements of cost to serve can be useful in developing strategies to increase customer value.

CLOSING CASE

ING Bank provides corporate, commercial and retail banking services to millions of customers in Turkey through its 327 branches. The bank had charted an ambitious plan to be the leading financial services provider. In 2010, ING's IT department was mandated to develop an effective CRM system to provide its sales team with a 360° view of its customers. The CRM system was integrated with the daily planning tasks of the sales team, including leads, feedback on sales and performance.

ING had to enhance its market position while investing in CRM by supporting 900 sales agents to create new business opportunities. It also facilitated the operations of corporate customers and attracted new customers via social media platforms such as Facebook and Twitter (now X). The bank enhanced its quality of service while improving software integration at low cost. Developing customisation options for customers proved to be critical as the organisation extended the tool into new verticals such as corporate and private banking, pensions and life insurance, and for corporate clients and small and medium-size enterprises (SMEs) (Lacey, 2012).

Training programmes for employees enabled them to offer seamless customer service. Integrating direct channels such as call centres and the internet with established touch points and existing channels allowed the sales team to maximise their customer contact time and undertake cross-selling by offering the right products. In addition, integrating social media networks with the CRM system helped the bank manage outbound calls, direct channels, call centres, etc. Lastly, the company included Facebook along with a Twitter fan page, blog and the employees' stories and the success of their products.

This process enabled ING Bank to use CRM effectively at minimum costs, allowing it to provide several benefits to various stakeholders. These benefits were enhanced by the use of digital and social media channels as they incurred significantly fewer costs (VeriPark, 2020).

SUMMARY

Customer centricity helps companies focus on increasing their share of customers. In this chapter we highlighted the difference between the concepts of market share and share of customers. We discussed the concept of the lifetime value of customers by focusing on the potential profits generated by customers in the future, with the understanding that lifetime value analysis is instrumental in identifying customers' current and potential value. We also underlined the importance of applying activity-based costing for customer relationship management initiatives to assess the cost of serving customers and their profitability.

Industry Best Practices

In a competitive business environment, understanding and prioritising customer relationships is essential for growth and sustainability. This means recognising each customer's unique value, navigating the balance between market share and share of customers, optimising service costs versus profit margins and focusing on customer-centric strategies. Here is a simplified breakdown.

Understanding Customer Value

- Economic Valuation: Assess customers based on their current and potential future value, considering purchasing patterns and referral possibilities. This helps in focusing efforts on the most valuable customer segments.
- Customer Segmentation: Differentiate customers by their economic contribution, and tailor marketing and service strategies accordingly to enhance engagement and repeat custom.

Market Share vs. Share of Customers

- Differentiating Metrics: Market share measures overall industry sales captured by a company, while share of customers looks at a company's proportion of an individual's total purchases in a category. Both are crucial but serve distinct strategic goals.
- Strategic Focus: Aim to increase the share of customers, especially among high-value segments, through personalised marketing and loyalty initiatives. This approach emphasises the depth of the relationship over the breadth of market capture.

Balancing Service Costs and Profit Margins

- Cost-to-Serve Analysis: Understand the costs of serving different segments, including both direct and indirect expenses, to identify where efficiencies can be improved.
- Margin Optimisation: Use cost insights to pinpoint profitable segments and adjust strategies, potentially shifting resources towards higher-margin customers or reducing costs for lower-value segments.

Consumer-Centric Strategies

- Personalisation: Use customer data to customise interactions, making experiences more engaging and fostering loyalty.
- Omnichannel Experience: Provide a seamless experience across all customer touchpoints, integrating online and physical interactions for a cohesive brand experience.
- Feedback Loops: Incorporate customer feedback into business strategies, product development and service improvements to better meet customer needs.
- Empowered Service Teams: Ensure customer service teams have the necessary tools and authority to solve problems effectively, promoting a culture of customer advocacy.

CONCLUSION

Adopting a strategic approach to CRM by valuing each customer, focusing on customer loyalty, managing service costs wisely and adopting customer-first practices leads to improved satisfaction, loyalty and business growth. When implemented effectively, these principles elevate customer relations and drive profitability and competitive advantage in the market.

DISCUSSION QUESTIONS

1 Discuss the role of customers across the different stages of the evolution of marketing concepts.
2 Discuss approaches for companies to institutionalise customer centricity.
3 Explain the role of activity-based costing (ABC) in assessing customer profitability.
4 Discuss the role and importance of cost to serve (CTS) in implementing CRM.

REFERENCES

Buzzell, R.D., & Gale, B.T. (1987). *The PIMS principles: Linking strategy to performance*. New York: Free Press.

Kaplan, R., & Anderson, S.R. (2007). *Time-driven activity-based costing: A simpler and more powerful path to higher profits*, Harvard Business School Press.

Lacey, R. (2012), How customer voice contributes to stronger service provider relationships. *Journal of Services Marketing*, *26*(2), 137–144. https://www.emerald.com/insight/content/doi/10.1108/08876041211215293/full/html.

Shapiro, B.P., Rangan, V.K., Moriarty, R.T., & Ross, E.B. (1987). Manage customers for profits (not just sales). *Harvard Business Review*, *65*(5), 101–108.

Sheth, J.N., Sisodia, R.S., & Sharma, A. (2000). The antecedents and consequences of customer-centric marketing. *Journal of the Academy of Marketing Science*, *28*(1), 55–66. https://doi.org/10.1177/0092070300281006.

VeriPark. (2020). Retail banking: CRM for retail banking sales agent. Retrieved November 19, 2021, from https://www.veripark.com/industries/retail-banking.

PART II

CRM Applications in Consumer and Business Markets

CHAPTER 5

CRM IN B2C MARKETS

CHAPTER OVERVIEW

This chapter will help you understand Customer Relationship Management (CRM) in business-to-customer (B2C) markets differentiating between services and product markets. The discussions cover:

1. Service quality themes used to provide customers with experiences that lead to satisfaction and enhance loyalty
2. The relationship between CRM and service recovery – understanding the role of CRM in helping organisations recover from occasional service failures
3. The attributes of service guarantee that improve customer satisfaction
4. CRM initiatives in select service businesses
5. CRM practices in select product-oriented businesses

Vignette

HDFC Bank serves more than 85 million customers, including retail and business customers, by leveraging multiple delivery channels – such as telephone banking, internet banking, mobile banking and text (SMS)-based banking – in addition to via its 8800 branches and 21,000 automated teller machines (ATMs) across 3836 cities and towns in India. The bank customises wealth management solutions to meet the financial aspirations of over 100,000 high net worth and ultra high net worth clients by partnering with them on their wealth ambitions. A relationship manager (RM) and a cross-functional team of experts in research, investments, insurance and estate planning support these 'wealth' clients. Each RM handles about 100 clients to ensure that each client has easy access to an experienced manager. As a result, the bank can offer a differentiated service to customers based on their financial needs, value and potential.

The RMs use digital tools to access all customer-related information, including client portfolios, at the click of a button. Reducing preparation time for

DOI: 10.4324/9781003518174-7

meetings and making meetings more productive is a win-win situation: the bank benefits through improved productivity, and clients benefit from spending less time explaining their issues or needs. This arrangement has also paved the way for opportunities to constantly understand clients' evolving needs and offer solutions to meet their requirements.

Based on its extensive experience, the bank has now extended its wealth management offering by launching a digital investment platform, HDFC Bank SmartWealth, as a new-age investment application (app). Targeted at first-time investors, the platform aims to democratise wealth creation through digital tools that allow users to make the right investment decisions and plan their financial journey.

OPENING CASE

Marriott International

Marriott International is the world's leading hospitality group, managing 30 brands and more than 8500 properties across 138 countries. Its collection boasts luxury hotel brands such as Ritz-Carlton, St. Regis, W Hotels and JW Marriott, as well as the very high-end Bulgari fashion house. The premium collection comprises the Marriott, Sheraton, Westin and Le Méridien hotels, among others. Marriott excels in customer service by delivering a seamless experience. Its experience strategy focuses on customer delight, and its personalised service encourages customers to remain loyal. Marriott Bonvoy, its loyalty programme, had more than 196 million members worldwide in 2023.

The leadership emphasises the strong links between employees and customers, with a belief that employee satisfaction is a key driver of customer satisfaction. This belief is deeply embedded in the company's core values (Carroll, 2011). The company connects with its customers through multiple channels, including direct mail, email, website, social media handles, online communities and personal contact during their stay at its properties. The social and digital channels capture the 'live moments' of customers as many share stories related to the extra care and benefits. For example, one woman shared the story of the care shown while her spouse was undergoing treatment at a hospital close to their hotel; and another family shared the positive experience of their stay in a Marriott hotel when they lost access to electricity at home during a local emergency. In another instance, the company invited a frequent guest to inaugurate a new gym in a property. These gestures make customers feel even more special. Marriott pampers its valuable platinum-tier guests. In addition to personalised services, they are offered customised gifts when they check in (Social Tables, 2021). Marriott has therefore improved its competitiveness and performance by prioritising customer experience and making them feel special. Capturing some of these special moments on digital and social media platforms has further enhanced this 'special feeling' (Swanborg, 2009).

CRM IN SERVICES

Service Quality Themes in CRM

Customer Relationship Marketing is essentially about building long-term and mutually beneficial customer relationships. Developing and managing relationships with customers takes on different dimensions due to the characteristics of services that distinguish them from tangible products. Listed below are the essential characteristics of services:

- *Intangibility*: Customers find it difficult to evaluate the quality of services offered to them because of the intangible nature of services. Unlike goods, services cannot be touched, smelt, seen or experienced through sensory organs, and hence it is difficult for customers to evaluate them.
- *Simultaneity*: Services are consumed as they are produced; therefore, the chances of error are greater than for goods that can be inspected for quality before sale.
- *Perishability*: Most services cannot be stored or inventoried. For example, if a flight leaves with a few seats vacant, they are lost. Similarly, if a hotel has unoccupied rooms on a given day, the potential revenue is lost.
- *Heterogeneity*: Most services are people intensive as they require employees to render a service in the presence of other customers. Therefore, the quality of the offering will vary, depending on the person providing the service, and standardisation is not easy to achieve.

The nature of services makes it difficult for managers to design, deliver and manage the quality of offerings. It has also been found that service firms devote most of their energy and resources to attracting new customers while efforts to retain existing customers take a back seat. This practice is needlessly restrictive and potentially wasteful (Berry, 1995). It is equally important for service firms to retain customers rather than merely acquiring them. Retaining the existing clientele forms the central theme of relationship marketing, which greatly emphasises attracting, maintaining and – in multi-service organisations – enhancing customer relationships.

Berry identified three situations in which relationship marketing is most applicable to a service firm:

1. There is an ongoing or periodic desire for the service on the part of the customers. For example, a telephone service is ongoing, while the service provided in a hospital is periodic.
2. Customers decide which service provider they want to use. For example, a customer may choose to go to a particular restaurant for dinner as opposed to simply taking the first available taxi in the queue outside the railway station.

3 There are alternative service suppliers, so it is common for customers to switch from one supplier to another, which is easy as it involves negligible or no switching costs for customers. For example, a customer may fly with an airline of her choice instead of signing up for electricity from a monopoly utility provider licensed to supply a city.

When conditions such as these exist, there is an opportunity for service firms to attract customers and strengthen relationships with them. Promising and delivering quality service are among the most important ways to differentiate dimensions that are meaningful to customers and difficult to duplicate.

Parasuraman et al. (1985) developed a conceptual model that defines service quality from the customer's perspective and identifies key service provider gaps potentially responsible for poor service. 'Perceived service quality' is defined as 'the degree and direction of discrepancy between the consumer's perceptions and expectations'. Later, Parasuraman et al. (1988) identified the following five dimensions that determine service quality:

1 Reliability – the ability to perform the promised service dependably and accurately.
2 Assurance – knowledge and courtesy of employees and their ability to inspire trust and confidence.
3 Tangibles – physical facilities and equipment, and the appearance of personnel.
4 Empathy – caring and the individualised attention a firm provides to its customers.
5 Responsiveness – willingness to help customers and provide prompt service.

However, these dimensions are not equal in importance for service quality. In most services, reliability and responsiveness emerge as the most important dimensions.

Product features and prices are relatively easy to copy in competitive markets. However, service quality is difficult to imitate as it is embedded in an organisation's processes and the skills and knowledge of its employees. Customer satisfaction, built over multiple interactions and experiences with a service provider, leads to loyalty (Figure 5.1). Nevertheless, customers are constantly lured by competitive offerings.

Customers assess the quality of a service by evaluating all five dimensions listed above. However, their relative importance varies. While the variation in importance depends on the service, the customers and their preferences, there seems to be some commonality. Customer studies have found a consistent order in the importance of these five generic service quality dimensions. Most customers give a higher weighting to reliability (32%), responsiveness (22%), assurance (19%) and empathy (16%), and a relatively lower weighting to tangibles (11%).

THE COST OF LOSING CUSTOMERS

Firms tend to underestimate or, even worse, ignore the cost of losing a customer. They assume that a lost customer can be replaced, and that one should not worry as long as the top line grows. However, this is flawed thinking as it does not look at the quality and implicit costs of losing customers (Reichheld & Sasser, 1990). If managers do not measure the actual cost of losing a customer, they will not be able to focus on reducing defections as they will not know

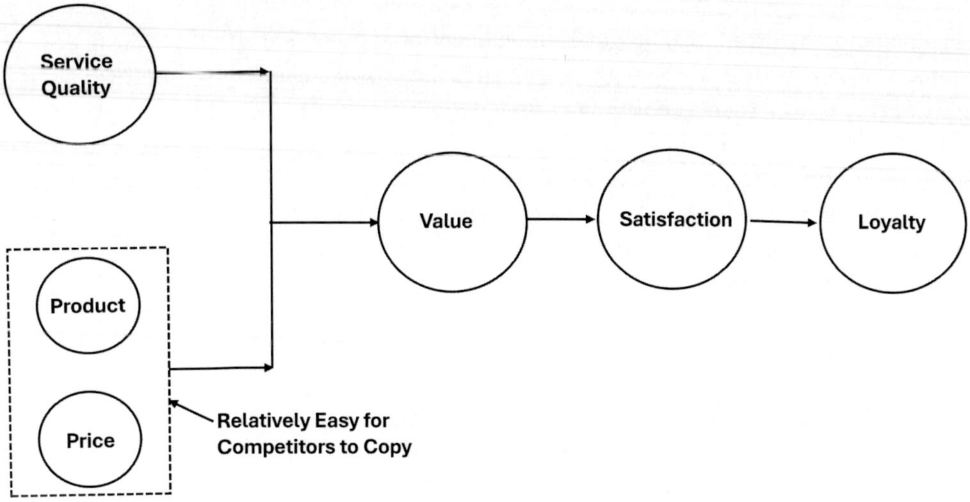

FIGURE 5.1 The Impact of Service Quality on Loyalty

the true worth of a customer. Customer defection is a key indicator of a drop in business performance. A few of the many ways in which a lost customer costs the firm are outlined below:

1. A lost customer reduces cash flows for the firm in the future. Served correctly, customers generate increasingly more profits each year they stay with a firm because of their increasing familiarity with the service it provides to them. This familiarity with the service then further increases the volume of business the customers choose to offer the firm. For example, as a customer grows more comfortable with using a credit card, she will use it more often for purchases as time goes by.
2. If a firm wants to maintain the same volume of business it has to attract new customers. Replacing an existing customer with a new customer costs up to five times more in advertising and other costs. Usually, in the beginning (or sometimes up to a year), the new customer tends to spend less than an old customer would have done.
3. Serving customers over time becomes more cost effective for firms as they discover new customer traits, likes and dislikes. Therefore, a firm can serve existing customers more efficiently than new ones.
4. Firms with long-term customers who have developed a higher level of loyalty can charge more for their products and services. For example, customers will often willingly pay more to stay at a hotel they know or consult a doctor they are used to rather than take their chances with some unknown hotel or a less familiar doctor.
5. Finally, highly satisfied long-term customers will likely refer new customers to the firm. This means that the firm must spend less on advertising and other expenses to attract new customers.

When a firm considers all the costs due to the loss of a customer, its managers become aware of the actual situation. They realise that continual improvement in the quality of service is not a cost but an investment in the form of a customer who is an asset that generates a much greater profit stream than the margin on a one-time sale. Estimating the costs of losing customers makes it easier for managers to justify the cost of continually improving service quality versus factors such as cost reduction with more tangible measures.

In addition to the direct impact on financials, lost customers can incur social costs in the form of positive reviews, feedback and stories. Similarly, unhappy customers share negative stories about their experiences. A negative review can potentially impact the perceptions of thousands of prospective and existing customers because many people now rely on online reviews and digital platforms such as Yelp before choosing a service provider, such as a restaurant.

MANAGING DEFECTIONS AND LEARNING FROM THEM

It is difficult to eliminate all customer defections, but firms should also not strive to keep all their current customers. Instead, a business should focus on retaining all its desirable customers – i.e., those who generate higher profits and potentially have high lifetime value. Early warning systems based on indicators such as complaints, reduced purchases, fewer interactions, etc. help assess the likelihood of customer defection. Analysis of churned customers provides insights that can be used to improve processes and initiate steps to improve customer retention.

Reichheld and Sasser (1990) underscore the challenges associated with customer defection, along with suggestions for an action plan.

1 Managing and moving to the goal of zero defections first requires mechanisms to find customers who are leaving or are likely to leave the firm. Sometimes, such mechanisms may not be present, and firms may have to invest in IT solutions that permit the capture of the defection data, in which case company staff will also have to be trained.
2 Defining defections is also an important task for any firm. In some cases, say a courier firm, a customer might not shift all their business to a competitor. However, if a customer shifts about 70% of their business, it should be looked on as a defection. In other sectors, such as retailing, defining defection in itself is a very tricky business because customers tend to be faceless and nameless. Even here though, a company can collect important defection information if it can introduce innovative mechanisms such as 'store cards'.
3 Once potential defectors are identified, it is important for a firm to try and win these customers back in order to prevent major erosion of its returns.
4 A more important reason for identifying defections and talking to defecting customers is to gain their insights, views from outside that are not available to the management on the inside.
5 Early defection is also a type of 'early warning signal' to the firm. It indicates causes for a customer leaving that may soon open the floodgates for others to follow.
6 Defecting customers usually express their reasons for leaving, which can help a firm to look at its service delivery mechanism and take corrective action. It also helps provide

the firm with clues about important environmental trends such as a rival undercutting it on certain products or introducing a new product or service, and so on.

7 Analysis of defections also helps a firm decide which service-quality investments will be profitable. This enables the firm to address any issues and make appropriate investments so that investments are not lost.

8 A firm should not keep all customers at any cost as there are many customers who may not be profitable to the firm. In such circumstances it is better for the firm to let them go. Information gained from defectors can point to common traits among customers who do not stay with the firm. This information must be used to clarify market characteristics to pursue and target advertising and promotions equally.

Keeping customer defections to a minimum should be a top priority for any business leader. A lower defection rate also indicates a higher level of customer satisfaction. However, when defections do occur, they provide a chance for a company to learn and enhance customer experience by analysing the flaws in its delivery process.

Ensuring quality delivery with zero defections requires the management to recognise the need to establish a culture and environment that emphasises 'zero defections' as a key goal. Achieving this goal requires empowering supporters of the zero defections culture at every level of the organisation, especially among the middle and frontline management. Adopting customer retention as a key performance measure helps focus efforts on preventing customer defection. An appreciation of the concept of the customer as an asset and aligning customer value with the company's strategic goals creates a positive impact. The firm also needs to create incentives to encourage programmes for customer retention. Employees must be rewarded for customer acquisition as well as retention. Successful managers understand the link between defection rates and financial performance of the firm.

Finally, we can say that defection is a reflection of a firm's quality of service. The best service firms aim to minimise defections and use them as a signal to improve processes and delivery. Focusing on a zero defections culture helps retain customers, with significant savings in customer acquisition costs and effort. Firms that lead the way in service quality can aim for zero defections.

SERVICE RECOVERY

It is vital to remember that, no matter how flawless and fabulous a company's service delivery is, mistakes might still happen due to the diverse nature of services. Errors are unavoidable in services that are frequently performed in the presence of customers. While businesses may not avoid all difficulties, they can learn to recover from them. Successful recovery can turn angry and dissatisfied customers into devoted ones. Personnel must be willing to make that extra effort and act promptly to reclaim clients for a successful service recovery (Hart et al., 1990).

Let us take a look at a real-life example. On a Monday morning, visitors signed in for a conference at a resort that regularly accommodates meetings and conferences. A party of holidaymakers was checking out simultaneously after spending the weekend at the resort.

During the chaos at the front desk, one of the outgoing visitors picked up the suitcase of an incoming conference delegate and went to the airport to catch a flight. When the delegate reported the loss, the resort manager correctly determined that the bag must be with the party that had checked out, and took down all pertinent details about the suitcase and its contents. He encouraged the delegate to attend the conference after assuring him they would be able to retrieve his luggage. He then dispatched a bellboy to the airport to do so while simultaneously purchasing a new suitcase of comparable worth and packing it with identical items. The manager handed the suitcase to the guest first, explaining that the resort accepted responsibility for what had occurred and wished to compensate him for his loss. When the bellboy managed to fetch the guest's suitcase at the airport, he was overjoyed. Finally, as compensation for the guest's ordeal, the resort management gave him both suitcases. The guest was very grateful for this gesture, and the resort earned a lot of business from him over the next few years, both directly and through recommendations.

It should be underlined here that the resort was not actually at fault because the customer had failed to secure his belongings before checking in. On the other hand, the manager rose to the occasion and made a courageous decision, averting a potentially humiliating scenario for the resort and turning it to its benefit.

'Service recovery' is the process through which businesses respond to and recover from negative customer experiences. Recovery is usually initiated after receiving customer complaints, which may be in person, posted on social media platforms and digital channels or received as emails. Companies can also carry out customer surveys and draw insights from employees. Customer perceptions about the complaint handling process are critical for retaining customers. Fast, efficient, effective and action-oriented service recovery directly relates to customer perception and future sales. More specifically, a good recovery process positively impacts the customer's intention to continue buying from the firm. Studies show dual benefits to organisations, namely retaining customers and maintaining more extended associations (Hyken, 2017).

There are numerous opportunities for service providers to recover from failures. Any problem that the frontline personnel close to the customer can identify and resolve is an opportunity to go above and beyond the call of duty, earn a customer for life and build extra goodwill. To begin with, no firm can afford to lose clients because, as mentioned previously, it is more expensive to replace an existing customer with a newer one. Firms that alienate and annoy their clientele will quickly discover that most customers will migrate to competitors that go out of their way to please them. Although some outstanding individuals can recover from service issues, businesses should not rely on such individual initiatives. Leaders must ensure that everyone, especially frontline staff, has the necessary skills and motivation and is empowered to make service recovery a priority.

The Service Recovery Process

Because of the nature of services, where service quality variances are the rule rather than the exception, zero defects are an unrealistic aim in service-oriented businesses. Despite stringent protocols, training, advanced technologies and quality controls, service companies discover that zero defects are an unattainable aim. Other circumstances, such as the weather and customers, are beyond the firm's control. It is also been observed that most responses to difficulties are knee-jerk reactions, which only perpetuate negative attitudes to a service. There could be various reasons for poor service, including an employee's lack of authority, lack of awareness of alternatives and so on. Employees must follow company regulations and operational procedures throughout the usual course of business when everything is running smoothly. However, during failures and in addressing complaints, managers must be comfortable with exceptions, allowing frontline employees to address issues as they see fit. However it is difficult to develop this kind of dual capability. It has been seen that, more often than not, firms that recover well from service disasters have considered the aspects outlined below (Hart et al., 1990).

Cost of Effective Service Recovery

Managers often underestimate the total costs to the firm when customers shift their business elsewhere. They concentrate on acquiring new customers who might represent unprofitable business, thus neglecting to take steps to retain their more valuable existing customers. The need for service recovery becomes apparent when firms measure how much it costs them when a customer defects to a competitor. Measurement of actual costs of service failure, including the cost of lost customers, will often attract the management's attention when they find that effective service recovery helps reduce customer attrition. Firms known for excellent service will go the extra mile to cover all the costs a failure incurs; and, if the inconvenience is so great that the firm cannot fully compensate the customer, the tone of the firm's response must indicate regret for the failure.

Encouraging Customer Input

Every customer's problem is an opportunity for the firm to prove its commitment to service, even if it is not to blame. In fact, when the fault lies with the customer and the firm has solved the customer's problem, the firm walks off with a grateful customer for life. The positive word of mouth generated for the firm is more impactful than any advertising campaign. All good recoveries start from identifying problems.

Complainers are the exception in any service: more often than not, dissatisfied customers are reluctant to complain either because they think the situation is hopeless or because they just do not want to create a scene. They quietly shift to another service provider, thus creating a dent in the customer base of the firm. The firm therefore needs to make it easier for customers to complain, using a preferred channel/method of their choosing – including apps, emails, review sites and social media – to make their voice heard easily. More formal 'listening posts' such as surveys and feedback are effective only if these are systematically monitored continually and action is taken on complaints and suggestions promptly.

Anticipate Needs for Recovery

Every business has potential trouble spots where the chances of things going wrong are relatively high. Firms can narrow the search for problems (read opportunities) by identifying and monitoring these areas of their organisation and addressing them in their service recovery strategy. Complex scheduling that involves the movement of people and goods is an area that tends to be problem-prone.

Another occasion where confusion is created in the minds of the people, resulting in unusual requests, is when firms introduce new services or products. By looking at problems that have occurred in the past, the firm can get a good idea of where (recurring) problem spots lie, and then prepare for service recovery.

Fast and Prompt Action

Identification of a problem before a customer comes to know of it is useful only if a firm responds quickly. As good news travels slowly and bad news travels very fast, the firm must resolve any problem a customer is currently facing before he/she becomes dissatisfied with the service and begins to spread that dissatisfaction. Service problems usually escalate; therefore, whatever opportunity the firm has to recover may be minimal or fleeting. In general, the firm's first priority should be to complete the service promptly. The urgent resumption of service and an apology are often sufficient to make amends, but not always. In some cases, the firm may need to go the extra mile to make up for the mistake. Such gestures will earn the goodwill of the customer.

Training and Empowering Employees

For a firm to effect service recoveries it must train its employees properly and empower them to act on their own as they deem fit in situations that warrant action. The firm must give employees the authority, responsibility and incentives to recognise, care about and attend to customer needs. Employees closest to the customer are often the first to learn about any problems and are in the best position to determine what can be done to satisfy the customer. Unfortunately however, these are also the employees who lack the power to act on their own in most cases. The problem has to travel through the organisation hierarchy; so, by the time the manager comes to know about and act on a problem, the opportunity to implement a service recovery has often passed. Therefore, the firm must recognise the need to train and empower frontline employees to act on their own in case of such emergencies.

A firm can help the frontline employees develop the communication and creative skills needed to deal with irate customers. Recovery skills also can be developed through simulated real-life situations. Employees need to understand the entire service delivery process and where they fit in it as this helps employees understand the system's interconnectedness and find a quick solution. The most direct way to develop this perspective is to rotate employees through different jobs and departments. While all employees must follow company rules and treat every alike, frontline employees are expected to be flexible to proactively take the initiative and improvise to deal with unexpected situations.

To develop good service recovery skills, the firm should give the employees the responsibility, authority and incentives to follow through with customers. Responsibility means the obligation to act and put things right and not just accept the blame for a problem. Good service firms also anticipate problems and tend to be prepared for them by having a set of rules to be followed in case of emergencies. Finally, from the employees' point of view, good service recoveries must be rewarded, publicised throughout the firm and held up as examples to inspire others to follow.

Closing the Loop

This is the final stage of the service recovery wherein, if a customer's complaint(s) lead to corrective measures being taken by the firm, it acknowledges the help it received from the customer. Firms often get the opportunity to improve their service delivery mechanisms because of customer complaints. If customers are informed about the corrective measures implemented as a result of follow-up on their complaint, they feel they are part of the extended quality control team. It also encourages them to point out other faults with the service delivery mechanism. If a problem cannot be resolved, the firm should explain why. Effective ways of closing the loop include contacting the customer with feedback, asking for even more feedback and letting the customer know how her suggestion is being implemented and the possible improvements it will likely bring about. These efforts tend to give customers a more positive impression than various forms of compensation.

Finally, we can say that service recovery is a part of the management philosophy that looks at customer satisfaction as a primary goal of business. It shifts the emphasis from what it costs to please a customer to look at the value it delivers to the customer and the value it gains in the process. This philosophy also entrusts frontline employees with using their judgement by training and empowering them. Errors will always occur in services, but a firm can turn such situations to its advantage by efficient recovery.

Service Guarantees

Buying an appliance or an automobile is almost always accompanied by a guarantee or warranty. However, we rarely come across a guarantee attached to a service. Most managers find it difficult, if not impossible, to offer service guarantees. This kind of thinking arises from the inherent characteristics of services. Human beings, as opposed to machines, generally deliver services. Services are produced at the same time as they are consumed, so it is difficult to standardise services. Also, customers find it difficult to assess the quality of services. However, customer satisfaction can still be guaranteed in services. If a firm promises a service guarantee, it will be forced to keep that promise. Managers will have to ensure that processes are in place and the firm can satisfy the customer as per the guarantee given. The firm then, because of the guarantee, is forced to improve the quality of its service delivery mechanisms, which in the long run is very beneficial.

Good Service Guarantees

Committing to error-free service can force a firm to provide it, thus improving its services. A strong service guarantee will encourage everyone to focus on delivering outstanding customer experience, every time. In turn this will help the firm improve its performance and gain market dominance. Most service guarantees really do not do the job they are supposed to do. Either they are limited in scope and difficult to use or they promise so much that the customer feels embarrassed to use them. A guarantee's power diminishes in direct proportion to the number of conditions it contains. A good service guarantee has certain attributes that make it beneficial for the service organisation implementing it (Hart, 1988), some of which are listed below:

- *Unconditional:* The best service guarantee should be unconditional, without exceptions, and customers should understand it quickly and easily without the need to consult others. If a firm cannot guarantee all elements of its service unconditionally then it should at least guarantee those elements it can. For example, a motor rental service should be able to guarantee that the hire car the customer picks up will be in perfect working order. On the other hand, it is not right to expect it to guarantee a fast ride as that depends on the road and traffic conditions.
- *Easy to understand and communicate:* A guarantee should be written in simple language and in such a manner that a customer reading it will get an idea of what to expect from the service provider. Specifying a 'five-minute' service is better than 'quick service' as it gives a customer a measure of what to expect.
- *Meaningful:* A service should be meaningful to the customer in two respects. First, it should guarantee those aspects of the service that are important to the customer. For example, a fast service may be more important to a customer at lunch than at dinner. Second, a good guarantee should be financially meaningful. It should offer customers a reasonable payout as fair compensation for services not rendered. If it is either too much or too little the customer will not be inclined to use the guarantee even after a service failure.
- *Easy to invoke:* The customer should be able to receive damages or compensation for shoddy service without having to put in too much effort. For example, a situation where a customer has to explain matters to three people over the phone and fill in two forms to get the compensation due to him/her from a firm is more likely to frustrate and annoy the customer further. This means that the firm must trust customers to be honest without asking for proof. Customers should also not be made to feel guilty about invoking guarantees. In fact, firms should encourage customers to invoke guarantees whenever the service is not up to the mark so that employees pull up their socks.
- *Easy to collect:* Finally, customers should not be made to work hard to collect any compensation that is due to them. The procedure should be quick and easy, and made on the spot if possible – for example, a prompt replacement meal for one that is served cold.

One should not promise customers something that is expected from the organisation or that the organisation is not capable of providing. Second, if a firm's guarantee is somewhat weak or does not involve significant compensation, it might not be invoked. Also, it ceases to have any meaning and will not serve the purpose it was initially meant for.

Benefits of Service Guarantees

A guarantee is an effective and significant tool for marketing services and raising the organisation's service standards to the levels required for ensuring successful implementation of the guarantee. A service guarantee compels a business to prioritise its clients and determine which aspects of the service they value the most. The firm must understand the consumers' expectations and the weight they place on different aspects of the service. This knowledge is critical to ensure appropriate procedures. For example, in a restaurant mostly patronised by customers for lunch, the guarantee of quick service is more importance than ambience.

A service guarantee is implicitly built into its service standards. When a firm guarantees a service, it sets clear guidelines on the quality of service that will be rendered. This forces the firm to define each employee's role, responsibilities, expectations and fit in the delivery process. As mentioned earlier, employees will have to be trained to honour guarantees. The absence of such standards will lead employees to raise customer expectations beyond what the firm is capable of delivering and any shortfall will damage the brand's reputation. Payouts/compensation that harm the firm financially will make employees take service guarantees seriously and work towards meeting the standards.

A service guarantee is a significant source of customer feedback (Hart, 1988). Customers invoke guarantees when they are not satisfied with the service rendered by the firm or feel the service they are receiving is not worth the price paid. A guarantee creates a goal, and its invocation by customers shows that the goal is yet to be achieved. Managers can easily identify shortcomings by analysing the feedback from dissatisfied customers. One of the benefits of having explicit service guarantees is that it forces the firm to acknowledge failures. Problems in service delivery are exposed and make it possible to explore options to prevent recurrence. Analysing its service delivery mechanisms helps the firm better understand its operational capabilities and factors that might limit them.

Finally, a service guarantee's most important function is to boost marketing. It encourages customers to opt for the firm offering guarantees because it reduces customer risk while making a choice. Guaranteed services can be easily bought without the need for extensive search for information as there is an option for redress when the service fails to meet expectations. A service guarantee will help gain marketing mileage under certain conditions. For example, the price of the service should be high as customers are not highly concerned about invoking guarantees for low-cost services. Sometimes a customer's ego may be on the line; or, if a customer has not used the service before, he will most probably choose to obtain it from a firm that guarantees it. If the negative consequences of a service failure are high, then a customer will most probably approach a service provider who offers a service guarantee. Other situations include cases where a firm depends on frequent customer repurchases or when the business is deeply affected by word of mouth – e.g. professional services like consultancy.

A service guarantee will be of benefit only if there is commitment to customers. If the aim is to minimise the financial obligations arising out of guarantees while trying to maximise marketing mileage, the firm will not succeed. It will neither improve its service capabilities nor prevent customer defections arising from dissatisfaction. Guarantees are the best way to identify operational weaknesses. Preventing guarantees from being invoked are lost opportunities for gaining knowledge.

It is not necessary for a firm to give explicit service guarantees at all times. If a firm has built a reputation for impeccable service, then giving a service guarantee would probably not matter much because customers expect certain standards. If a guarantee is part of a firm's image, then dropping it would probably hurt it. Finally, suppose an organisation is oriented towards customers in such a way that every employee is inculcated with the absolute customer satisfaction philosophy. In that case, errors will be few and the employees are empowered to do whatever possible to rectify shortcomings, so the firm will not have much to gain from service guarantees. However, such firms are very rare. Sometimes, it is impractical to guarantee a service if customer satisfaction is strongly influenced by variables that are beyond the service provider's control. Breakdowns are inevitable. However, the reason for the breakdowns should be shared with customers as most will be willing to understand the reason. A firm whose operations do not match standards and is incapable of enforcing guarantees should not offer guarantees. In cases where such firms do offer guarantees, the most likely outcomes are bankruptcy arising from financial compensation to customers or employee discontent at being made to keep guarantees that the firm cannot deliver.

Service guarantees allow firms to rewrite the rules of competition by changing the service delivery process as competitors conceive it. This puts their competitors at a serious disadvantage and, if they are unable to match guarantees, they can compete only on price. Service guarantees, by improving the firm's service capabilities in all dimensions, can provide it with a source of competitive advantage and a strategy to differentiate itself from its competitors.

CRM IN SERVICE INDUSTRIES

Let us now look at the CRM initiatives undertaken in some service-oriented businesses. A significant feature that distinguishes these organisations from other businesses such as those involving packaged goods, electronics, appliances and durables is their opportunity to interact and engage with clients on a regular basis. Customer engagement is not a one-off event; it is recurrent and may last a long time, particularly in the case of financial services, hospitality and air travel. As a result, an organisation must be perfect in its service delivery methods, quickly resolving any potential issues.

Hospitality

The hospitality industry includes hotels and restaurants of various types and vacation resorts, and is largely people-based and driven by people. Interactions between service providers (hotels in this case) and customers (guests) typically take place over a long period – essentially the time during which the customer enjoys the hospitality of the service provider. Right from the customer's initial contact with the hotel (whether through an app, an online travel agent, by phone or through a high-street travel agent) to book rooms to their arrival at the hotel, their stay and finally to check-out there is continual interaction between customer and hotel employees. Therefore, people (employees), physical environment (ambience of rooms, lobby, restaurant, swimming pool) and process all play significant roles in determining customer satisfaction.

Service providers in the hospitality industry understand the need to cultivate long-term relationships with their customers. The main philosophy here is to cultivate understanding and caring for customers throughout the organisation by anticipating their needs. The idea is to retain customers and make them visit regularly. The customer retention approach calls for exceeding the customers' expectations by providing service of a quality that goes beyond the 'value for money' proposition and ends up delighting them.

Customers tend to be primarily of two kinds – corporate visitors on official business and guests on personal visits. While for the former, the customer's organisation needs to be contacted and people-to-people relationships developed, relationships with the latter can be strengthened by a 'package providing a pleasurable experience'.

The hospitality business can be looked on as a process with various service quality standards and benchmarks established by the firm acting as a guide to better service standards. The employees' main task should be not only to meet customer expectations but also to exceed them repeatedly. As customers differ hugely in their tastes and preferences, it is imperative to customise services to meet these diverse needs. The primary step is to identify the customer well. Many hospitality organisations have built up world-class systems that routinely harvest information from multiple interaction points. This data is then analysed and shared with different departments within the organisation to help the personnel better serve their consumers by customising services. Customisation to cater to individual tastes, likes and dislikes is one of the ways hospitality organisations achieve their goal of customer satisfaction.

Employees are a vital resource in hospitality businesses as they deal with customers directly. Therefore, employee morale, well-being and training all impact the services provided. The best organisations offer excellent training to their frontline staff and rotate them throughout the organisation in various departments to ensure that employees understand their tasks' value and place in the service delivery system. Most businesses that provide superior services have well-defined staff procedures and enough feedback and appraisal. With the engagement of top management, firms must ensure that all employees understand the firm's mission and the service culture it reflects.

The hospitality industry was one of the early adopters of reward schemes, with customers rewarded for using a firm's services through loyalty programmes. The more a consumer utilises a business's services, the higher the benefits. Customers earn reward points for their purchases and these points can be redeemed for complimentary stays or services. Regular customers are prompted to join exclusive clubs with benefits such as concessions on services, free stays for children and a choice of hotels in various holiday locations.

Hotels communicate frequently with their guests through digital channels including apps, newsletters and magazines. These efforts are directed towards earning the goodwill and allegiance of their customers, and typically result in positive word-of-mouth publicity, especially if the guest is satisfied. Referrals are critical in the hospitality industry. Loyal customers are valuable to the hospitality industry as, in addition to their spending during stays, many of them contribute to additional revenue through referrals.

Telecom

The telecom business provides a range of services, from basic communications to value added services such as internet, data and mobile services. The liberalisation of the telecom sector has led to a significant increase in competition that has expanded in lockstep with user growth. The hyper-competitive mobile services sector in India has transitioned from a dozen players in 2010 to an industry dominated by two players, Reliance Jio and Airtel, who account for almost 81% of the country's mobile user base of over 924 million. Reliance Jio is also the world's largest mobile operator in data traffic consumption. This shift from voice to data usage with significant use through mobile devices has also transformed the customer experience.

Customer defection is easy and mobile number portability (MNP) ensures that customers retain their contact number when switching to another service provider. This has forced telecom operators to look at innovative ways to attract and retain customers. Innovations to develop new services and price promotions are commonly used to attract customers, while retention programmes focus on improving customer loyalty.

The fundamental idea in any CRM programme is to retain customers and increase their lifetime value by boosting loyalty. The key tasks involve providing high-quality service and superior use experience by constantly investing in the latest technologies and capacity to cater to peak loads. Rapid technological evolution requires deep pockets to make significant financial commitments regularly. Service providers copy each other in competitive markets so their offerings are evenly matched. Differentiation can be achieved through superior customer experience and added value.

Customer needs are evolving rapidly along with the development of new technologies such as 5G cellular networks. Therefore, firms must study evolving customer needs to offer packages designed specifically to meet their requirements. Defection is very easy in the telecom business in the absence of exit barriers. One way to prevent defections is to proactively identify valuable customers through analytics of transactions, interactions and usage behaviour. Customer retention teams use data mining tools to predict potential churn and reach out to valuable customers, understand them and try to retain them.

Firms have adopted the latest developments, including artificial intelligence (AI)-based chatbots for customer self-service, app-based support and robust contact centre processes. Omnichannel options are provided to offer information about services, help customers get started with the service, explain different payment options available, buy new services and resolve complaints. Firms use loyalty programmes to retain and grow profitable users, who are rewarded with differential and bundled packages, free airtime and access to premium streaming services. The organisational structure and systems therefore need to be geared to support such initiatives. Leading players invest in regular training to enable their employees to offer service excellence. Many link variable compensation to customer-related metrics that drive customer satisfaction and loyalty. Programmes for reducing customer churn, and for service excellence, benchmarking with world-class service providers and investment in improving user experience are very common. Such initiatives are likely to prevent defections, reduce complaints, generate goodwill and finally pose entry barriers while boosting profitable growth.

Banking

The banking and finance industry has been experiencing increasing competitive pressure due to deregulation and globalisation. It has witnessed consolidation through mergers, acquisitions and closures. Banks now have greater flexibility in offering competitive interest rates for both asset and liability products. They are also pivoting away from the earlier transaction-based banking, which focused exclusively on branch automation, towards a comprehensive relationship orientation to create long-lasting, profitable engagement with customers. This has resulted in various improvements in the way financial services are delivered to customers, with a strong emphasis on digital technologies.

Banks adopted ATMs to reduce dependence on branches. Enabling account holders to conduct transactions from convenient locations (including shopping centres, offices and residential neighbourhoods) 24/7 significantly boosted customer experience. Convenience has been further enhanced by home banking, phone banking and internet banking. Applications for all services, including loans and credit cards, have been automated and digitised by all leading banks. For example, a customer can speak to a relationship manager for a customised loan.

While the availability of channels such as physical branches, ATMs, phones, internet and mobile applications has improved the options for customers, it has simultaneously created opportunities for banks to understand, analyse and improve their understanding of customer usage behaviour and tailor their offerings. Leading banks regularly invest in enhancing customer experience, offer a wide range of products, enable self-service options through digital tools (including chatbots) and constantly structure their services to the convenience of their customers.

The State Bank of India's YONO (You Only Need One) mobile app is an integrated digital banking, investment and shopping platform. It is a convenient and integrated self-service solution that serves customers' banking and lifestyle needs over mobile devices. YONO allows access to e-commerce sites for buying products/services, booking tickets, paying bills, making investments and transferring funds on the move. Features such as 24/7 online banking services, instant account opening, quick loans, card-less cash withdrawal and a spend analyser have transformed YONO into one of the most convenient and popular solutions for customers while improving their experience through a seamless and pleasant digital journey with the bank.

Many companies, including the State Bank of India, have found that their biggest obstacle is not the technology itself but convincing customers to adopt and use it. Customers must have a clear sense of their role in the self-service process, must see a clear benefit and must feel they can actually use the technology. Self-service technologies are not for everyone as they can lead to frustration and even anger at being unable to get support when facing problems.

A successful CRM strategy in the banking industry usually considers the following aspects. The first step is to define the customer relationship – with emphasis on the primary channel. The frontline personnel who initiate the customer contact and provide support play a key role in determining the initial experience and customer expectations. Not all customers are equal as retail banks typically have the greatest skew in customer profitability as well as potential. Therefore, categorising customers based on transaction volumes, value, channels, products and services provides a more comprehensive 360° view for strengthening relationships with the most valuable customers. Appropriate policies and relationship pricing to reward profitable customers serve as incentives for them to remain loyal. Initiating customer contact programmes from time to time and analysing the results can gauge the requirements of customers. Such initiatives usually improve service quality and boost customer satisfaction.

Air Travel

Airlines are incredibly capital-intensive businesses that require a sizable initial investment. This expenditure is recouped over time by passenger and freight services. As with hospitality businesses, airlines have the potential to connect and engage with customers throughout the customer journey. Global competition and the apparent ease with which customers can switch carriers have compelled airlines to focus on improving long-term relationships with their customers. They therefore employ a variety of techniques to acquire and keep clients, including the following:

- Airlines use differential pricing, offering tiered service levels to different customer segments, and maximise capacity utilisation. Business-class passengers pay significantly more and enjoy preferential treatment from the moment they board the flight to arrival at their destination. These include a streamlined check-in process, more space, more comfortable seating, a broader selection of entertainment options and personal choice of food and beverages.
- Almost all airlines now offer a frequent flyer programme. Members earn points for each flight they take with the carrier and earnings grow through a combination of the miles flown and the amount spent. These points can then be redeemed for a wide range of partner services and discounts on airfares.
- Airlines experience disruptions in flight schedules for various reasons, including bad weather, technical difficulties, airport congestion and delayed preceding flights, leading to connecting flights being missed. Although they may not be at fault, most airlines take responsibility for such disruptions and arrange for food, accommodation, transportation and other services for passengers to mitigate the negative experiences.

All airline employees are trained to deal with the challenges inherent in the aviation sector. For instance, managing aircraft delays and disruptions, angry clients and misplaced baggage is challenging. Employees are required under the service concept to maintain a cheerful demeanour while dealing with such issues, and frequently need empowerment to deal with novel situations during journeys. For example, a passenger may fall ill unexpectedly during a flight. Reservations and customer information services make extensive use of information technology. Mobile applications and information desks are critical in conveying accurate, trustworthy and current information regarding flight connections, timetables, reservations and other related information. CRM will continue to play a key role in determining future performance in the airline business.

Healthcare

Healthcare services have been using CRM initiatives by adopting customer-centric practices. Investment in digital technologies is helping service providers easily retrieve data relating to both patients, non-patient clients, physicians and consultants, among others.

Successful implementation boosts organisation performance and growth, as illustrated by the experience of Apollo Hospitals, an Indian multinational healthcare group, with the digital feedback management system (FMS), which helped the organisation systematically study and resolve customer pain points. The mobile app-based system enhanced customer experience by helping Apollo Hospitals gather all-round feedback from patients, attendees, staff and doctors (Jha, 2016). FMS helped synchronise patient data across relevant medical departments accessed by the patient. The online applications provided a unified customer view on the dashboards of different departments. This user-friendly system helped the organisation quickly resolve customer issues and provide them with excellent service. Systematic data collection, retrieval and integration supported by analytics thus enhanced the customer experience with Apollo Hospitals to boost customer retention (CXOToday, 2018). The application helps patients as they now have convenient access to all details related to their appointments, consultations, prescriptions and diagnostic test reports on their mobile devices.

Reliable, responsive and empathetic doctors and frontline personnel are key criteria when patients and family members choose doctors and healthcare service providers. Customers in India therefore seek feedback from review sites and digital platforms like Practo during their information search process for choosing hospitals and doctors. So, while digital technologies are being leveraged to enhance customer experience, core healthcare services must continue to provide excellent patient outcomes.

Insurance

CRM in insurance is built on a foundation of trust and reliability as this service is used primarily to cover risk. Trust is developed through a track record of helping customers when they face a crisis and reach out to the firm to help them process claims.

Insurance firms have adopted technologies and leveraged digital channels to provide customers with instant access to information and support. Field advisors and surveyors need up-to-date information to help customers with claim processing. Self-service channels, including the internet and digital tools, are used across the customer decision journey for comparing features and players during the buying process, signing up, premium payments and claim processing. Leading insurance players regularly create new products that combine risk mitigation and investments to meet growing customer needs.

Insurance is inherently a low engagement service. Customers tend to remember their insurance providers when they have to pay their premiums periodically or when they make a claim, which are not necessarily the best times to be reminded of a service provider. ICICI Lombard, a leading insurance firm in India, created a mobile application, ILTakeCare, to improve customer engagement by creating opportunities for more regular and positive interactions. In addition to helping customers keep track of their insurance policies, enabling payment of premiums and processing claims, the app offers a 'health vitals' feature through facial scan using a smartphone camera. A 10-second scan provides details such as heart rate and variability, oxygen saturation, respiratory rate and blood pressure. This app is therefore a very convenient way for customers to keep track of their health parameters. It is also a very positive way of continual engagement with regular users.

CRM IN PRODUCT MARKETS

Consumer Durables

Consumer durables are often used for extended periods before a subsequent purchase. Typically, interactions with customers are limited and mostly during purchase or after-sales service. Due to the limited potential for interactions, the likelihood of a customer defecting to another firm is high, particularly if the customer is having difficulty using the product. As a result, companies in the consumer durables business focus on developing long-term, individualised connections with their customers. Loyalty is built up mostly through interactions and not through promotions alone. Both customers and dealers are equally important in the quest for market share. The idea is to enhance and build personalised relationships with customers and dealers with benefits that might be tangible or emotional.

As customer interaction with the firm is quite infrequent and lower than in other industries, this makes it difficult for the firm to get close to the customer. These firms depend a lot on advertising to attract customers to their brands. Most of the information the firms know about their customers is captured during their initial interaction while purchasing the product from a store. This can be partly through details provided by the customer while completing the warranty card. Some firms also ask customers to complete a short questionnaire to collect demographic and lifestyle-related information, which is used to segment the customer base appropriately. The growing preference for buying from e-commerce sites, including Amazon worldwide or Flipkart or Croma in India, has resulted in consumer details being held by these intermediaries. So, brands such as Samsung, Sony, LG and Voltas now try to get customers to share information while filling out warranty cards or during service/product use.

Leading firms pay a lot of attention to customer support through service centres. Regular check-up camps provide an opportunity to help customers and get close to them.

Many CRM initiatives in the consumer durable segment target both customers and dealers. Consumer durable firms also run loyalty programmes, such as Titan Encircle in India and Sony Club, which customers are automatically enrolled in when they make a purchase. These programmes help maintain regular contact with customers through mailshots, newsletters and social media, informing them about new product launches, upgrades, discounts and other promotional offers specially targeted at them. Businesses promote offers and deals to entice existing customers to purchase other products in their portfolio and upgrade their existing products, and exchange programmes are often run to encourage customers to switch from older durables to more advanced models.

Numerous businesses have also established call centres and customer care centres to address client issues. Training programmes for dealers and members of the sales and service teams are crucial components of any customer endeavour. Businesses have increased their market share through cross-selling and up-selling methods. In the consumer durables industry, word of mouth, referrals and branding are critical. However, organisations that can establish good relationships with consumers through various CRM initiatives stand a high chance of success.

Automobiles

Firms in the motoring sector have implemented many innovative CRM programmes. Purchasing a vehicle such as a car or motorbike tends to be a major decision for customers because of the high costs involved. Major players in the automobile sector aim to build long-term relationships with customers over the lifetime of the vehicle and encourage them to buy another from the firm when replacing their vehicle. Therefore, it is important that the firms signal to the customers the importance they attach to them and their relationship. This often includes recognition of the customer as a member of an exclusive group, with all efforts made to win her trust by clearly understanding what the customer expects and aligning the firm's offerings with the needs of the customer.

The relationship begins as soon as the customer purchases the vehicle. Regular maintenance, servicing and replacement of parts after wear and tear ensure performance and reliability. Conveniently located service centres with trained personnel and modern equipment for servicing and repairs are a must in this competitive industry. Feedback on the performance of their vehicles is gained by firms 'listening' to their customers during contact, such as servicing and warranties through firm-owned channels. Market research firms can validate the customer data collected during service delivery. Such validation helps the firm understand customer perceptions of the brand based on their experience with the vehicle.

Complaint resolution is a key driver of customer satisfaction – the faster customer complaints are resolved, the greater the customer satisfaction will be. Many firms monitor satisfaction through periodic interaction using various channels such as newsletters and emails, and increasingly through review sites and social media 'listening'. Customer insights are used to design new products as well as upgrades. A full understanding of all customer usage and interactions with the firm improves customer centricity. Strategy, structure, values and a customer-oriented culture enable superior performance. Senior management needs to be involved not only to make sure that the customer-oriented culture permeates the whole organisation, but also to empower employees and train them suitably. Often automobile firms have an internal cross-functional group that acts as the 'customer's voice' to review business operations and problems from the customer's perspective to enable customer orientation.

Automobile firms keep in touch with their customers through emails, newsletters and social media channels. Some firms might organise customer 'carnivals' at regular intervals to inform existing and prospective customers about their products and give them a feel for their vehicles by offering free test drives.

Tie-ups between automobile and finance firms help customers finance their acquisitions at reasonable interest rates. Dealers are also considered an important link in the entire customer delivery mechanism. Lately, dealers have been offered incentives such as foreign trips, higher commissions, etc. to induce them to make greater efforts to sell vehicles.

All these measures have helped automobile firms retain and acquire new customers. Many customers, if satisfied with the firm's product, might upgrade to a new vehicle from the same firm.

Good after-sales services not only help firms come close to customers and build credibility about their service and commitment towards customers but also help improve sales. Word-of-mouth publicity and goodwill generated from such customer-oriented efforts ultimately helps firms improve their performance.

SUMMARY

If CRM practices are embedded companies can provide pleasurable customer experiences leading to long-standing customer loyalty. Further, CRM is closely related to service recovery, so it can help organisations recover from relatively poor customer experience. The best means of achieving this is via social media platforms, digital channels, email, etc. CRM can also ensure that the organisation's operations align with the set procedures. This conformity is especially useful when the firm faces service failures and customer complaints and resolves problems immediately. If this capability is developed further, the organisation's employees can be trained to respond almost reflexively to issues that might need the focus of CRM practices.

Another important lesson to be learned from the study of CRM is that instantaneous responses to customers' questions can be generated at systemic and systematic levels. Such systemic and embedded development can reduce the costs incurred due to the loss of regular and long-term customers. Additionally, an effective CRM system can function as an anticipatory mechanism to protect the organisation from customer defections. Finally, effective CRM practices can lead to deeply embedded relationships between customers and the organisation that can be sustained by ensuring that the customers' needs are perfectly understood and used as the basis of the various policies, offers and interactions the company has with its customers. In all, CRM is a multi-oriented discipline, function and asset to the organisation that can streamline its marketing, human resources (HR) and production departments simultaneously.

Industry Best Practices

In the competitive world of business, nurturing and managing customer relationships are key to ongoing growth and success. Effective relationship management involves building trust, recognising the impact of losing a customer, promoting Customer Relationship Management (CRM) initiatives and applying strategies that work across all levels. The following methods help increase loyalty and make a business's relationship efforts stand out.

Building Trust and Likeability

- Encourage Word of Mouth: Positive experiences shared by satisfied customers can attract new ones and build trust due to their genuine nature.
- Create Memorable Interactions: Make every encounter with the brand positive and memorable. Personalising experiences and exceeding expectations can leave a lasting impression that sets the brand apart.

Understanding Customer Loss

- Economic Impact: Acknowledge that losing a customer affects more than just immediate sales—it impacts their lifetime value, referral potential, and the brand's reputation.
- Recovery Strategies: Have strategies in place to win back customers by addressing their complaints with personalised solutions and showing genuine commitment to their satisfaction.

Advocating for CRM

- Industry-Specific Benefits: Advocate for CRM by emphasising its benefits tailored to each industry, such as improved customer retention, service efficiency or personalised marketing.

- Data-Driven Insights: Use case studies and return on investment (ROI) analysis to demonstrate the value of CRM investments, helping to secure stakeholder support.

Strategies at Every Level

- Meta-Level Strategies: Adopt broad strategies that shape the company's CRM approach, such as fostering a customer-centric culture, integrating advanced CRM technologies and setting long-term goals.
- Micro-Level Strategies: Pay attention to the execution details, such as customer segmentation for targeted marketing, training staff for better engagement and using feedback for improvement.

Businesses can improve customer loyalty and gain a competitive edge by focusing on building trust, understanding the consequences of customer loss, effectively advocating for CRM, and applying both broad and detailed strategies. These best practices help exceed customer expectations, creating strong and enduring connections between the brand and its customers.

DISCUSSION QUESTIONS

1 Discuss the role of CRM in enhancing customer value through customised services.
2 Discuss the various processes to ensure that effective CRM leads to customer retention.
3 Discuss the advantages of following the CRM practices boost the company's marketing efforts.
4 Discuss the relevant means of tracking the CRM practices of an organisation.
5 Discuss how a company can maintain strong and effective long-term relationships with its customers using CRM practices.

REFERENCES

Berry, L.L. (1995). Relationship marketing. In A. Payne, M. Christopher, M. Clark, & H. Peck (Eds.), *Relationship marketing for competitive advantage: Winning and keeping customers* (pp. 65–74). Butterworth-Heinemann.

Carroll, B. (2011). How Marriott says 'thanks' to build customer loyalty. Retrieved November 19, 2021, from https://customerthink.com/how_marriott_says_thanks_to_build_customer_loyalty/.

CXOToday. (2018). Apollo hospitals using Microsoft AI to improve cardiac care. Retrieved November 19, 2021, from https://www.cxotoday.com/tag/apollo-hospitals/.

Hart, C.W. (1988). The power of unconditional service guarantees. *Harvard Business Review*, July, 54–67. Retrieved November 20, 2021, from https://hbr.org/1988/07/the-power-of-unconditional-service-guarantees.

Hart, C.W., Heskett, J.L., & Sasser, W.E. (1990). The profitable art of service recovery. *Harvard Business Review*, *68*(4), 148–156.

Hyken, S. (2017). Collect data through the customer service center to improve the customer experience. *Forbes.* Retrieved November 21, 2021, from https://www.forbes.com/sites/shephyken/2017/01/28/collect-data-through-customer-service-center-to-improve-customer-experience-cx/?sh=71d64265c6f0.

Jha, S. (2016). Apollo hospitals uses big data analytics to control hospital acquired infections. *Economic Times*. Retrieved November 13, 2021, from https://cio.economictimes.indiatimes.com/news/case-studies/apollo-hospitals-uses-big-data-analytics-to-control-hospital-acquired-infections/55023676.

Parasuraman, A., Zeithaml, V., & Berry, L. (1985). A conceptual model of service quality and its implications for future research. *Journal of Marketing*, *49*(4), 41–50.

Parasuraman, A., Zeithaml, V.A., & Berry, L.L. (1988). SERVQUAL: A multiple-item scale for measuring consumer perceptions of service quality. *Journal of Retailing*, *64*(1), 12–40.

Reichheld, F.F., & Sasser, W.E. (1990). Zero defections: Quality comes to services. *Harvard Business Review*, *68*(5), 105–111.

Social Tables. (2021). Why Marriot's marketing strategy is above the rest. Retrieved November 19, 2021, from https://www.socialtables.com/blog/hotel-sales/marriotts-marketing/.

Swanborg, R. (2009). CRM: How Marriott broke down customer data siloes. Retrieved November 20, 2021, from https://www.cio.com/article/280848/enterprise-software-crm-how-marriott-broke-down-customer-data-siloes.html.

CHAPTER 6

CRM in B2B Markets

CHAPTER OVERVIEW

After reading this chapter, you will be able to understand:

1. The characteristics of business markets, the role of decision-making units and complex business buying process
2. The importance of Customer Relationship Management (CRM) in business-to-business (B2B) markets by understanding the role of customers and technology in the decision-making process
3. Key account management (KAM) and appreciate its necessity for customer retention in B2B markets
4. Customer value aspects such as substantiating customer value propositions, determining customer value in advance and documenting customer value and exceptional performance in the business market

Vignette

Tata Steel, founded in 1907, adopted a customer-centric approach to meet the needs of the competitive market by re-engineering its marketing and sales strategies. Transforming its product portfolio reduced the share of high-volume, low-margin products such as semi-finished steel from 54% to 3%, while high-value flat products used in automobiles and consumer durables increased from 40 to 65% by 2000. The company initiated a branding programme for products bought by contractors and builders from its distribution network to develop application-specific products for roofing, reinforcing and general engineering requirements. Branding improved product identification and boosted brand recall while ensuring a price premium of 5% over rival offerings. In the enterprise segment, characterised by growing competition and price wars, the company adopted an innovative partnership approach to retain and grow the share of business from existing, profitable customers to escape the downward spiral of price pressures (Kotler et al., 2022).

DOI: 10.4324/9781003518174-8

Tata Steel initiated a multi-year, multi-phase customer value management (CVM) programme with the top 25 of its 1500+ business customers to find a long-term solution to combat product commoditisation, and switched selected customers from transaction selling to strategic partnerships to improve both competitiveness and performance. Joint study teams helped streamline multiple interfaces across the entire value chain to eliminate value drains, harness value creation and share opportunities collaboratively. CVM aided Tata Steel's growth into one of the most reliable, responsive and trustworthy partners for these industry-leading customers in automobiles, durables, office furniture and construction. Instead of reducing prices to match competitive offerings, the company collaborated with its strategic partners to jointly identify opportunities for cost reduction in its value chain while exploring value creation opportunities through new product development.

OPENING CASE

Bühler: Insights for CRM

Bühler is one of the world's leading manufacturers of food-processing machinery and plant. Established in 1860 by Adolf Bühler, the Swiss company has two major businesses – grains and food solutions and advanced materials. Its grain-processing technologies and solutions focus on food-processing equipment and plant. Its process engineering and die-casting business focuses on protecting the environment with energy-efficient vehicles, technologies and buildings. The Bühler Group, with a turnover of 3 billion Swiss francs in 2023, operates in 140 countries and employs over 12,500 people to serve more than 30,000 customers worldwide.

Its machinery and plant are used by leading global manufacturers and marketers of branded processed consumer foods – including Nestlé, Mars, Hershey, Cadbury, Ferrero, General Mills and Barilla – for a wide range of products such as chocolates, biscuits, coffee and pasta. Indeed, 75% of the world's chocolates are produced using Bühler's machines. The company is also a leading systems and equipment provider for the rice and wheat processing industry in Asia. As a trusted milling solutions provider for its clients, the company is known for its value-added services and solutions. Bühler Insights, a connected platform for customers of grain milling, generates higher returns for the mills through a structured approach to save energy and increase yield and revenue (Buhler, 2025; Kotler et al. 2022). It offers a detailed analysis of grain mills – in terms of plant performance, yield, availability and operating cost optimisation – that enables mill owners to increase overall efficiency and revenue. Integrated service solutions include minimal interruption production, reduced lead time and improved plant productivity. These value-added solutions help the company build stronger relationships with its clients while maintaining a competitive advantage.

THE CHARACTERISTICS OF BUSINESS MARKETS

In business markets, the buying and selling of goods and services occurs between business organisations. A company may purchase raw materials from another firm or corporation for additional processing or buy finished items or even services to resell to consumers under its brand name. For instance, Indian multinational Britannia Industries purchases flour from numerous mills to manufacture biscuits to be sold in consumer as well as institutional markets.

> The business market comprises of all the organizations that buy goods and services for use in the production of other products and services that are sold, rented or supplied to others. It also includes retailing and other wholesale firms that acquire end goods for the purpose of reselling or renting them to others at a profit. In the business buying process, business buyers determine which products and services their organizations need to purchase and then find, evaluate and choose among alternative suppliers and brands.
>
> (Kotler & Keller, 2016, pp. 201–202)

The business market is bigger in size than the consumer market. Each consumer item involves many processes using various raw materials. For example, to produce a car, the manufacturer must procure parts and components (such as tyres), sub-assemblies, paint, batteries, upholstery and other items from different suppliers or firms. Therefore, many sets of business purchases are made just for items the consumer buys. Although business markets share several aspects with consumer markets, a few key characteristics make them unique. These include:

- Market structure and demand
- The nature of the buying unit
- Types of decisions and decision-making processes
- Major types of buying situations in B2B contexts
- Participants in the business-buying process
- The business-buying process
- The importance of personal relationships.

Market Structure and Demand

Typically, there are innumerable buyers, viz. individuals or households in the consumer market. However, they purchase in smaller quantities. On the other hand, a business market usually contains fewer but larger customers who buy in bulk. The ability to buy large quantities increases their power over sellers. Similarly, business markets are more geographically concentrated as many buyers choose to operate in clusters that provide easy access to talent, resources and infrastructure. For example, chemical manufacturers are more concentrated in the western part of India, while many software firms are located in Bengaluru (Bangalore) in the south.

The demands in business markets are 'derived demand', derived from how much the firm plans to sell to its customers. For instance, Toyota's demand for engines, tyres and paint will depend on the volumes it hopes to sell to consumers in India and elsewhere. Many business markets have inelastic demands – i.e. the total demand for many business products is not affected much by price changes in the short run unless that is linked to consumer demand. Finally, business markets have more fluctuating demands because a small change in consumer demand can cause a large change in business demand. Thus, the demand for many business goods and services tends to change much faster than the demand for consumer goods or services.

The Nature of the Buying Unit

A business purchase usually involves more individuals in the decision-making process and a more professional purchasing effort. As the quantity and value of purchases increase, the number of people involved in the purchase also tends to increase. Purchase of a software solution such as Salesforce for a retail bank's 8000 employees will usually involve managers representing various departments, including sales, marketing, customer services, IT, purchase and finance. Organisations recruit specialists for contracts and purchasing whose entire professional role is dedicated to buying in the business context. The key players involved include technical experts, management and business markets experts, and highly-trained sales personnel.

Decisions and the Decision-Making Process

Business buyers procure products and services for use by their organisations, so they end up making more time-consuming and complex decisions than retail buyers. In addition to the higher volumes and value of purchases, many products, such as an MRI scanner for a hospital's oncology department, involve complex economic and technical considerations. In the buyer's organisation, interactions take place continually between many people across different departments before a decision is made on purchasing. This results in making the business buying process more formalised and structured to handle the complexity.

Decisions are made using a well-defined process after considering multiple criteria involving the assessment of quality, cost and delivery of products. Usually, the process takes a considerable amount of time for deliberation. In the business buying process, buyer and seller are also much more dependent on each other. Therefore, it is common to find sellers working directly with their counterparts in the buying organisations. They help the buyers make decisions by identifying and defining any problems, providing more information on relevant products and informing them about customisation. It is essential for sellers to build close, long-term relationships with their customers. From the point of view of stimuli for business buying situations, the major factors that influence the buying process include the four marketing Ps – i.e., product, price, place and promotion – along with other factors such as economic, technological, political, cultural and competitive forces.

Major Types of Buying Situations in B2B Contexts

Numerous purchasing scenarios arise in business-to-business transactions. They differ from each other with respect to the kind of complexity associated with the decision-making process. The role and involvement of the decision-making unit (DMU) also varies.

Straight re-buy occupies one end of the spectrum. This involves the buyer reordering something from a past supplier without any modifications. The purchase department, based on the list of past suppliers and their performance, routinely places these orders. Many manufacturing firms have an automated reordering system triggered by a drop in inventory levels. In addition to saving time and effort, this automated process ensures timely delivery of parts for operations.

In **modified re-buy**, the buyer modifies product specifications, prices, terms or suppliers, which involves some additional decision-making efforts. Suppliers may get involved, depending on the modifications to the order.

When a firm buys a service or a product for the first time, it is referred to as a **new task situation**. In this case, if the cost or risk associated with the purchase is high, the number of participants in the purchase process increases. Initially, a lot of information about the purchase, the market, suppliers, etc. is collected. Suppliers actively engage with different members of the buying unit to highlight the benefits of their offerings. Decisions involve product specifications, a shortlist of potential suppliers, budget, payment terms, order quantities, delivery schedule and terms, etc. The importance attached to these factors varies and influences the outcome.

In many situations, buyers prefer to buy a packaged solution from a single supplier instead of buying components from various suppliers and then integrating them. This is known as **systems buying**, and helps the organisation avoid the tedious process of making multiple decisions involved in a complex buying situation. 'Systems selling' is a key business marketing strategy for winning and holding accounts. The contract often goes to the firm that provides the most comprehensive solution to meet the customer's needs. Leading software firms (such as SAP and Oracle) market enterprise resource planning (ERP) solutions to customers, which include large banks and insurance firms. In addition to software solutions, these firms help the buying firms through professional services for change management and the training of end users and boost the implementation of various processes.

Participants in the Business-Buying Process

Major purchasing decisions are made in corporate organisations by the 'buying centre', which consists of individuals, units or departments from across the firm – each with a stake in the purchasing decision being made. These stakeholders exert a distinct influence on the purchasing process, all playing different roles while fulfilling specific responsibilities. Individuals who perform one of the following five roles in the purchase decision-making process are included in the buying centre:

1 **Users:** They are members of the organisation who will ultimately use the product or service. They initiate the buying process and help define the product specifications to meet their requirements.
2 **Influencers:** They consist of all members who usually have the technical capability to help define specifications and enlist criteria for evaluating alternatives.
3 **Buyers:** They have formal authority to select sellers and negotiate terms of purchase. Vendor selection, negotiating, contracting and ensuring compliance with agreed terms and conditions (including quality and delivery) are some of their major roles in the procurement process.
4 **Deciders:** They have the formal or informal power to select or approve the final suppliers. Sometimes, buyers may take this role in routine purchases.
5 **Gatekeepers:** They control the flow of information about the products and services being purchased for use by others within the organisation. Often, they have an impact on the decision-making process.

The buying centre may not be a formally identified unit, but is usually a set of roles that different people assume for different purchases. Sometimes in small firms one person might assume all the roles and be involved in all stages of the buying process. The marketer in the selling organisation must know about all the participants involved in the decision making, their relative influence and their evaluation criteria. Sometimes, informal participants may actually make or strongly impact the buying decisions. Business buyers are influenced by environmental, organisational, interpersonal and individual factors, as well as economic factors and accountability. The greater the accountability, the more attention is paid to details. Finally, it can be said that buying decisions result from the complex interactions of ever-changing participants in the buying centre.

The Business-Buying Process

Business-to-business purchasing follows a complex multi-stage process. It typically comprises the following eight stages and usually spans a longer time horizon:

1 **Problem recognition:** An individual manager or department head recognises the problem or the need that can be met by acquiring certain goods or services. Depending on that person's influence, a proposal may be carried further.
2 **General need description:** In this stage, the firm describes the broad characteristics and quantity needed of the required item(s).
3 **Product specification:** The buying organisation specifies the technical characteristics of the required product(s).
4 **Supplier search:** In this stage, the buyer tries to identify a list of potential sellers.
5 **Proposal solicitation:** Qualified suppliers are invited to submit proposals.
6 **Supplier selection:** The decision-making unit reviews the proposals and selects a supplier or suppliers.

7 **Order-routine specification:** The buyer decides and specifies the details of the order, including technical specifications, quantity required, expected delivery time, return policies, warranties, etc.
8 **Performance review:** This is the final stage where the buying organisation formally evaluates the experience with the product and rates all suppliers before deciding whether to continue, modify the order or drop them.

Advances in technology have had a dramatic effect on the B2B marketing process. Increasingly, business buyers are purchasing products and services through online marketplaces or auction sites. This gives buyers access to new suppliers, lowers purchasing costs and hastens order processing and delivery. Business marketers in turn are in touch with customers online to share marketing information, sell products and services, provide customer support services and maintain ongoing customer relationships.

THE IMPORTANCE OF CRM IN B2B

B2B marketers often aim to develop long-term relationships with customers. They leverage opportunities for close interactions with different sets of decision makers and influencers. Today, business customers demand greater responsiveness, reliability and quality consciousness from their vendors. The business-to-business landscape has changed dramatically due to ever-evolving customer needs and to factors such as the internet. The rapid rise of e-commerce and online marketplaces has created more options for customers. Buying firms are able to access instant information on demand and supply situations. Suppliers provide product-related information including quality, availability, price and delivery conditions online to help buyers make more informed choices. The proliferation of digital service providers has also enabled vendor comparison on various parameters to be readily accessible to buyers. These service providers also act as intermediaries. Online auction sites and e-marketplaces empower buying firms to specify requirements for sellers to compete for the order. Companies can now plan for daily trading to reduce their inventory and obtain competitive prices for their purchases. All these innovations have given rise to a situation wherein it becomes very easy for customers to switch from one supplier to another.

Industrial customers use a range of purchasing strategies in today's business environment. They may purchase commoditised, low-value products from the open market when they do not perceive much difference in the quality of the offerings of various suppliers in the marketplace. In such situations, suppliers compete for sales by outbidding one another and offering superior services based on delivery time and support. For high-value, mission-critical items, business customers usually opt for long-term close engagement with selected vendors. Supplier partners are selected more carefully in these instances, and customers use different supplier management strategies to cut costs and enhance product quality and responsiveness from their vendors. In addition, they demand greater value addition, tighter integration with their processes and systems so as to lower the total cost of ownership, higher service levels and more cost-effective solutions.

Thus, fierce competition for the top customers, rising customer acquisition costs, maturing markets, the commoditisation of many products and services through e-commerce and lower vendor switching costs have forced vendors to focus on building customer loyalty. They seek to develop and nurture long-term and mutually beneficial relationships with their customers. It is not uncommon to find suppliers signing long-term contracts (up to ten years) for products and services. Vendors also agree to integrate their systems with the customers to reduce the lead time required for making purchases. In many industries, the top-ranking companies have taken the lead and implemented CRM concept, which has resulted in a clear competitive advantage for them. The following are some of the strategies that firms in the B2B markets have adopted to sustain competitive advantage (Bansal & Gupta, 2000):

- Focusing on key customers and building strong relationships with them.
- Proactively generating high levels of customer satisfaction with every interaction.
- Anticipating customer needs by careful study of the environment, customer processes and behaviour. The firm can then respond to these needs even before the competition becomes aware of them.
- Building closer ties with customers, sometimes by integrating their systems.
- Finally, creating value perception – customers must see their relationship with vendors as something that brings value and adds to their competitive advantage. Otherwise, customers will take their business elsewhere.

Mjunction and GeM Portals

India's mjunction, a B2B e-marketplace within Tata, was set up in 2001 as an online auction portal to sell steel. It has steadily transformed into an end-to-end value service provider in over a dozen categories, including steel, coal, oil, minerals, real estate and forest produce, among others. Its e-bidding platform connected buyers and sellers directly, bypassing intermediaries, and thus added value to both buyers and sellers with faster inventory conversion, fair prices and access to multiple buyers and sellers.

Regulatory requirements for transparency, met by online auctions, attracted the attention of the Indian government and public sector companies, which soon turned into key segments for mjunction. The transaction value on its platform rocketed from $0.01 billion in FY02 to $14.7 billion in FY20.

Mjunction has leveraged the evolving business landscape, driven by the growing adoption of digitalisation, and has transformed itself into an integrated e-marketplace. Its technology-based trading solutions are integrated with support services such as transport, procurement and finance. Its tie-up with multiple banks facilitates end-to-end supply and demand solutions with funding options for clients.

Mjunction's advanced offering – mjPRO – is a cloud-based procurement service that combines artificial intelligence (AI) and machine learning (ML). In 2018, the company shifted from software licensing to cloud-based software as a service model for its e-procurement application. The model, which offers pay-per-use, helps clients save on upfront capital investments in hardware and licensing, and allows them to configure systems to align with their procurement workflow and rules. Insights from the platform's analytical tools help clients improve their procurement process and save costs. Mjunction's services span the entire B2B e-commerce spectrum, from sales, sourcing, procurement and finance to loyalty solutions (mjunction, 2025).

The Indian Government e Marketplace (GeM) platform, set up in 2016, facilitates online procurement of products and services by public entities. It provides tools for e-bidding, reverse e-auction and demand aggregation to boost transparency, efficiency, value for money and speed in public procurement. The rapidly growing platform enabled orders worth $5 billion in 2021, clocking a compound annual growth rate (CAGR) of 93% over five years (2016–2021). The total value of orders rose to over $50 billion in FY2023–24 procured through 6.3 million orders. The mandated buying of goods and services on the GeM platform for public organisations and government departments makes it necessary for sellers targeting public institutions to establish their presence on the platform.

Digital platforms like mjunction and GeM are levelling the playing field for suppliers, especially small and medium enterprises (SMEs), while improving choice and reducing buyer information asymmetries.

CUSTOMERS AND TECHNOLOGY

Customers

Typically, a small percentage of a B2B firm's customer base (20% or less) accounts for more than 70–80% of its revenue and profits, so it is essential for the firm to identify these key customers. Identification of key customers is based on the following two factors:

1. **Lifetime value**: It is important to assess what the customer will potentially contribute to the seller throughout their relationship. Factors that need to be considered include estimated annual revenues, cost of acquisition, cost of retention and potential retention rate. Estimating the future value of the customer based on expected business is often very difficult in business markets. However, it will be a critical determinant of the firm's success in managing relationships with its most profitable current customers.
2. **Strategic importance of the customer**: A firm must also assess the customer's contributions in maintaining its competitive edge. Some customers are important simply because they are major players in the market. The supplier's reputation is enhanced by serving such customers, so they cannot afford to lose these leading players as they play a key role in helping the seller firm achieve its current business goals. However, a customer who is currently a large buyer may have a comparatively low lifetime value if it is not very profitable and draws resources away from the firm's most profitable and loyal customers.

Technology

Technology plays a critical role in relationship development in today's business environment by easing the information flow along the value chain. Commercial customers increasingly invest in technology to improve their collaboration with supplier partners. As customer demand becomes much more evident across the extended supply chain, it enables suppliers to be more responsive to their customers' needs while also allowing businesses to reduce excess inventory and stock obsolescence. Improved customer data flow also helps companies monitor purchase behaviour more carefully and take proactive steps to establish brand equity. At a later partnership stage, businesses start sharing data with vendors to analyse and forecast demand.

Technology is transforming how connections are formed and managed. More specifically, digitisation has increased and is seen explicitly in the extensive use of mobile devices and digital solutions with capabilities for new, innovative, seamless and faster customer service across all elements of the B2B value chain. Real-time responsiveness and the easy use of mobile apps have significantly influenced B2B activities. Logistics management solutions from leading players in India, such as Delhivery and Porter, use retail tracking apps for all B2B shipping to connect their e-commerce customers with their retail consumers and business buyers. Live tracking of shipments via apps using smartphones and the internet for all customer requirements is making these companies very competitive while helping their customers grow.

Several developments in the digital space have supported improvements in customer experience for B2B businesses. Redesigning customer experience processes to enhance satisfaction and loyalty transforms firms that outperform competitors. Digital tools aid this transformation through applications that facilitate real-time connections with customers for problem resolution and self-service.

The use of digital platforms boosts loyalty among B2B customers. For example, there could be 30,000 employees serving a large global client base in an IT company. These employees might report different issues while serving this client. These are then shared with other relevant employees in real time so that they are aware of the client's specific requirements. These digitised incident management platforms thus widen the focus of employees as they can immediately learn from any incident and prevent other incidents occurring with the client. This reduction in incident occurrence maximises positive customer experience and increases loyalty.

The effective adoption of digital technologies in the B2B context requires a deeper understanding of the customer experience before aiming for improvement. It is imperative to understand the B2B customers' buying behaviour and use this understanding to enhance the customer experience. When the customer base is heterogeneous and comprises firms with very distinctive requirements, it requires dealing with customers on a one-to-one basis. For example, a large bank planning to optimise its lending process for its business customers started by understanding the perspectives of multiple stakeholders (including the company head, finance head and managers responsible for risk management, sales and customer service) to develop a deeper understanding of their buying process and decision making. These insights helped the bank explore options to offer customised solutions aligned to its business customers' needs.

Another bank developed two tracks based on its customers' journey: (1) an express track that allowed faster approval for low-risk, accessible deals requiring less verification and smaller teams; and (2) an advanced track for more complicated deals involving auditing and risk assessment after extensive discussions with senior managers. Risk assessment, chosen to differentiate the tracks, could be deployed with the help of digital platforms that provide instant access to an applicant's details. Subsequently, the stakeholders' views were instituted while connecting with other relevant parties via digital media. Digital channels expedited the process and enhanced the customer experience as the work was delivered to the client on time in line with specifications and requirements (Maechler et al., 2016).

The following two sections will explore the concepts of key account management (KAM) and customer value in business markets. These elements of technology and CRM were adopted by Volvo for its commercial vehicle business, which has a portfolio of buses, trucks and earth-moving equipment used by transporters, freight operators and the construction industry. Volvo's marketing, sales and service teams use advanced automation to provide content and support to prospects, buyers and users. Long-standing customer relationships, dealerships and service centres engage with the company through online channels and digital platforms. According to Johnston (2011), this programme aimed to provide Volvo's stakeholders with relevant and appropriate product- and service-related information to support customers in the following ways:

- Employing new online marketing processes and analytics. Integrating CRM for online interactions with customers helps gain a 360° view of each customer, such as a freight operator who has a few dozen Volvo trucks. Customers receive an integrated view of their own dealings with Volvo, while dealers and employees receive actionable insights.
- Redesigning the digital channels helped engage more closely with leads. Online communications and interactions were synced with customer details.
- Data related to leads were integrated with sales (including online sales), warranties, credit, surveys, social media, lead results and analytics. This process was automated and synced with online activities through streamlined and automated processes. Regular updating ensured that relevant data was used for the evolving customer profiles and usage.
- Automation increased the lead data distribution to the internal sales team as well as the dealer partners.
- The company integrated this new process in all online customer activities, communications and interactions.

All these initiatives ensured real-time reports on managing the leads and resulted in an increase in sales of up to 30%. The key learning is that technology for marketing automation that improves the customer experience can significantly boost business performance. Speedy response and feedback to stakeholders are imperatives that can be accomplished by leveraging digital technologies (Johnston, 2017).

KEY ACCOUNT MANAGEMENT

Key account management is one of the most widely used and successful customer retention and development strategies. It has been recognised as an important part of the customer relationship management programmes in business markets. KAM is an organisational approach that B2B suppliers employ to maintain relationships with critical clients and provide quantifiable and tangible business results.

Key Accounts

A key account is defined as a customer in the business market who has been identified by a selling organisation as of strategic importance to the achievement of the supplier's corporate objectives (Millman, 1995). In the literature, the term 'key accounts' tends to be used interchangeably with other terms such as 'national accounts' and 'major accounts'. Definitions of national and major accounts typically focus on the geographical spread and size of customers, emphasising criteria such as sales turnover, profitability, centralised planning systems, etc. Millman (1995) classified national accounts as a sub-category of key accounts. However, not all key accounts need to be national. Not all customers are equally profitable or equally important. In fact, when accessing a new market, some sellers and vendors identify certain customers as key accounts not due to their profitability or potential lifetime value (which may be low) but due to other criteria such as prestige or reference value. All key accounts are of strategic importance to the seller. However, they may vary widely with respect to other variables like firm size (e.g. small or large) in comparison with the seller or operations (viz. local vs. global).

Using KAM for Customer Segmentation

Analysis of existing customer portfolios helps a firm categorise customers according to their performance and value to the firm. Many managers attempt to segment customers based on their profitability. The trickiest part in this kind of analysis is allocating and defining the costs that should be included in the analysis at different levels of aggregation. Instead of spreading the total costs across all customers, it is essential to estimate the real costs of serving each customer as they require different levels of service, promotion mix, sales strategies, customisation, etc. Such analysis requires a focus on the true costs, especially the incremental costs, over and beyond the routine order processing and service support. For example, customisation may be costly to achieve; however, a sales manager, in his eagerness to get an order, may promise very high levels of customisation without knowing the total cost of that customisation. Therefore, an account that could have been profitable now contributes very little to the selling firm.

Such a scenario is very common and is an outcome of the firm's inability to capture true costs to serve its customers. Other customer-related information that marketing managers may find useful with respect to accounts and its management include:

- Growth in profitability along with sales.
- Interactions, buying behaviour, usage and characteristics of decision makers in each key account.
- The cost of serving these customers vs. their contribution.
- The risks and potential financial impacts of losing a key account.

CRM solutions incorporate account management modules that offer scope for such detailed analysis. They generate financial performance reports on a regular basis and help assess the future profit impact of a key account decisions and changes in the trading environment.

Managers can also perform sensitivity and scenario analyses to assess opportunities and threats, which helps identify changes that make a customer unprofitable.

KAM is also used for sales and business development planning after relevant segmentation to select the right accounts team for mapping opportunities to drive the success of KAM in an organisation (Ryals, 2012).

Customer Retention Strategy

In relationship marketing the emphasis shifts from the *transactional model*, which involves seeking and acquiring new customers, to the *relational model*, which involves enhancing value to secure repeat business while moving towards full partnership. In the relational model, *retention* is seen as a strategy that involves building customer loyalty through higher levels of customer satisfaction. Customers are divided into groups to identify the value they place on long-term relationships before setting the KAM process for customer retention strategies.

Leaders encounter several challenges while formulating customer development plans. One of them is related to contrasting opinions across different departments arising out of differences in perspectives. For example, marketing and selling functions place different emphasis on the key aspects of relationships with customers, leading to them losing sight of potential frictions in interface when customers engage with the supplier firm. Similarly, the differing priorities of marketing and purchase functions can create challenges. While marketing focuses on areas such as customer service, branding, public relations, etc., purchasing focuses on improving supply chain efficiencies through cost-cutting initiatives, vendor development for quality improvement and partnership, etc.

Another important aspect of KAM is the receptivity that sellers and buyers display towards such programmes. The parties may not wish to get close to each other or may not be willing to commit to such an arrangement. The potential for mismatch between the objectives and aspirations of buyers and sellers may prove important, especially when developing long-term relationships. While a seller may see a new account as a prospective long-term customer, the buyer may view it as a one-time purchase or use it to obtain more competitive quotes from other sellers. It is better to fully understand customer behaviour and use receptivity to KAM strategies as a major segmentation variable. Each account may require a different allocation of resources to the relational mix as part of the account plan.

KAM as a Growth and Development Strategy

Most businesses concentrate their KAM efforts on customer retention and ensure their operations remain stable. This strategy, however, is insufficient in response to the long-term structural shift in the business environment. The more critical task in this situation is to capitalise on the potential of key accounts and use it to raise the share of profitable customers. A business can successfully implement KAM as a growth and development strategy if it has the diagnostic tools necessary to understand the customer's business and add value to the firm. A critical component of successful KAM is balancing client retention and increasing the share of revenue from retained clients. KAM is an organisational approach based on the premise that relationships are not static and evolve. Each interaction is a result of the customer–supplier relationship. In turn, the interaction influences the relationship and its growth. Millman and Wilson (1995) created a six-stage model that is a useful tool for examining sources of competitive advantage and characterising managerial behaviour. The model's stages are outlined below.

1 Pre-KAM: In this stage it is essential for the firm to identify those accounts that have the potential to move towards key account status so that it does not waste time and money on those accounts that do not have that potential. At this stage, selling strategies are concerned with making basic products or services available, and information about the customer is also gathered in order to determine whether or not they have the potential become a key account.
2 Early KAM: In this stage a firm explores opportunities for closer collaboration with its customers by examining their motives, behaviour, culture, strengths and weaknesses. The firm then highlights the potential benefits they may enjoy as 'preferred' customers. A detailed understanding of three aspects is very important at this stage: (1) the decision-making process; (2) the nature of the decision-making unit; and (3) the buyer's business and problems. Internally, the firm will have to look at promoting the importance of a particular account to the firm as a whole. In addition, the firm will have to promote the importance of benefits such as non-standard offerings to members of their own firm. The focus of the sales effort is on building trust through consistent performance and open communication.
3 Mid-KAM: As the relationship between firm and customers deepens, the level of trust and the range of problems that are addressed increase, as does the amount of contact between the firm's employees and its customers. This implies that the sales personnel's role in the customer relationship will decline and the top management's role will increase. The relationship may fall short of exclusivity and the activities of competitors within this account may require constant review.
4 Partnership KAM: This represents a mature stage of key account development. The supplier is often viewed as an external resource of the customer and the sharing of sensitive commercial information becomes commonplace. Joint problem resolution is the main focus at this stage of the relationship development.
5 Synergistic KAM: At this advanced stage, key account management goes beyond the partnership level, and the two organisations tend to see each other as parts of a larger entity creating joint value in the marketplace.
6 Uncoupling KAM: This is the final stage wherein the partnership comes to an end. Partnerships that are ill conceived or that have outlived their usefulness and served their purpose should not be allowed to continue beyond a certain point. Sometimes short-term relationships might prove to be more profitable than long-term relationships. Getting out of ill-conceived relationships and into a new one will minimise substantial economic, political and emotional costs associated with building a relationship that was never destined to last. However, managers view this as a painful stage for the parties concerned.

The above model of key account relational development implies that fundamental changes are required in the approach to customer needs by selling companies. In the initial stages of KAM development, managers might seek to focus on product/service attributes and, in the later stages, they move towards more sophisticated offerings that solve a wide range of problems.

KAM helps sellers achieve a deeper organisational level understanding of their customers. Strategies evolve and differ for each stage of the relationship with customers. As supplier firms improve their understanding of customers based on their experiences, they have more opportunities to adapt to each stage of their relationship. Thus, KAM may be viewed as an important initiative aimed at developing long-term, mutually beneficial relationships.

KAM is very effective, with a proven track record of success across multiple sectors in manufacturing, service and technology. The following steps will be helpful in successfully implementing KAM.

1. **KAM requires organisational change not a sales approach:** Companies that consider KAM to be another sales technique do not succeed. It requires a change in the organisational approach to dealing with customers, so it impacts other functions in addition to sales. KAM is a commitment and a dedicated undertaking for priority customers. The promises to these customers must be delivered precisely to execute KAM. Operations, delivery and supply chain must be actively involved to support key customers. The key to success is to train the operation and supply chain employees and the sales department in KAM.
2. **Top-level buy-in:** The involvement of top leaders is required to successfully execute organisational change involving cross-functional coordination and collaboration. Active participation of the chief experience officers (CXOs) during programme evaluation shows the signal commitment to the programme.
3. **KAM champion:** Appointing a senior leader as a KAM champion drives the implementation effectively. The KAM champion will need top management support to make organisational changes and draw on organisational resources to implement customer-centric programmes. In addition to being passionate about KAM, the champion must excel at influencing skills and exhibit energy and enthusiasm. Tetra Pak, a leading global food processing and packaging solutions company, has two KAM champions who travel to its businesses worldwide to sell the message about KAM within the organisation.
4. **Selection of key accounts:** It is imperative to identify the key accounts carefully to succeed in the KAM programme. The secret to success is to start with a few exceptional accounts as it will be easier to add more at a later stage. Large enterprises typically start small (with up to five key accounts), experiment, learn and then evolve to grow their base of key accounts. For example, Xerox now manages over 100 key accounts.
5. **Assign and train key account managers:** Many firms identify their key accounts and then convert their sales manager's role into one of relationship manager to handle the account. However this is not the most effective strategy as KAM requires a different mindset and approach centred on how client firms and their stakeholders work. A firm's best sales staff may not be effective people managers to influence customers and internal teams. Training in skills to develop business acumen, financial knowledge, people management, negotiation and influencing help transform managers into key account managers.

6 **Develop the right metrics:** Identifying the right metrics is also important for the successful implementation of KAM. A leading software firm includes performance metrics that mirror the objectives set for clients to highlight accomplishments of account-level strategies, financial performance of the account (e.g., revenue, profitability), repeat business, resource utilisation, and productivity and metrics on client and employee satisfaction. Its account scorecard also captures intangibles like the number of references by account, brand enhancement value, contribution to knowledge and competency assets.

7 **Establish and enhance benchmarks:** Key account management is a dynamic process that should be refreshed regularly to evolve over time. Developing benchmarks for improvement through customer meets and industry best practices enhances value for both partners.

To conclude, KAM can have a significant influence on an organisation's performance. However, a clear implementation plan, as outlined in the above seven steps, is needed to successfully transition to KAM. This process is worth exploring and has been successfully adopted by leading firms in the B2B space (Schmitt, 2013).

CUSTOMER VALUE MANAGEMENT IN B2B

Value has emerged as the key element in business marketing because of the dominant role of functionality or performance of the offering made by the seller. Businesses discover that viewing supplier–customer relationships as isolated exchanges is not enough. It is also imperative to differentiate the offering from competitors. This differentiation can be created by focusing on those benefits that are relevant to the customer. Growing competition can be managed by continually offering superior customer value propositions.

The essential element that companies need to consider for value propositions is that offerings must focus on key customer requirements and expectations. These benefits may consist of technical and social aspects and customers' values. Additionally, these value propositions can be enhanced by offering only elements needed by the customer segments. Leading companies such as Tata Steel, Bühler and Tetra Pak have adopted customer value management processes for differentiating their offerings while increasing their share of customers' wallet through long-term relationship-building initiatives.

Many suppliers list all possible benefits of their offerings to all customers. However, this simple listing of benefits will not effectively communicate the real value to each specific customer seeking highly differentiated propositions tailored to their business requirements. Therefore, understanding customer requirements is the starting point for developing value propositions. This process would also help companies sustain profitable growth (Anderson et al., 2006).

The concept of a value chain where a firm in the business market is part of a larger ecosystem in delivering value to the end customer is becoming central to ensuring sustained competitiveness. Anderson and Narus (2004) represented business market processes as comprising three distinct elements with corresponding value opportunities, as shown in Figure 6.1.

Understanding Value	Creating Value	Delivering Value
Crafting Marketing Strategy	Managing Market Offerings	Gaining Customers
Understanding Firms as Customers	New Offering Realisation	Sustaining Reseller Partnerships
Market Sensing	Business Channel Management	Sustaining Customer Relationships

FIGURE 6.1 Customer Value Management in Business Markets

Adapted from Anderson and Narus (2004).

Value in business markets is the worth in monetary terms of the economic, technical, service and social benefits a firm receives in exchange for the price it pays for a market offering (Anderson & Narus, 2004). This value can be created only when the problem is clearly defined. Managers are under constant pressure to reduce costs and offer lower prices. A focus on value reduces this constant search for matching lower price offerings. It involves the following aspects:

1 **Substantiate Customer Value Proposition:** Several value propositions are offered by suppliers. However, they lack the people, processes, tools and experience to substantiate their claims, so customers often dismiss these propositions. The suppliers must therefore demonstrate the feasibility of any value proposition they want to undertake for the customers. This proposition can be conducted by using the 'value word equation', which uses words and mathematical operators to assess the differences in performance among offerings. This equation provides the best choices of appropriate value proposition for the resources available. Thus, value estimates can be collected from the businesses. This estimation can be determined after coordinating the suppliers' and customers' views and requirements.
2 **Determine Customer Value in Advance:** Prospective customers must understand the cost savings and added value when choosing a supplier. Suppliers can easily demonstrate this value proposition to customers through value case histories and value calculators. Value case histories are documents that indicate the cost savings and the added value that customers would receive after using a particular supplier's offering. Value calculators and value assessments are essential tools for sales teams to determine potential customers' value after using a supplier's offerings.
3 **Document Customer Value:** After determining and demonstrating value propositions to potential customers, it is important to document these processes. These documents aim to express monetary along with technical, economic, service and social benefits the customer would receive from the supplier's offerings. The supplier must also document the cost savings and incremental profits companies might receive after providing these offerings. These documents help refine customer value models and develop value case histories. They also enhance the credibility of supplier offerings and support managers in receiving credit from potential customers. More importantly, in developing the documents, suppliers gain knowledge and experience of and confidence in their offerings.

This confidence provides further refinement in customer value propositions and offerings, which are developed for various kinds of customer ad categories. Further, for systematic documentation, the following elements should be considered:

- *Economic Benefits:* Monthly consolidated invoices are developed after invoicing each customer transaction. Transactions are also processed according to the customers' yearly cost savings.
- *Technical Advantages:* These are very important and need to be recorded as catalysts in the value proposition. Faster operations and seamless technical support add to company revenue and profits. They also generate high up-time and quicker cycle times for the organisations.
- *Unique Service:* This exceptional service must be recorded explicitly by companies as it acts as a key differentiator and facilitates in gaining competitive advantage. For example, a supplier that uses natural raw materials would save costs and position the organisation as an eco-friendly company that acts uniquely.
- *Social Benefit:* This is gaining greater importance for businesses because customers approve of companies that work for the benefit of society. Companies must document this benefit to act as critical differentiators.
- *Exceptional Performance in Business:* Systematically structured, constructed and delivered customer value propositions significantly influence and contribute to business performance. Precisely, these value propositions are fundamental elements of the primary business strategy. For example, Tetra Pak has developed unique value propositions that are distinctive, measurable and sustainable. It also meticulously records the impact of value propositions on business units in terms of their performance.

Customer value propositions can significantly impact business performance. However, developing value propositions is not a one-time task delegated to marketing. It requires continuous work to invest in innovations, adopt the latest technologies and assess the impact on helping business customers win in competitive markets. As dynamic markets evolve rapidly, customers and competitors change; so value propositions that worked successfully in the past will no longer be relevant.

To reiterate the above, Anderson and Narus (2004) define value in business markets as the monetary worth of the economic, technical, service and social benefits a client firm receives in exchange for the price it pays for a market offering (e.g., rupees/dollars per unit, per litre or even per year). Benefits represent net benefits; that is, all costs incurred by the customer (except price) are deducted to calculate the net benefits. The market offering comprises two elements – value and price. Value is what a client firm gets in return for the price paid. Finally, value considerations take place within a competitive context, so customers can choose, including an option to make the product instead of buying it. The essential concept of value is represented in the following equations:

$$\text{Value} = \text{Benefits} - \text{Costs (other than price)}$$

$$V_f = B_f - C_f \quad (6.1)$$

where V_f = Value of the offering by firm *f*; B_f = Benefits of the offering by firm *f*; and C_f = Costs incurred by the customer firm in obtaining the desired benefits.

$$\begin{aligned}&\text{Customer Incentive to Buy (CIB)} = \text{Value} - \text{Price}\\&\text{CIB}_\text{f} = V_f - P_f\\&\text{CIB}_\text{f} > \text{CIB}_\text{a}\ \text{(CIB for the Alternative)}\\&(V_f - P_f) > (V_a - P_a)\end{aligned} \quad (6.2)$$

The final equation indicates that the customer firm will be motivated to purchase an offering only if the customer is incentivised to buy (CIB) – i.e., the difference between the value and price of the offering is more significant than the CIB of the alternatives. It is important to note that, in business markets, the value of an offering does not change with an increase or decrease in price. Instead, a change in price changes the customer's incentive to buy. If the price does not change a value, what makes it change? The answer lies in Eq. (6.1). Value changes when the market offering provides the same functionality or performance while the cost to the customer changes. The cost to the customer does not include the price. For example, a product with the same performance specifications as a competing product but with lower operational costs provides higher customer value.

Alternatively, value changes with the functionality or performance changes while expenses remain the same (price is not part of this cost). Value analysis is instrumental in business markets where purchase costs are a significant component of the overall costs and motivates customers to pressure suppliers to reduce prices. Value analysis, conducted by suppliers, helps customers focus on total costs and not just acquisition costs. A thorough understanding of the drivers of benefits and costs to customers helps identify the key aspects of suppliers' offerings that contribute to customer value.

CLOSING CASE

Federal Express: Customer Value Proposition

Federal Express (FedEx), the American multinational courier delivery service provider (headquartered in Memphis, Tennessee), is known for its exceptional global credibility. The company wanted to create a niche in the air cargo market (Conlon, 2004). It wished to target the small package market for shipping, which would help the company increase its profit and would need less space while shipping. They named this service the 'courier pack' (CP) as the cost was low ($4.25) compared to the standard $10.60. The CP was therefore profitable for both company and customers.

The primary customers for CP were from the service industry, with around 15.5 million shipments every year, which accounted for 1.87% of the company's market. FedEx introduced a marketing plan of $100,000 to promote CP services, and identified that it had to increase business by 25% to break even quickly. This increase in business was directly associated with the flights used for carriage. FedEx identified that it would need flights that could carry 10,000 pounds (around 4536 kg) of such packs after acquiring many CP customers and generating business from them.

FedEx faced intense competition from the airfreight industry. Competitors included Air Cargo (which had thousands of freight forwarders) and Emery and Schulman, renowned for their postal services in the US. Interestingly, FedEx had its known 'Priority One' service that delivered services overnight, even weightier packages, for just $23.56. There could be brand cannibalisation within FedEx because CP and the company's priority service aimed to deliver shipments overnight at reasonable rates. Many airlines in the US also provide express postal services to customers. They were also competing with CP, so there was intense competition within and outside FedEx for CP to excel and grow (Lovelock, 2003).

After understanding the intense competition, let us now explore the various customer value propositions FedEx offered and delivered to succeed in this complex environment. CP used an acquisition strategy to gain a competitive advantage; the company acquired rush service providers. CP might have used a customer retention strategy as it could be cost effective and beneficial in the long run. However, it realised that acquisition was easier to measure and more feasible as CP was at the nascent stage with a meagre market share. FedEx wanted a unique differentiation strategy for CP to gain a competitive advantage and high value, benefits and incentives for customers to select its services. FedEx already had sales teams in major cities in the US, and used them to promote CP primarily on a B2B basis. CP located various industries that provided the highest profit per CP usage. CP selected B2B as FedEx realised that its primary customers were also from the B2B industry. These customers quickly associated FedEx with B2B as they assumed the company was essentially linked to office-related services.

FedEx also determined that office equipment and orientation would be other areas to grow in this strategy and environment. CP thoroughly analysed the profiles of its B2B customers in terms of their transactions with FedEx. These customers were from various industries. CP created a ratio of the number of packs used every month in an account and the balance was tabulated for each industry associated with CP. It was found that office equipment and printing made significant contributions to the company.

The demand in the market increased as CP was considered cheaper than other service providers. Customers with packets weighing less than 2 pounds wanted to use CP services. More importantly, when there were fewer than 26 boxes in a week, CP even reduced the price to $10 from $12.50. This reduction was to encourage customers to use their services and provide them with business to reach their break-even point. However, CP reduced the minimum quantity needed to place an order. CP used this strategy as more customers would use the service, it would receive bulk orders and customers could receive discounts on those orders. CP also expedited and increased its delivery speed while retaining the existing distribution systems and processes to reduce costs, working on ground freight and flights to speed up processes within the existing infrastructure. The procedures were expedited because customers expected speedy delivery, and customer satisfaction was directly related to the prompt delivery of products.

To conclude, FedEx's CP faced several challenges from both the industry and the company itself, but managed these challenges by working on customer-centric strategies and well-developed customer propositions. The company developed cost-effective processes and approaches and achieved higher profits with little investment in infrastructure by determining critical areas within the business and allocating appropriate resources, including employees who could help it achieve its business goals (Lovelock, 2003).

SUMMARY

In this chapter, we explored the nature of business markets, the role of the buying unit and the business buying process. After briefly highlighting the role of technology, we focused on key account management (KAM) and customer value management. Further, we learnt about the role of multiple stakeholders in the business buying process, and saw the expertise and experience required to achieve long-term affiliation with consumers. The chapter also highlighted the importance of value propositions expected by business customers. In conclusion, we could see that B2B markets require differentiated approaches to customer relationship management.

DISCUSSION QUESTIONS

1. Discuss the key differences between B2B and B2C in scale, operation and organisational philosophy.
2. Discuss the means and techniques a company must develop in finance, logistics, operations and talent to ensure it possesses the optimal B2B programme.
3. Discuss the importance of KAM as an integral element of B2B for customer retention and growth.
4. Discuss the opportunities and threats of CRM in B2B in the digital context.
5. Discuss the importance of customer value propositions for B2B.
6. Discuss the means of maximising customer value propositions for B2B contexts.

REFERENCES

Anderson, J., & Narus, J. (2004). *Business market management: Understanding, creating and delivering value* (2nd edn). Upper Saddle River, NJ: Pearson Prentice-Hall.

Anderson, J., Narus, J., & Rossum, W. (2006). Customer value propositions in business markets. Retrieved February 24, 2017, from https://www.vlerick.com/en/research-and-faculty/research-for-business/marketing-sales/vlerick-sales-excellence-centre/activities/article-summaries/customer-value-propositions-in-business-markets.

Bansal, S., & Gupta, G. (2000). Building customer loyalty in business-to-business commerce. In J. Sheth, A. Parvatiyar, & G. Shainesh (Eds.), *Customer relationship management: Emerging concepts, tools and applications*. New Delhi: Tata McGraw-Hill.

Buhler (2025), 'Buhler Insights - Our Platform for Digital Services' Retrieved February 15, 2025 from https://www.buhlergroup.com/global/en/services/digital-services/buhler-insights.html

Conlon, G. (2004). CRM delivers for FedEx. Retrieved November 19, 2021, from https://www.destinationcrm.com/Articles/CRM-News/CRM-Featured-Articles/CRM-Delivers-for-FedEx-44636.aspx.

Johnston, J. (2011). Case study: How Volvo uses advanced automation to deliver relevant buying stage content to customers and keep the sales force advised. Retrieved November 20, 2021, from https://docplayer.net/6009577-Case-study-how-volvo-uses-advanced- automation-to-deliver-relevant-buying-stage-content-to-customers-and-keep-the-sales-force-advised.html.

Johnston, J. (2017). Volvo construction equipment: Hitachi solutions. Retrieved April 21, 2017, from http://www.customereffective.com/volvo-construction.php.

Kotler, P., & Keller, K.L. (2016). *Marketing management* (15th edn, Indian adaptation). New Delhi: Pearson India.

Kotler, P., Keller, K.L., Chernev, A., Sheth, J.N., & Shainesh, G. (2022). *Marketing management* (16th edn, Indian adaptation). New Delhi: Pearson India.

Lovelock, C. (2003). *Federal Express: Early history*. Harvard Business School.

Maechler, N., Sahni, S., & Oostrum, M. (2016). Improving the business-to-business customer experience. Retrieved November 20, 2021, from https://www.mckinsey.com/business-functions/marketing-and-sales/our-insights/improving-the-business-to-business-customer-experience.

Millman, T. (1995). Key account management in business-to-business markets. In A Payne (Ed.), *Advances in relationship marketing*. London: Kogan Page.

Millman, T., & Wilson, K. (1995). From key account selling to key account management. *Journal of Marketing Practice: Applied Marketing Science*, *1*(1), 9–21. https://doi.org/10.1108/EUM0000000003877.

mjunction (2025), 'mjPRO' Retrieved February 15, 2025 from https://www.mjunction.in/services/eprocurement/mjpro/

Ryals, L. (2012). How to succeed at key account management. *Harvard Business Review*, 13 July. Retrieved November 20, 2021, from https://hbr.org/2012/07/how-to-succeed-at-key-account.

Schmitt, J. (2013). Segmentation, your key to successful sales territory planning. Retrieved November 20, 2021, from https://www.salesforce.com/content/blogs/us/en/2013/04/segmentation-is-key-to-successful-sales-account-planning.html.

PART III

Technological Tools for Customer Relationship Management

CHAPTER 7

Components of e-CRM Solutions

CHAPTER OVERVIEW

After reading this chapter you should be able to understand:

1 The CRM architecture that emphasises the importance of a balanced approach to combining operational and analytical technologies
2 Data warehouse and data mining that provide the foundations for functional and analytical CRM
3 Campaign management, sales force automation, customer service and support as the main modules of a comprehensive CRM offering
4 Interactive technologies, especially digital technologies, that are revolutionising CRM

Vignette

Westpac, one of Australia's big four banks, uses specialised 'Know Me' software to enhance its customer experience. The software encourages one-to-one contact at each touchpoint in the customer journey for online and offline channels. The bank benefits from the Know Me initiative in two ways. First, the volume of consumer data – including customer notes, social media posts and online clickstream data – has increased dramatically. Second, with 60 million online interactions monthly, the bank holds large datasets of customer experiences from online and mobile banking. The company uses the information to connect with customers via personalised channels for reminders about credit card payments, topping up superannuation funds, deals for travel insurance during international transactions and even messages that appreciate the customers initiatives for paying off home loans. The bank's 'next best bid' program automatically analyses all data sources and provides live and real-time contacts, deals and offers based on customer requirements and the bank's offerings. Its 'service-driven contact' generated over 812,000 best offers and experiences for customers within nine months of its launch, resulting in a 37% rise in new product adoption.

DOI: 10.4324/9781003518174-10

Nearly 500,000 consumers were approached through the contact centre, resulting in a 60% adoption of new offerings. Targeted online messages, appearing on 80% of customers' online banking profiles, produced an additional $7.8 million in sales. The deals programme delivered $22 million in annualised sales, more than double the initial target.

OPENING CASE

Caterpillar's e-CRM Initiatives

Caterpillar, a global leader, designs, creates, engineers, manufactures and markets construction and mining equipment. Its offerings (including machinery, engines, financial services and insurance) serve diverse customers across the globe through an extensive dealer and service network (Caterpillar, 2017). Its key customers include businesses involved in mining, construction and transportation. The company leverages digital platforms to engage with customers by integrating social and digital media into every activity to add value to all customer interactions and experiences with its products.

Caterpillar utilises digital tools for social media listening, customer support, promotions and sharing content on thought leadership. Social listening helps pay attention to customers sharing experiences about their products, perceptions, perspectives, issues and challenges they face. Root cause analysis helps understand the potential sources of these issues that can potentially influence customer preferences. Customer conversations, treated as a critical asset, form the basis for developing action-oriented strategies. The pull strategy leverages social media to engage in dialogue and strengthen customer relationships.

The company provides customers with content that helps them use Caterpillar's products more effectively. Incorporating digital technologies into products and services increases productivity, lowers costs and improves safety for Caterpillar's customers. Digital tools for managing equipment and monitoring conditions connect physical products with an intuitive digital experience. Gathering and transforming data into actionable insights offers customer value throughout the product's lifecycle.

The switch from physical to digital interactions between the company and customers is accelerating with the advent and rapid adoption of social media and smartphones. It has forced traditional firms, including Caterpillar, to reconsider its electronic Customer Relationship Management (e-CRM) strategies.

Customer-facing functions such as marketing, sales and service are adapting to this change in customer behaviour, and digital tools are facilitating the transition, beginning with digitally savvy customers. In this chapter, we will focus on the elements of e-CRM used to engage with digital-savvy customers (Nelson, 2012).

INTRODUCTION

Technological advancements in recent times have enabled business organisations to automate their processes. Automation has resulted in better performance for businesses through reduced costs and cycle time and improved productivity.

We will focus on understanding the core technologies more conceptually in managing customer experiences. We will specifically emphasise interactive technologies in customer-facing functions, including marketing, sales, and customer service and support. The growing role of artificial intelligence (AI) and machine learning (ML) for analytics as the foundation for CRM, and 'data lake' and 'data warehouse' storage and processing will also be covered.

CRM technologies enable an organisation to combine, merge and centralise all relevant information to efficiently manage interactions with prospects, leads and customers. At the same time, the customer also feels happy and satisfied. Better decisions are made when the main front-end marketing, sales and other processes are integrated with the supporting back-end processes in CRM. However, it is important to keep in mind that technology is just an enabler. If an organisation must reap the benefits of CRM, investments in technology alone do not suffice. The company should also be customer focused with proper CRM processes in place.

CRM is a broad term encompassing many strategies, processes and technologies that work in tandem to get as close to customers as possible. CRM solutions are built to:

- Aid in developing profitable, mutually beneficial and long-term relationships with customers.
- Interact with customers to get closer to them at every point of contact.
- Maximise the company's share of the customer's wallet.

To deliver customer pleasure, firms need to understand what they want and then deliver consistently. This requires a system to gather all possible data about the customer from every touchpoint – i.e. online, by phone, by emails, on social media and in person. New insights emerge from analysing this unified view of customers by integrating their personal, behavioural, contextual and transactional data. As firms utilise this customer understanding, they can offer an exceptionally personalised experience.

Initially, when CRM technology was in its infancy, basic tools were developed to address certain aspects of customer-facing functions. These solutions adopted a piecemeal approach and usually operated as standalone point solutions with limited ability to integrate with the company's internal processes or databases. Some of these products included standalone sales force automation, campaign management software, service systems and so on. However, a comprehensive approach to CRM inevitably makes it essential to integrate back-office and front-office activities to share information seamlessly across all tiers of the marketing effort. The CRM architectural framework discussed here helps us understand the different solutions from a holistic perspective (Shahnam, 1999). It emphasises the importance of a balanced CRM approach that combines both operational and analytical technologies. The framework has three primary components:

- Operational CRM – involving process management technologies.
- Analytical CRM – involving business performance management technologies.
- Collaborative CRM – involving business collaboration management technologies.

Operational CRM

Operational CRM automates horizontally integrated business processes involving front-office customer touchpoints. These technologies connect all parts of a firm that impact the 'moments of truth', such as when a customer reaches out to an employee. This might include a query from a customer regarding a product or service, placing an order, contacts while an order is being fulfilled (e.g. installation) after-sales service and support. Typical CRM solutions in the operational category include marketing automation, sales force automation, mobile sales, customer service and field service solutions. The back-office side of operational CRM solutions requires plugging into the enterprise resource planning (ERP) system for order management and the supply chain management (SCM) system for order processing for manufacturers. Traditional transaction processing and other legacy systems are also important elements of operational CRM systems.

Operational CRM automates marketing, selling and service-related processes. Marketing automation utilises prospect- and customer-related information to create, manage and measure marketing communication. Automation enables campaigns and communication approaches to be developed for multiple channels such as television, in-store displays, online, radio, mailshots, social media, etc. Managing a coordinated communication programme across channels boosts unified messaging across campaigns. Automation simplifies the management of campaigns on different platforms. Implementation of event-based triggers, such as an online search for home loan rates, enables the interactions at the top of the customer's buying funnel to focus on creating awareness and taking the prospect forward in the purchase process.

Sale force automation manages relationships with existing customers and helps attract potential customers. Identifying prospects, creating leads, qualifying the leads and closing the deals at scale improves the productivity of the sales team while providing a satisfying onboarding experience to new customers. Automation provides the relevant customer data to the sales team to effectively manage the prospects and convert them to customers.

Service automation is directly linked to managing customer experiences with support and service. Customer interactions for their contact details, support, installation, renewals, reminders, queries, resolution and so on span multiple channels, including home and site visits, emails, contact centres, websites, chatbots, blogs and review sites. The exchanges are recorded in the service database as a complete repository of customer history. Successful firms leverage this information to develop deeper understanding of their customers' needs and experiences with their products and products.

In the course of its day-to-day transactions and interactions, firms collect large amounts of customer data. Extraction of actionable insights from this data requires analytical techniques.

Analytical CRM

This component of the CRM ecosystem analyses the data created on the operational side of the CRM effort for business performance management and improvement. Predicting customer behaviour, identifying relevant customer segments, identifying potential customers and so on are some activities that could be performed with the knowledge gained from analytical efforts. Data mining applications perform this analysis and extract relevant and valuable customer knowledge. Modelling individual customers' preferences and behaviours is a prerequisite to offering tailored products. Historical data required for mining applications is stored in a central data warehouse.

Companies leverage analytics to understand customers' spending patterns, affinity and segmentation in the following ways:

1 *Customer analytics* lays the foundation for developing customer knowledge by collecting and analysing customer data to gain insights on customer behaviour. It involves using various tools to collect and organise different data types and a methodological framework for analysing the data. Modelling to determine the value of different segments in the portfolio of existing customers and their profiles, preferences and buying behaviour is the starting point for developing a comprehensive action plan.
2 *Marketing analytics* helps improve decisions related to marketing, such as identifying which advertising campaign or platform generates higher returns. Marketing analytics focuses on tracking and analysing data from marketing efforts and expenses to achieve multiple objectives. These include improving brand awareness, sales, market share and profitability. Leading firms use marketing analytics to: improve customer experiences; increase the return on investment (ROI) of marketing efforts; craft future marketing strategies; identify new market opportunities with high potential; assess marketing performances at different geographic levels (e.g. district, state and national); and for campaign planning and management.
3 *Sales analytics* help plan, simulate and predict sales volumes and profits. Analysing the organisational sales process and tracking the conversion of opportunities into leads and deals boosts the sales cycle. Modelling, understanding and predicting sales trends and outcomes help leaders identify potential improvements in the process and the performance of salespeople and teams. Sales analytic systems help discover, diagnose and run predictive programs and tweak parameters, measures or dimensions as part of an analytic or planning exercise.
4 *Service analytics* plays a significant role in improving performance by helping customer service teams monitor key metrics such as customer satisfaction scores, average ticket

response time, first-time resolutions and overall support volume. As service directly impacts customer satisfaction, quality, cost, user experience and complaints, it enhances customer experience while improving brand equity.

5 *Channel analytics* focus on customers' usage experience and behaviour across touchpoints and channels, including online, personal interaction, mobile, etc.

Analytics enable firms to optimally manage customers and offerings to boost performance.

Collaborative CRM

The third arm of this CRM architectural framework facilitates interactions between customers and companies, and between members of the company around customer information, to:

- improve communication and coordination,
- raise customer switching costs, and
- increase customer intimacy and retention.

Collaborative CRM technologies including voice, conferencing, email, web-based, chats and other interactive methods.

Synchronisation and integration of interactions among customers and channels communication are key aspects of collaborative CRM. Engaging with customers consistently serves to enhance customer retention and loyalty. Internally, it creates a collaborative network across different departments of the firm, including sales, marketing, finance, operations and support. Customer information is shared among these departments to help the company understand these individuals better. Marketing analysis to understand customer preference (including features, price and cost of use) help teams in research and development (R&D), product development, finance and operations to collaborate and succeed in the marketplace by creating competitive products and services. Some of the many advantages of collaborative CRM include:

- Strengthening customer relationships – improving the customer experience by sharing real-time information within the business to solve issues and address concerns builds lasting relationships with customers.
- Enabling seamless interactions across channels – collaborative CRM helps firms manage interactions across all touchpoints and media platforms for customers to effectively use the channels while customising usage based on their requirements.
- Service cost reduction through the adoption of self-service technologies (SSTs), including digital applications (apps) and AI-driven automation tools like chatbots, which offers convenience and 24/7 access to customers while lowering the firm's costs for customer support.

As collaborative CRM integrates customers, processes, data, knowledge and strategies, it supports the firm's ability to serve and retain customers effectively and efficiently.

It should be noted that there is considerable overlap between the operational and collaborative CRM efforts, with a single tool taking care of these functions. Collaborative CRM is primarily geared towards increasing customer and company interactions. In contrast, operational CRM is geared mainly towards capturing information about customers at contact points and getting the main work done.

Comprehensive CRM technologies facilitate the creation of a CRM ecosystem, and all three CRM efforts are equally crucial for a balanced CRM solution.

CRM solutions have evolved along with the rise in computing power and developments in telecom technologies that accelerated the rollout of 4G and 5G networks facilitating high-speed data transfer. These developments have resulted in the emergence of cloud service models and solutions that offer CRM in a software-as-a-service (SaaS) mode.

As social media impacts customer experience through posts, reviews and opinions that have moved beyond text to images and videos, customer feedback systems are being transformed. Companies are increasingly leveraging digital and social media platforms to engage with customers.

DATA LAKES AND DATA WAREHOUSES

Data lakes and data warehouses are important constituents of data infrastructure and CRM technology ecosystems. They provide the foundational infrastructure for a secure end-to-end system that stores, processes and analyses raw, unprocessed and treated and transformed data for analytical applications to derive timely, actionable insights. Firms use several channels to interact and engage with customers. However, as the channels proliferate, it becomes increasingly difficult to integrate data from all customer touchpoints. Data lakes emerged as a solution to store the vast amounts of data being generated in the form of texts, numbers, images and videos from business applications, mobile apps, the Internet of Things (IoT) devices, social media, emails, chats, etc. that provide the core data consistently to help decision makers utilise analytics, machine learning and artificial intelligence.

The growing importance of digital channels of communication and interaction has created opportunities and challenges. Clickstream data on digital channels – including browsing behaviour, time spent on webpages and social media handles, abandoned shopping carts and exits from chats – creates data that enables the company to understand visitors, prospects and customers. It is then possible to treat each customer as an individual by catering to her personal tastes, preferences, likes and dislikes. Data about customer interactions in near real time helps in personalising the interactions. For example, a company may find a user switching out after browsing for some time. The system automatically detects the prospect's interest in a particular area (e.g. travel insurance). It can then reach out to the user, understand her requirements and create a tailored offering that is aligned with her specific needs.

Data lake solutions help consolidate raw data to make it accessible in an integrated and secure manner for decision making. They store a wide range of data types, from unstructured to semi-structured and structured. Flexibility and scalability enable data lake solutions to perform complex analyses and handle a variety of processing tools.

In contrast, a data warehouse stores relational data, such as treated data that has been transformed with a specific purpose in mind e.g. operational reporting. Data warehouses produce more standardised forms of business intelligence analysis and serve a defined use case, for example customer profitability. A data warehouse is a subject-oriented, integrated, time-varying, non-volatile collection of data that is primarily used in organisational decision making (Chaudhuri & Dayal, 1997). Although physically different from traditional databases, data warehouses are maintained primarily for decision support.

Data warehouses play an important support function in marketing campaigns. Campaign management is the process of planning, executing and assessing outbound campaigns. The data warehouse provides the empirical data needed to determine the ideal size of a campaign market, identify customer prospects and evaluate the success of a campaign based on the responses. As a company undertakes many campaigns in various segments, it collects a lot of data about prospective customers, people targeted in the previous campaigns and how they responded to the various forms of communication utilised by the company. This historical data supplied by the data warehouse in conjunction with a campaign management tool makes it easy for the company to identify prospects based on their previous behaviour. Thus, the company can target the right customers, increasing the marketing campaign's effectiveness.

In short, we can say that a data warehouse is an important constituent of a balanced CRM ecosystem. It aids in critical decision support by consolidating and integrating crucial customer information along with other information (such as demographics, competitor information, etc.) from various sections of the company. A well-designed data warehouse goes a long way towards building and aiding successful CRM applications.

Typically, data warehouses are maintained separately from the organisation's operational databases. Operational databases are optimised for an organisation's day-to-day transactions, similar to order entry and banking transactions that are bread-and-butter, day-to-day operations. These repetitive, structured tasks consist of short and atomic transactions. For example, a bank customer can access her account from multiple channels, including automated teller machines (ATMs), mobile banking and banking apps. Therefore, they contain only the relevant information, such as the balance of funds in the customer's account, at any particular time. Redundancy is reduced to optimise these databases for speed and minimise concurrency conflicts.

On the other hand, a data warehouse contains historical and other data collated from all parts of the organisation. These databases might have redundancy as they are optimised for decision support, not speed. They tend to be orders of magnitude larger than the operational databases, ranging in size from hundreds of gigabytes to terabytes. The decision maker (typically a manager) can make ad hoc queries requiring access to millions of records. Query throughput and response times are more important than transaction throughput.

Earlier, various parts of an organisation were served by different databases, each designed for a specific purpose. For example, a company's marketing and finance departments may have different databases. Decision support requires data from such heterogeneous sources to be consolidated into one extensive database for analysis. Second, external sources that might not be found in an operational database may also be needed for decision support. Different sources may contain data of varying quality or inconsistent representations, codes and formats, which must be reconciled. Data warehouses are usually constructed separately from operational databases to consolidate the organisational repository.

Data warehouses may be implemented on standard or extended relational database management systems called Relational Online Analytical Processing (ROLAP) servers, or

Multi-dimensional Online Analytical Processing (MOLAP) servers if the data is stored in multi-dimensional form.

Data warehouses may involve considerable time, effort and money, so many businesses are opting for smaller data warehouses – 'data marts', which are departmental subsets focused on selected subjects. For example, a marketing data mart might include customer, product and sales information. These data marts can be rolled out faster; but, in the long run, integrating all these data marts into a data warehouse might prove to be a major problem.

Data Warehouse Architecture

The function of a typical data warehouse includes extracting data from multiple operational databases and external sources. This data is then cleaned for consistency using transformation tools, and data from various sources can be integrated. Further, there are tools for loading data into the data warehouse, periodically refreshing it and probably purging it to other, slower archival mediums. There might also be many departmental data marts. Data in the warehouse is stored and managed by one or more warehouse servers, presenting multi-dimensional data to various front-end tools such as query and reporting, operational CRM or data mining tools. Finally, there is a repository for storing and managing metadata and tools for monitoring and administering the warehousing system.

The data warehouse architecture is composed of the following three tiers:

- *Bottom tier:* This consists of data warehouses connected to a dataset server because this architecture is based on a relational database system. Data is fed into the tier via backend tools and utilities in this system. These tools and utilities are used to retrieve, extract, clean, load and refresh the data warehouse's functions.
- *Middle tier:* An OLAP server is implemented in the data warehouse in this tier. This server is essentially the ROLAP associated with a relational database management system. This ROLAP maps the data at two levels – multi-dimensional and standard relational operations. The MOLAP model is directly related to the multi-dimensional data and its associated operations in an organisation.
- *Top tier:* This comprises the front-end client layers. These work on the queries posed by clients, as well as on reports, tools, analyses and data mining.

DATA MINING AND CRM

Recent advances in data gathering and storage technologies, along with the steep fall in prices, have made it possible for companies to gather and store large amounts of data. Large companies generate gigabytes of data daily through everyday transactions. Analysing such large quantities of data requires very different approaches from the traditional data analysis approaches adopted in disciplines such as statistics, AI, machine learning and others. It has given birth to Knowledge Discovery in Databases (KDD), more popularly called *data mining*, which is the non-trivial process of identifying valid, novel, potentially useful and ultimately understandable patterns in data (Fayyad et al., 1996). Others look at data mining as a set of *tools and techniques* that operate on and extract implicit patterns from data.

Data mining differs from several traditional data analysis disciplines in the following ways:

- Data mining is an interdisciplinary field, taking its input from diverse but related disciplines such as statistics, AI, machine learning and large databases, among others.
- Data mining tools and techniques can help analyse very large databases. Therefore, many techniques that were available to researchers earlier cannot be used without modification to suit these large datasets.
- Data mining techniques give the search methods some degree of search autonomy, resulting in the automated or semi-automated nature of discoveries.
- Data mining usually involves data that has been collected while undertaking day-to-day business transactions. Such data usually has less bias than data that has been specifically collected for the purpose of analysis. However, limitations in attributes might often be insufficient to carry out some desired analysis.
- Lastly, data mining aims to facilitate the involvement of the end user (e.g. manager, etc.) in the discovery process without the need for trained experts to run the various techniques or interpret the results.

Matheus et al. (1993, p. 903) described the problems faced when analysing data: "The grand challenge of knowledge discovery in databases is to automatically process large quantities of raw data, identify the most significant and meaningful patterns, and present these as knowledge appropriate for achieving the user's goals."

Data mining tools and techniques operate on large databases and extract patterns that are implicit in them. Knowledge extracted from databases by data mining algorithms is primarily of two types – predictive and descriptive:

- Prediction involves finding out the future state of a variable using its past values and the values of other related variables. For example, a bank manager might want to find out whether a specific customer will default on a loan repayment. The chances of a specific customer defaulting can be found using a classification algorithm, which would assign the customer to either the defaulting or non-defaulting set.
- Description involves identifying the properties that describe the data under consideration. For example, the manager of a retail store might want to know the change in profiles of customers with changes in age, income and family size.

Data Mining Tasks

Data mining tasks are operations that extract predictive or descriptive knowledge from large datasets. The main tasks are outlined below.

Classification

Classification is a process that maps a given data item into one of several predefined classes (Weiss & Kulikowski, 1991; Fayyad et al., 1996; Yoon, 1999). In CRM, classification is used for various purposes, including behaviour prediction and product and customer categorisation. Classification is used in campaign management to identify prospective customers for a new product from a database of existing customers.

Regression

Regression is the operation of learning a function that predicts the value of a real valued dependent variable based on values of other independent variables (Fayyad et al., 1996). Suppose the effectiveness of an advertising campaign is measured in terms of brand recall; and suppose a marketing manager has a priori belief that the ad's effectiveness is dependent on the total advertising budget and the media channel used. In that case, they can estimate the effectiveness of the campaign in terms of budget and other related variables that might be important. If a new campaign is proposed for launch, the manager can estimate how effective it will be based on the above estimated regression equation. The campaign budget and other parameters can then be fine-tuned to achieve the required degree of effectiveness.

Link Analysis

Link analysis seeks to establish relationships between items or variables in a database record to identify patterns and trends (Simoudis, 1996; Yoon, 1999). Link analysis can also trace connections between items of records over time. Market basket analysis (MBA), an important link analysis application in CRM, seeks to establish relationships between product items characterising product affinity or buyer preferences. For example, a manager in a typical retail chain focuses on display and merchandising decisions, so would prefer to display only those products that are likely to be purchased. Optimising shelf space with products that are the most likely to be sold would help the manager increase revenue and profitability. If the marketing manager mines for association rules – those that identify which items sell together – these rules could then be used to reconfigure the display space to accommodate principally those items that sell together. By doing so, the store manager can improve sales.

Segmentation

Segmentation aims to identify a finite set of naturally occurring clusters or categories to describe data (Anderberg, 1973). Segmentation is done in such a way that cases belonging to a segment or cluster are more similar with respect to the clustering criteria. At the same time, they differ significantly from cases belonging to other segments. Knowledge of market segments is very important to a marketing manager as, based upon this knowledge, marketing campaigns are run, advertising budgets are allocated, store locations are decided, offers are made and a variety of other marketing activities are conducted. However, before investing resources, segments have to be identified and their characteristics (including factors that influence demand) need to be determined. Clustering algorithms are used to segment datasets based on the required criteria into groups with members that are homogeneous.

Deviation Detection

Deviation detection (DD) focuses on discovering the most significant changes in the data from previously measured, expected or normative values. Many CRM and other packages routinely check critical parameters as they change with the market scenario. If the parameters change above a value as defined by the user, this is reported to the manager for appropriate action to be taken.

Most data mining tasks are exploratory in nature. They highlight potential relationships that may exist between variables but, in most cases, are unable to ascertain or explain the reason for the occurrence of a detected pattern. However, their usefulness comes from the fact that they can point to the possibility of obscure and hidden relationships between variables. The use of data mining approaches must be guided by the questions that need to be asked. Two or more data mining tasks used in proper conjunction on a large database would give a manager rich preliminary insights into the phenomenon and probably reveal hidden relationships otherwise impossible to recover.

Data Mining Tools and Techniques

Data mining tools and techniques are algorithms and methods used to carry out the above data mining tasks. They differ in the type of data handled, assumptions about the data, scope and interpretation of the output. It should be noted that a single tool (say, a neural network) could be used to carry out many tasks (e.g. segmentation, classification, etc.). Similarly, a data mining task could be performed using two or many tools (e.g. variety can be achieved by decision trees, neural networks or rule induction).

The main elements of data mining are extraction, transformation, data loading in a data warehouse, maintaining data in a versatile database, determining access to analysts and experts, analysing the data using various tools, and illustrating the data in terms of visual and graphical representation. This process uses classes, clusters, associations, patterns, statistical analysis, neural networks and machine learning.

Data mining techniques are consistently emerging and evolving. We provide a brief outline of some of the more important data mining tasks that are part of many of the data mining packages currently available.

Decision Trees

Decision trees are tools that divide examples into finite numbers of classes, considering one variable at a time and categorising the entire dataset based on it (Yoon, 1999). In other words, they assist with planning and making choices by invoking rules for classification and segmentation.

Rule Induction

Rule induction is the process of invoking general rules that apply to many cases from a database of specific examples. These rules may be of the classification or the predictive type, or rules that perform link analysis.

Case-Based Reasoning

Case-based reasoning (CBR) methods (Yoon, 1999) try to simulate how a human being thinks. Typically, when an example is presented to a CBR solution, it tries to match it with other examples in its repository, and retrieves the case that is most similar to the current case. The decision is then made based on extrapolation – i.e. fitting the decision made in the most appropriate case. The power of CBR packages depends largely on the indexing method used to store cases and the matching method used to retrieve relevant cases.

Visualisation Techniques

Visualisation techniques allow users to view data from various angles using graphic display techniques like charts, diagrams, displays for multi-dimensional data and so on. Used in conjunction with other data mining techniques, visualisation techniques are ideal when users do not know what and where to look for in the data and to discover new knowledge. Managers with no technical knowledge can easily understand the properties of a dataset if it is presented in visual form. Most data mining packages include at least one visualisation tool.

Nearest Neighbour Techniques

Nearest neighbour techniques (Yoon, 1999) use a set of examples to approximate a classification model. Suppose a case has to be classified into a predefined class. These techniques try to find 'neighbours' of this case – one or more case with almost similar properties to the specific case under consideration. A similarity measure is used for this purpose to find the 'closest' example in terms of certain parameters. It then assigns this new case to the class that has the maximum representation among its neighbours.

Clustering Algorithms

These divide the database into different groups called 'clusters' such that intra-cluster similarity is the maximum and inter-cluster similarity is the minimum (Anderberg, 1973; Jain et al., 1999). Research in clustering has been conducted in several fields, resulting in diverse approaches with their own advantages and disadvantages. Market segmentation using a clustering algorithm is almost the first thing that every manager undertakes to gain more knowledge about a particular market.

Analytics packages obtained from vendors usually come with many different tools that might be used for various tasks as outlined above. However, it must be kept in mind that the choice of algorithm to be run on the data depends not only on the data that is available but also on the questions you seek to answer. If you want to know whether or not a customer will repay a loan, it is more appropriate to run a classification algorithm. On the other hand, if you want to know which items sell together in a retail outlet, it may be more appropriate to run an association rule-finding algorithm.

As transactions occur, the contents of the data warehouse continue to grow – whether by adding new data or updating existing data. A data mining solution for a particular CRM application must therefore be capable of catering to such dynamism. Running the same algorithm over the entire database repeatedly is an expensive proposition with regard to both time and resources. Tools with incremental knowledge updating capabilities can help in dealing with such situations. Finally, tight integration between the front-end CRM solution (such as a campaign management solution) and the back-end data mining solution helps ensure consistency and timely dissemination of information throughout the company. This could be leveraged to make more informed and better decisions.

Several data mining tools are available on the market. These tools were developed with standard functions backed by business-specific analysis and intelligence. A few examples are outlined below.

- *RapidMiner* is popular as it provides advanced analytics without the need for any coding expertise. It uses Java for data processing, visualisation, predictive analysis and integration with free, open-source tools such as R programming and Waikato Environment for Knowledge Analysis (Weka). This software for machine learning and data analysis delivers more advanced-level analysis for visualisation and predictive analysis. It uses modelling techniques, clustering, classification and regression to analyse customer data and information.
- *Python-based Orange and Natural Language Toolkit (NLTK):* Python is a well-known, popular and easy-to-use tool for data analysis, text analysis and machine learning features encapsulated in the visual programming interface. Orange and NLTK are open-source tools based on Python's software language for data mining, machine learning and data scraping to address customers' specific needs.
- *KNIME* (the Konstanz Information Miner) is another free and open-source analytic, reporting and integration platform used for data processing, extraction and transformation. It is an efficient tool for financial data analysis, machine learning and data mining, and is used extensively for generating business intelligence reports.

These tools provide insights for effective business decisions that drive growth (Thompson, 2022).

In the following we outline a few examples where CRM, aided by results from data mining tools, has made a difference to a company's profitability by enhancing its ability to retain customers (Berry & Linoff, 2000).

Churn Modelling in Mobile Services

As the mobile service market has attracted many players, competition has increased rapidly with no corresponding increase in the number of users. Customers, lured by promotional offers, would switch easily suppliers. In addition, better services and bundled offers on the latest smartphones increased churn (i.e. customers ceasing or likely to cease using a company/provider). As the cost of acquiring a new customer is much higher than the cost of retaining an existing one (by about five times), churn has a negative impact on profitability. Churn models are therefore developed to predict the likelihood of defection and identify customers who may churn out.

Using the attributes of customers who left a company recently, decision tree models or other classificatory models could be built that help in extracting the attributes of 'churners'. These models are applied to the existing customer base to identify current customers with attributes similar to those already churned. The possibility of churn in this segment is much higher compared to the other customer segments. These customers, once identified, could then be targeted and induced to remain with their present telecom company through better offers. It should be noted that the characteristics of the churn segment continue to change with time. The decision tree algorithm should therefore be constantly updated with data on customers who churned recently to keep the model up to date. Telecom service providers could reduce churn using such models (i.e. encourage loyalty).

FEATURES OF A GOOD LOYALTY PROGRAM

'Encircle', the loyalty programme of Titan Company, is one of India's most popular and engaging loyalty programmes. It aims to help the company get to know its customers well and to treat them as they expect to be treated. Obviously, a loyalty programme going beyond customers' expectations is considered good, so Encircle's vision is one of 100–0, going beyond customers' expectations and expecting nothing in return. Customers are therefore given the choice to engage with any of Titan's brands and earn or redeem points. Customers enjoy this freedom of choice and, in return, the company can improve customer satisfaction and generate loyalty. A good loyalty programme must therefore have some factor that makes it unique and offers an enjoyable customer experience. In turn, it will help the company or brand achieve loyalty from customers and create an experience for a lifetime.

Market Segmentation

Data mining is commonly used for customer segmentation. Data allows companies to develop relevant and meaningful segments based on demographic, psychographic and behavioural variables. Conversions are improved, promotional campaigns are made effective, lists of interesting markets are developed, appropriate customisation can be achieved, and relevant customisation and personalisation can be achieved to ensure business success.

Customised Products

Data mining facilitates the development of customised products designed for market segments, which helps companies predict the features that the customers may like and prefer. Companies can then develop innovative products that meet customers' requirements. Data mining also helps companies determine any gaps by studying customer demand. Products are developed based on customers' apparent needs, uniqueness, distinctiveness of the products, unique markets, lucrative design, high impulse price and low cost in order to increase profits. Companies should therefore use data mining analysis to develop innovative products that customers cannot imagine.

Warranties

Lastly, data mining is integral to predicting the number of customers who will pay for warranties and guarantees. For example, QuickSprout used data mining to improve sales and data by analysing the number of customers who would return products. The company also knew about net sales and settlements made by the organisation. Based on this, it then determined guarantees, customers who paid cash for the promise, adjusted guarantees, etc. Companies can thus deliver more value by leveraging data-driven analytics to boost revenues (Patel, 2015).

Understanding Buying Patterns in Supermarkets

Supermarkets sell hundreds of diverse stock-keeping units (SKUs), often at very competitive prices, and profits are often tied to the volume of sales they generate. Initially, data scanners were used to speed up the checkout and payment process. Vast amounts of data are generated by these scanners at checkout counters, which are now increasingly self-checkouts. Supermarkets can use this data very profitably to understand their customers' buying behaviour.

'Association rules' are implication rules that use the co-occurrence of items in a transaction as the baseline. They have the following form:

Item A implies Item B with support *x*% and confidence *y*%.

This means that items A and B occur together in *x*% of the total customer transactions in the database, and that *y*% of the transactions that contained A also contain item B.

Algorithm mining of such association rules has been developed to help find items and sets of items that sell together. This knowledge can be profitably used to:

- Design discount coupons
- Design display space
- Manage inventories
- Differentiate item combinations that do not sell together, etc.
- Remind customers of items that they want to buy together.

Examples often quoted in the data mining literature are beer and diapers (nappies). One US store running an association rule-generating algorithm found a rule that 'beer implies diapers'. This was a surprise to the store manager because it was thought that beer and diapers are such diverse items in terms of use that customers generally do not buy them together. However, on further probing, it was found that this pattern occurred most often on Friday nights, which might be related to young couples going out during the weekend (for which they bought crates of beer) while leaving their infants in the care of babysitters (for which they needed diapers). It is very difficult to find such a causal relationship using normal data analysis methods. Sales subsequently rose dramatically when the manager displayed these two disparate items together on Friday nights. The manager used the knowledge mined from customers' buying patterns profitably.

Data Mining in Financial Services

Banks and insurance companies know an enormous amount about their millions of customers. These services have experienced dramatic changes in the last two decades, especially in increasing competitive intensity, the adoption of digital technologies and shifting customer preferences and behaviour. Many incumbents are finding it tough to retain their profitable customers.

Financial service providers have an advantage as customers must provide several details, including demographic information, when signing up to meet mandatory Know Your Customer/Client (KYC) requirements even before availing themselves of the services. In addition, all transactions and interactions with the service provider are automatically captured by the operating systems. Banks typically offer a wide range of products (e.g. savings accounts, deposits, loans, credit cards, etc.), while insurance firms have different kinds of products for life, health, motor, property and travel insurance targeted at retail consumers. These companies routinely attempt to cross-sell or up-sell their products. For example, a customer seeking health insurance may be offered travel insurance or auto insurance. Cross-selling to existing customers, based on a deeper understanding of their evolving needs, is simpler, easier and faster than searching for new customers.

One of the problems businesses face is a lot of wastage in communications. If a company routinely sends messages about new product details to all its customers, it is likely to incur high costs as response rates for these are usually very low even among existing customers. A better option is to identify those customers who would likely respond favourably to such offers. Predictive analytics is used to identify such high-potential customers. Favourable prospects are identified by segmenting the database (using classification algorithms) into subjects who are likely to respond favourably to such marketing efforts and those who are likely to respond unfavourably. By communicating only with the favourable segment, companies are likely to increase their hit percentages considerably while reducing the cost of campaigns substantially.

Data mining helps in a CRM environment by providing the insights and knowledge needed to understand customers and predict their behaviour from past interactions. Integrating the data mining tools that run on data and front-end CRM tools substantially improves a company's ability to serve its customers by providing timely and relevant information to its employees.

CRM solutions play a crucial role in improving services while offering a high level of customisation. We now look at the main components of any comprehensive CRM solution, namely:

- Marketing campaign management
- Sales force automation
- Customer service and support.

MARKETING CAMPAIGN MANAGEMENT

Marketing campaign management involves planning, executing, tracking and analysing promotions over the entire life span of the marketing campaign, from the inception of an idea to assessment of the result. Demands on the marketing function have increased considerably in recent times, mainly due to increased market competition as technological advances have made it possible for competitors to catch up with innovators quickly. Customers have become increasingly demanding and expect better service as they have better access to information and can compare products and services from the comfort of their homes. The web revolution has made the internet a channel of mass personalised communication, but has simultaneously increased the complexity of and demands on the marketing profession. Marketing managers routinely run campaigns of varied types as part of their overall communication programme to inform customers about their offerings and generate sales. Campaigns are run to:

- Launch a new product or product range
- Increase the visibility of a product through advertisements
- Re-launch an old product with improved features
- Targeted specific segments of the market
- Highlight specific occasions (e.g. promotions during holidays and festivals)
- Build brands.

Typically, a marketing manager must plan, coordinate, execute and assess these campaigns. In addition to these tasks, many marketing campaigns might be conducted simultaneously – especially in multi-product, multi-location firms. The need to present a unified face to the customer and build a brand image in the customer's mind has become more critical and challenging with the increasing number of communications channels as different customers prefer different modes of communication.

There is a genuine need for support for planning, coordinating, executing and evaluating marketing campaigns. CRM vendors have introduced specialised marketing campaign management solutions primarily targeted to meet this need. Such solutions help a marketing manager plan, design, execute and measure the effectiveness of marketing campaigns. They help segment customers and develop targeting and positioning strategies for each segment; define products that match customer requirements; help in pricing and selecting distribution channels for those products; and implement communication strategies to build brand awareness, generate interest and motivate purchase. Recent products have enabled managers to exploit the internet as a channel to establish dialogue with customers. Some campaign management tools not only take care of campaign efforts but also integrate with sales and other functions. They integrate with the company data warehouse to access and utilise more information about customers.

The key roles of campaign management solutions are outlined below.

Workflow

This is the process of managing and coordinating the activities of a campaign, from planning, designing and budgeting to execution and tracking. The campaign may consist of many stages and a different message might be sent for each step. The software should support multiple campaigns as each campaign might be across various communication channels. Initially, the company might email prospective customers informing them of a new product and asking them to check out the company's website. Depending on the response from customers, further communications (such as emails, telephone calls or direct visits by sales personnel) could be planned. Managing such a workflow requires a tremendous amount of back-end support in coordination and book-keeping. The campaign management solution should therefore be capable of providing such support.

Segmentation

Segmentation is the process of identifying groups of customers around whom marketing efforts can be focused after analysing the existing customer base. These groups can be based on demographic, psychographic or behavioural characteristics. Segmentation is used to fine-tune the campaign and target the right prospects and customers. The customer database from previous campaigns that contains information about how they responded to previous offers is usually stored in a data warehouse (as discussed earlier). To utilise such information already with the company, campaign management software interfaces with the data warehouse and extracts the relevant customer details. Some analytic capability is also present in most campaign management packages, which allows managers to segment the database and identify the most appropriate target segments for a campaign. Further, data mining can uncover more specific characteristics of the target segment, such as the preferred mode of communication (e.g. email) or preferred product colour, etc. Segmentation capability is a very important functionality that all campaign management software should possess as it helps the marketing manager fine-tune the deliverables of the campaign.

Customer journey mappings are being undertaken to visually illustrate the customers' pathways related to purchase and non-purchase. This journey determines when and where the customer interacted with the company when they used the digital platform and when a physical location was used. These journeys differ for different customer segments so marketers create journey maps for each customer persona.

Outbound Communication Automation

This helps marketers segment customers based on automated lists that detail the customers scheduled to receive outbound communication such as emails, SMS alerts, reminders and app notifications. These schedules are decided well in advance by companies. Instead of developing checklists and preparing the delivery of messages, companies use automation. Emails include autoresponders and a follow-up message after a customer completes a form. The key purpose is to send the right message and content at the right time. Invitational emails about webinars, events or unique campaigns to specifically targeted prospects and customers generate high response rates. Such communication speeds up purchasing as they enable customers to complete the sales journey effectively.

Message Personalisation

This is used to personalise communications and re-target prospective customers. This content also delivers the message that 'you know them'. This message can incorporate some parts of the browsing history of the customers, which would determine companies' knowledge about the customers. Ad targeting can also be used and companies' banner ads can be used on customers' search browsers. For example, Busted Tees, an online t-shirt company, increased its email revenue after stopping generic emails which would have reached customers' spam folders. Instead, the company started sending personalised, time-based emails in proper time zones based on customers' browsing activities and history. Similarly, Pinterest emailed content collections to single women congratulating them on upcoming weddings.

Omnichannel Communication

Customers seamlessly use multiple media platforms and devices for communication, including laptops, smartphones, social media platforms and other digital channels. Companies use these platforms to develop automated marketing tools and provide a seamless customer experience. In this way, companies can capture data about the customer journey, patterns and behaviour, and use these elements to enhance their customer relationship and provide personalised messages, content and solutions. An omnichannel strategy is essential for this task over various digital media platforms. Lastly, the consistency of the content and messages is imperative for these multiple channels to remain connected with tech-savvy customers.

Marketing Analytics

These provide data about individuals' attitudes towards company campaigns and the content, messaging and product preferences used in those campaigns. These analytics also provide leads to the companies and profound insights on customers regarding important trends. This information is displayed to marketers on their dashboards in real time so that marketers can learn lessons and develop strategies instantly. These analytics also show the relationship between the various marketing channels (social media platforms, blogs, email marketing), search engine optimisation (SEO) and performance, supplemented by the real stories and results related to customers. This information is used in campaign management primarily for audience segmentation, content development, email automation, message customisation, omnichannel communication and customer interactions (Horwitz, 2016).

Personalisation

Today, most companies try to personalise their offerings to customers based on their likes, dislikes, preferences and characteristics. Distribution of personalised content to a customer over a preferred communication channel is emerging as an essential element of campaign management solutions. For example, if a customer prefers to be contacted by phone directly and usually responds if discounts are offered, such information can be used to personalise offerings to that customer.

Execution

Execution is delivering an outbound message to a market segment or target over a specific delivery channel. For example, a company might send an initial email to prospects identified by segmenting its customer database. Some customers may respond to this, while others may not. The company may then provide more details for those who respond by calling them on the telephone (through salespeople from a call centre) or visiting them personally (sending a salesperson). For others who do not respond, a different message could be sent, focusing on the following questions (among others):

- How do we schedule the message to the recipients?
- Who will deliver the message?
- What channels should we use?
- When should the customer be contacted?
- What content will be delivered in each contact?

The campaign management software should manage and schedule such interactions with individual customers.

Response Management

This is the ability to track a customer's response to the marketing message or deliver a particular offer to the customer. The marketing manager should follow the reactions to the campaign by channel and assess the actual performance. This would include each element of the campaign during or after the execution period and determining actual sales and ROI so that the marketing manager can judge each campaign's effectiveness. In addition to these features, most solutions enable reporting of campaign results in simple tabular and graphical formats. After completion of the campaign, the history and details are sent to a data warehouse to be reused for later campaigns.

Response Modelling

Most campaign management solutions provide a response modelling feature whereby models developed in current campaigns can be used in future segmentation and targeting efforts. Based on previous campaign results, suppose a 'good' model is found that reasonably forecasts a customer category's responses. In that case, the model can be run for other segments to find better prospects, who can then be made the targets of subsequent campaigns. This feature of response modelling also enables a manager to make reasonable forecasts of future sales emanating from each campaign.

We have presented some of the functionalities in almost all campaign management solutions. A powerful campaign management tool is one that can not only schedule and perform routine campaign management activities; it can also target specific customers based on analytic capabilities it possesses from the data culled from a data warehouse. This is then dynamically linked to all customer touchpoints, and the information it provides to managers enables them to plan, design, execute and analyse the responses most effectively.

SALES FORCE AUTOMATION

The sales function is a vital front-end aspect with numerous customer interactions. Therefore, it has a crucial role to play in any CRM effort. Customers contact sales representatives (reps) to learn more about a company's products. It is up to the representatives to convert these enquiries into orders, which means that the sales force should have all the information that would finally result in a purchase. Many IT solutions aim to help reps undertake their work.

Although these solutions appear under different headings, they can be grouped under the general term 'sales force automation' (SFA), which can be defined as implementing several processes designed to help sell products in less time and with less effort. Digital technologies are a significant enabler as sales force automation makes the sales processes more efficient and effective by reaching out to the right customers. These tools automate routine reports, contracts, scheduling, communication tasks and other non-contact activities, thus freeing up time for sales personnel to focus on prospects and existing customers. The time spent with customers is made more productive by facilitating the easy transfer of information between the sales team and personnel in other departments, such as operations and legal for contracting.

Sales force automation is one of the most challenging processes because of the dynamism of sales (changing products, sales models, etc.). It is a relatively independent activity owing to the considerable time sales reps spend with customers, especially in business-to-business (B2B) markets. Customers may be very demanding and, among other things, may want and expect the following:

- Timely and accurate information about products and product features
- Information about sales orders
- Prompt and dependable answers to questions
- Follow-through on commitments within promised time frames
- Regular contact and follow-up.

This makes the requirements of any solution very demanding; and, at the same time, flexibility is required. The sales cycle typically goes through the steps shown in Figure 7.1.

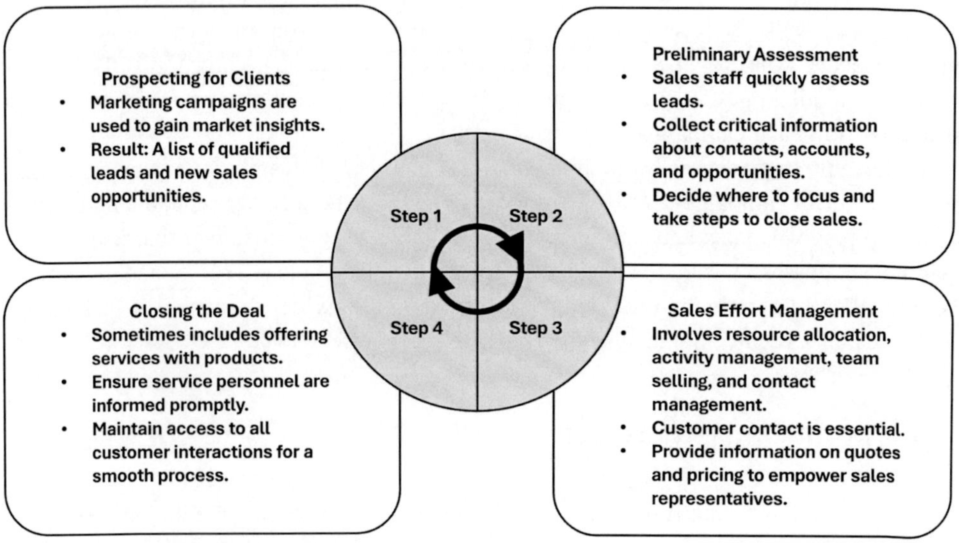

FIGURE 7.1 Efficient Marketing Campaign Use

Below are some of the basic functionalities of virtually all SFA solutions.

- They interface with campaign management software to provide sales reps with a comprehensive view of ongoing and completed marketing campaigns. They should then get lists of prospects, leads and qualified leads generated from internal and external sources.
- Some SFA solutions guide the sales representatives through conversations with prospects during their first contact. This helps prompt the right questions and provide correct and up-to-date information about the firm's offerings.
- They enable sales heads to manage their teams, oversee expenses, deploy representatives to different territories, forecast revenue, proactively address market trends and overcome shortfalls in sales targets through reassignment. Solutions such as Siebel and Salesforce provide forecasting and business planning support to senior sales managers. Reporting features enable managers to assess the current performance of their team by providing key performance indicators (KPIs), summaries, graphical analysis and details to make rapid, well-informed decisions.
- They enable contact management; business contacts in customer organisations are personnel with whom the sales personnel make initial contact for any sale. They may be at various levels in the hierarchy of client organisations. Some may be simply individual contacts in the purchasing role, while others may be decision makers who influence choice. Sales representatives maintain details of their key contacts in client organisations. However, many important characteristics about contacts (for example, whether the contact is a key decision maker, his preference, brand perceptions and usage experiences, etc.) can be lost, especially if they are part of the sales rep's tacit knowledge. If a different rep is assigned to this territory, he will not have the advantage of such information and will have to start afresh. As the number of contacts keep on rising, it becomes increasingly difficult to manage them. SFA solutions today provide contact management features wherein critical information about each customer contact is stored in the system and easily available. In addition to the usual details, specific information on contacts and organisations are also stored. Sales representatives can access such information through their mobile devices anywhere while on the move, and accordingly modify their sales pitch.
- Account management functionality enables sales professionals to build a deep understanding of target accounts with a complete history of all the interactions the sales organisation or partner's sales organisation has had with that account. Sales personnel can then schedule and track account-related activities, track product and service delivery, and establish new business opportunities with an existing account.
- Territory management enables the company to manage and execute sales activities based on territory. This functionality allows the sales department to automatically route opportunities, accounts, contacts and moves to the right team members based on flexible and configurable business rules. For example, business enquiries to a call centre can be routed automatically to the relevant sales representative based on the customer's address. If the caller is an existing client, the rep who previously closed the deal could be given the assignment. Assignment rules should therefore be flexible enough to be based on geography, industry, product interest or virtually any criteria the sales manager chooses.

To ensure that sales personnel make the most of the above functionalities, they should be easy to use and access, with features such as graphical user interfaces (GUIs) to enhance understandability. Proper use of these functionalities can reduce many of the routine back-end operations (like preparing reports) that sales personnel routinely undertake, leaving them more time to spend with their customers.

CUSTOMER SERVICE AND SUPPORT

A company's interactions with its customers do not stop after it has closed the deal and delivered the product. For example, customers might have difficulties using the product or the product may not function as expected. In such cases, the company has to provide good after-sales service and support. Customer service and support (CSS) has of late assumed considerable importance in CRM solutions, with many CRM vendors (e.g. Siebel Field Service, Oracle Service, etc.) offering standalone CSS packages, while others integrate CSS functionalities with other CRM applications. Here we provide a brief introduction to the CSS aspect of CRM, outlining the essential functionalities – service cycle and capabilities.

Service Cycle

Consider a company that markets a range of consumer durables: when a customer buys one of its products from an outlet, the company's online store or through an e-commerce site, service representatives are sent to install the product. The product usually comes with a warranty or some free maintenance clause. If the customer has any problem with the product, she will reach out to customer support through an app, online chat, toll-free number or an SMS to the contact centre. After obtaining the necessary details from the customer, service personnel are assigned to attend to the call. Alternatively, the service wing of the call centre may guide the customer to resolve the problem if it is minor. If self-service is feasible, the firm will save a lot of time and effort, and the customer can continue using the product. Calls may also be taken through a website. Interactive websites may have some features for problem diagnosis and resolution. The cost of using the web to empower users to resolve their problems can be five times lower than that of a service personnel visit.

If the problem is serious and cannot be resolved by the customer, service representatives are assigned to the problem. Assignment of appropriate service personnel based on skills, product or product-line expertise, workload, territory, etc. is an important function performed by the CSS suite. First, the service personnel should be able to quickly obtain information about the customer purchase, warranty status and service history of the product. Second, based on the call, he should be able to assess the possible cause of the problem and accordingly carry appropriate spares. The solution should be available to him while performing the service. Finally, the service personnel should be able to invoice the customer on the spot, collect payment and issue a receipt. The full service cycle therefore consists of:

- Logging the initial service request by the customer
- Verifying the contractual coverage (e.g. warranty and annual maintenance contract)

- Assigning and sending out appropriate field engineers
- Supporting field engineers through access to the organisation's database of available spare parts
- Actual repair or replacement
- Billing of customers.

Capabilities of CSS Solutions

Many CRM solutions provide varied functionalities that support all stages of the service cycle. Some of the more essential capabilities include:

- Multiple channel access
- Solutions knowledge base
- Managing requests
- Contract and warranty status
- Field service support
- Management of spares and depot repairs
- Billing.

Customer service and support, traditionally regarded as a cost to the company, can be made very efficient and effective by CRM solutions that provide CSS capabilities. The cost of delivering services is reduced, and improved efficiency and service levels is possible by disseminating relevant information to customers and service personnel to aid informed decision making.

Customer service and support are further understood in social media and digital contexts because many companies navigate their service through these platforms. As customers have started using these platforms extensively, companies can leverage these channels to stay connected and engaged with customers. Unboxing videos, community support channels and product enthusiasts (influencers) are useful content that brands can amplify to boost customer experience. In a digitalised world, companies can provide excellent service by leveraging the power of digital connections.

THE ROLE OF INTERACTIVE TECHNOLOGIES

Digital technologies have revolutionised how tasks are performed. They are bringing in better and more efficient methods of managing all business processes. Distance and time differences no longer matter. Customers have instant and reliable access to essential information. Knowledge can be disseminated efficiently and instantly. The development of digital technologies has led to new, better and faster ways to improve business operations. Companies have used such technologies to cut costs, improve processes, deliver better services and get closer to their customers. The development and deployment of interactive technologies and the proliferation of digital tools for communication have made it possible for companies to interact more closely with their customers and, simultaneously, get to know them better. This section will look at some interactive technologies that have made an immense difference to how CRM solutions are deployed and used. In particular, the following discussion will focus on digital technologies because they are the ones that are revolutionising CRM.

Interactive Technologies

Enabling bi-directional interaction through dialogue between a firm and its customers permits the use of more than one sense (sight, sound, etc.) for communication. Easy-to-use interactive technologies engage users to be more involved and permit more information to be communicated. For example, consider the website of an automobile brand. One way to communicate its offerings is to have a web page with just a few pictures about the cars on offer and their specifications. While conveying essential information to users, such sites are not interactive. Communication is just one way; the user is not able to respond to this information, so the company loses out on critical feedback from users regarding opinions about the product. A better way of communicating the same offering is to use more interactive web technologies. Significant advances have made it possible for companies to develop websites using Augmented Reality and Virtual Reality (AR/VR) to offer a three-dimensional (3D) view of a particular car, to look at it from various angles, change the colour and other accessories, and even take a virtual test drive in a simulated environment. Such interactivity conveys the features of the car better than any words or pictures can express. At the end of the experience, the user can be asked to respond to a few questions for feedback. This improved communication and engagement creates a positive impression about the product.

Interactive technologies have therefore become an integral part of CRM solutions. They consist of interactive websites, kiosks, customer experience centres, etc., and provide many advantages, including the following:

- *Better communications* provides detailed product features to customers and enables them to obtain a good idea of what the product has to offer, thereby enabling informed decisions. The company also benefits as an informed customer will appreciate the product better before making a decision. Customer expectations will be grounded in reality.
- Interactive technologies offer customers a chance to *voice their opinions* on products and services more proactively. Getting such feedback is the first important step in service and product improvement, ultimately affecting customer satisfaction.
- The company can *empower customers with sufficient knowledge* about products and their care, and enable customers to solve minor problems they face without directly involving service engineers or other personnel. Thus, a company makes considerable savings in services and can concentrate resources on solving more critical issues. For example, a company can guide a user step by step in *preliminary fault diagnosis*. The customer could then resolve minor complaints following instructions from a website or recorded voice, while the engineer is better equipped with prior knowledge to solve a more complicated problem. Using an interactive web page to provide such services has been shown to cost five times less than giving instructions over the phone.
- Since the company can improve communication, call duration and transaction times are reduced significantly, allowing operators to handle more calls and contacts. Thus, the

company realises significant savings and improves contact centre productivity while improving customer satisfaction through faster problem resolution.

The Evolution of Interactive Digital Technologies

Here, we will primarily look at the evolution of user interface technologies. The first generation of modern interfaces was based on proprietary programming that ran natively in the operating system on the client (the computer utilising resources from a remote computer or server), thereby reducing network bandwidth. Although they were interactive, the need for a significant amount of software installed on the clients led to high installation, maintenance and upgrade costs. Because of their proprietary nature, they could also be used only within the company or a few selected customer interaction points. Customers could not access such interactive user interfaces from the internet, thus blocking the primary customer segment.

In the next stage, standard HTML clients accessed application functionality on the server. The server generated the user interface for the application functionality as a static HTML-based document downloaded from the web. However, since standard web browsers are sessionless and have no application functionality (in other words, they are a dumb client), interactivity was limited. Each user interaction needed the client to send the entire document back to the server and refresh it, causing inefficient network usage, a jarring user experience and deterring user adoption.

The advent of thin client solutions using standard open technologies such as ActiveX and Java for implementing lightweight clients constitutes just the presentation layer of applications. These technologies provide a high level of client interactivity but only require software to be installed on the client's devices. Many web browsers now support ActiveX, Java and other interface technologies to improve customer interactivity.

The advent of digital interactive technologies has transformed the way companies connect with customers by creating opportunities for interaction and immersion. Digital tools and platforms now facilitate real-time interaction and engagement with users through interactive technology that permit users to actively participate and influence digital content to create dynamic and immersive experiences. Touchscreens, gesture recognition, voice commands or motion sensors enable users to interact with digital content in an intuitive, responsive and engaging manner. Brands are leveraging the power of these interactive technologies to engage with customers and develop consumer insights. For example, L'Oréal's Beauty Genius virtual makeover simulator tool allows users to get a realistic idea of how a colour will look on them by virtually applying cosmetic products such as lipstick, mascara, foundation or highlighter using a webcam or a mobile phone camera.

CRM applications can be used both within the company and by customers. Clients' and users' requirements and content to be delivered could differ significantly. Applications that are accessed by customers using their infrastructure need to be interactive but, at the same time, must be built using available technologies (such as Java, CGI, etc.) so that they can be accessed easily. Download times for applets (small Java programs running on clients) must be kept as low as possible. However, these applets significantly increase interactivity. A compromise is downloading the applets from the server as and when needed.

If organisations use the applications, proprietary software can be used. Client-side interaction is usually preferred as it enables the operators to access information quickly because server load is reduced. On the other hand, it requires a significant amount of software to be installed on the clients, making initial start-up periods quite long as software must be loaded on each client throughout the organisation. A compromise is to use a thin client version that uses the web to interface with the server.

The interactive web technologies used in CRM solutions include ActiveX, CGI, Java and Netscape Plug-ins.

- *ActiveX:* Microsoft developed this as a set of technologies that helps integrate software components using any language in a networked environment. It includes ActiveX scripting, documents, controls and server framework. ActiveX control is a Windows-based program that is distributed from the web page. The controls can do anything that any program on Windows can. Thus, the interactivity can be increased through appropriate programming.
- *Common Gateway Interface (CGI)* is one of the standard external applications for interfacing with information servers. It is equivalent to letting the world run a program on your system. Therefore, the client here takes most of the load and the server is accessible and performs the processing of transactions and critical information.
- *Java* is a set of three technologies – Java programming, Java virtual machine and Java byte code – that allow applications to compile only once and run on different platforms. This means it is platform-independent; programs can be downloaded to the client's machine and run there.
- *Netscape Plug-ins* are software programs that usually extend the Netscape navigator's capacity in a particular way – for instance by viewing movies and playing audio samples within the navigator.

In all the technologies listed above, the primary idea remains the same – i.e. run a program at the client's end and make it as interactive as possible. No delay will be associated while processing as it uses the client side to run. Once the processing part is over, it can send the same over the web to the server.

CLOSING CASE

Amazon Go

Amazon's physical grocery concept store, Amazon Go, has enhanced the customer's entire shopping experience through its mobile app (Rao, 2016). The company uses machine learning, sensor technology, artificial intelligence, computer vision, machine vision and other digital technologies to provide a seamless, self-enabled instore buying experience.

Shoppers scan their smartphones on entering the store, and the company's 'just walk out' technology detects when the customer selects products from the shelves or returns them. The technology keeps track of customers' virtual cards through their smartphones. After completing their shopping and leaving the store, customers are billed for the final amount via their Amazon.com account.

Amazon has been a pioneering customer-centric global e-commerce firm. The Go initiative is just another example of the company leveraging the latest digital tools and technologies to boost customer experience and strengthen its relationships while disrupting the physical retail store experience.

CONCLUSION

This chapter focused on technological tools that have helped accelerate the acceptance of CRM. We started with CRM architecture, which emphasised the importance of a balanced approach to combining operational and analytical technologies. We then learned about data infrastructure, including data lakes and data warehouses that are required for data mining and analytics to support operational, analytical and collaborative CRM. Finally, we focused on the main components of CRM solutions and the emerging role of interactive digital technologies.

Industry Best Practices

- Integration of a holistic, customer-centric approach using operational CRM to automate customer interactions, analytical CRM to gain deeper insights and collaborative CRM to enhance communications as part of adopting a holistic CRM strategy.
- Better customer understanding and decision making: Organisations can improve decision-making processes and gain deeper understanding of customer behaviour by merging operational and analytical CRM.
- CRM technologies are revolutionising customer interaction: CRM solutions have undergone a revolution thanks to developments in internet-based technologies like ActiveX, CGI, Java and Netscape Plug-ins. These technologies increase customer interaction and engagement while enhancing customer experience and generating insightful feedback that spurs innovation.

From interaction and insight generation to strategic implementation and efficiency improvement, the integration of cutting-edge CRM strategies and technologies greatly improves customer management processes. These strategies are therefore a must for any progressive company as they have been shown to increase important business KPIs such as profitability, customer retentions and satisfaction.

DISCUSSION QUESTIONS

1 Explain the differences and similarities between operational and analytical CRM.
2 Explain the advantages of data warehousing for CRM analytics.
3 Explain the role of data mining for CRM.
4 Explain the importance of campaign management.
5 What could be the main challenges to adopting CRM technologies in an organisation?

REFERENCES

Anderberg, M.R. (1973). *Cluster analysis for applications*. New York: Academic Press.

Berry, M.A., & Linoff, G.S. (2000). Mastering data mining: The art and science of customer relationship management. *Industrial Management & Data Systems*, *100*(5), 245–246. doi:10.1108/imds.2000.100.5.245.2.

Chaudhuri, S., & Dayal, U. (1997). An overview of data warehousing and OLAP technology. *ACM SIGMOD Record*, *26*(1), 65–74.

Caterpillar. (2017). Earth moving solutions. Retrieved March 6, 2017, from https://www.cat.com/en_IN/support/technology/earth-moving-solutions.html.

Dudley, E. (2025). How Caterpillar Uses Social Media to Overcome Customer Barriers. Crafted Agency Article. Retrieved from https://craftedagency.com/blog/how-caterpillar-uses-social-media-to-overcome-customer-barriers

Fayyad, U., Piatetsky-Shapiro, G., & Smyth, P. (1996). From data mining to knowledge discovery in databases. *AI Magazine*, *17*(3), 37–37.

Horwitz, L. (2016). What is Amazon Go? Retrieved November 19, 2021, from https://searchcustomerexperience.techtarget.com/definition/Amazon-Go.

Jain, A.K., Murty, M.N., & Flynn, P.J. (1999). Data clustering: A review. *ACM Computing Surveys (CSUR)*, *31*(3), 264–323.

Matheus, C.J., Chan, P.K., &Piatetsky-Shapiro, G. (1993). Systems for knowledge discovery in databases. *IEEE Transactions on Knowledge and Data Engineering*, *5*(6), 903–913.

Nelson, A. (2012). How caterpillar constructs a strong B2B social media strategy. Retrieved November 19, 2021, from https://www.sforce.com/blog/2012/10/how-caterpillar-constructs-a-strong-b2b-social-media-strategy.html.

Patel, N. (2015). 10 ways data mining can help you get a competitive edge. Retrieved November 19, 2021, from https://neilpatel.com/blog/data-mining/.

Rao, L. (2016). Amazon Go debuts as a new grocery store without checkout lines. Retrieved November 19, 2021, from https://fortune.com/2016/12/05/amazon-go-store/.

Shahnam, E. (1999). The customer relationship management ecosystem: Application delivery strategies. Retrieved November 17, 2003, from https://silo.tips/download/meta-delta-application-delivery-strategies.

Simoudis, E. (1996). Reality check for data mining. *IEEE Intelligent Systems*, *11*(5), 26–33.

Thompson, R. (2022). 12 best data mining tools & techniques for powerful data analysis. Retrieved January 12, 2025, from https://www.invensis.net/blog/data-mining-tools-techniques.

Weiss, S.M., & Kulikowski, C.A. (1991). *Computer systems that learn: Classification and prediction methods from statistics, neural nets, machine learning, and expert systems*. San Francisco: Morgan Kaufmann.

Yoon, Y. (1999). Discovering knowledge in corporate databases. *Information Systems Management*, *16*(2), 64–71. doi:10.1201/1078/43188.16.2.19990301/31178.10.

CHAPTER 8

CRM Product Offerings

CHAPTER OVERVIEW

After reading this chapter you should be able to understand:

1. The criteria used to evaluate technological solutions for Customer Relationship Management (CRM)
2. Product offerings targeted at large enterprises as well as a few solutions popular among small and medium enterprises (SMEs)
3. The growing popularity of on-demand CRM solutions that offer software-as-a-service (SaaS)

Vignette

The Auckland-based travel company Kiwi Experience offers hop-on-hop-off bus services and small group bus tours to travellers in New Zealand. It creates flexible guided tours and customised plans to match each tourist's budget and itinerary. Even though customers are part of small groups, all travellers can customise their plans with multiple options to select destinations to visit and time to spend at each destination. Such flexibility permits customers to join, leave and rejoin the tour. The travel experience includes transportation, food, accommodation, sightseeing and adventure activities at scenic destinations. Offering unique, personalised and memorable experiences to each traveller has helped the company emerge as a leader in this competitive sector. Kiwi Experience epitomises innovation in the backpacking industry by focusing on customer experience.

DOI: 10.4324/9781003518174-11

OPENING CASE

Blendtec – Customer Orientation

Blendtec, a leading brand of blenders for home and commercial use, was founded in 1975 by Tom Dickson in Utah, USA. The company's innovative, cutting-edge design and construction have helped build its reputation for advanced, powerful blenders of high quality and durability. The innovative company gained popularity for its 'Will It Blend?' viral marketing campaign, which featured the founder blending non-food items such as iPods, iPhones, marbles, golf balls and remote controls. The company has been experiencing steady growth due to its commitment to quality and customer satisfaction. While the company generates most of its revenue from retail channels, it has successfully used digital channels to differentiate itself by driving website and social media traffic and engaging visitors to boost brand awareness.

Blendtec grew further and provided open and engaging customer and partner solutions. In 2016, the company selected Microsoft Dynamics CRM to deliver exceptional customer service using machine learning, the Internet of Things (IoT) and analytics capabilities (Kresch, 2016). The company configured MS Dynamics' technology solution suite, including Power BI and AX, to connect with customers and partners and streamline its order fulfilment and customer support processes that drive its engagement strategy. This connection and engagement, aided by technology integration, has improved and strengthened the firm's relationships with its key stakeholders.

THE NEED FOR CRM SOLUTIONS

The growing importance of technology-led CRM makes it imperative to understand the CRM solutions and offerings organisations implement to strengthen their relationships with customers.

CRM solutions automate the customer-facing functions of marketing, sales and service, and play a significant role throughout the customer's journey with a firm. The marketing functionalities help create awareness among prospects; the sales functionalities power the sales pipeline; and the service functionalities help provide exceptional customer support. Thus, CRM solutions help firms achieve their goal of strengthening relationships with customers.

Analytics, leveraging data from customer interactions and transactions, helps anticipate and predict customers' needs and expectations. These insights help firms develop new products and redesign services to stay competitive.

Successful implementation of CRM solutions requires close coordination between the marketing, sales and customer service functions of the firm. It is imperative to understand some of the essential features of CRM solutions that will make them attractive for firms planning to invest in technology solutions. We will also highlight a few key functional and technical requirements for CRM solutions.

Essential Features of CRM solutions

1 *Simple and Easy Integration:* CRM products must be simple for employees to use while integrating with their daily activities.

2 *Remote and Mobile Access:* This has become necessary as it provides opportunities to access the solution on the move and from anywhere.

3 *Multi-Channel Support:* As organisations rapidly adopt an omnichannel presence, they expect all solutions, including CRM, to be enabled across all touchpoints, including phone, mobile, chatbot, emails and social media. Customers use multiple channels to interact with organisations, so they expect firms to cater to their needs and interact with them through their preferred mode of interaction.

4 *Integrated Analytics:* CRM products should provide managers with data-driven decision-making abilities through analytics, primarily to support marketing, sales and service-related decisions.

5 *Adaptability and Personalisation:* These facilitate the development of customised solutions for adapting organisational processes that enhance customer value.

6 *Compatibility with Existing Infrastructure and Ease of Integration:* Compatibility with existing information technology (IT) infrastructure is an important criterion when purchasing piecemeal CRM solutions for sales force automation, campaign management or a complete suite of CRM solutions. The compatibility issue becomes even more critical when the CRM solutions are integrated with a firm's IT infrastructure, such as data warehouses, supply chain management solutions, etc. If the solutions use open-source code and compatibility is high, integration expenses are lower. Under such circumstances, it is preferable to opt for compatible software. On the other hand, there will be times when the advantage of the software outweighs the added expense of an integration effort. In such cases, compatibility may not be much of an issue, but selecting the right solution to perform the appropriate task will be the relevant criterion.

7 *Scalability:* Scalability is the ability of a system to cater to higher loads without any deterioration in performance. For example, a transaction processing system can be highly scalable if it maintains the same performance from a 1000 to a million transactions. A CRM solution should be highly scalable because one expects the business to grow. Digital solutions to support omnichannel interactions should be designed to handle exponential growth. Scalable cloud-based solutions offer the opportunity to match the load with low incremental investments.

8 *Flexibility in Incorporating Changes and Upgradability:* This is an important criterion as all organisational requirements may not be anticipated during the initial implementation. With increased usage, experience and business growth, new requirements are identified, so the solution should be flexible and incorporate these changes.

9 *Initial and Lifetime Costs:* Price is an important criterion in the context of a wide range of pricing options, especially for SaaS solutions. Initial costs go beyond the price charged and

include the implementation costs of training, customisation and later upgrades. Therefore, lower cost of ownership is a key criterion for selection.

CRM solutions have proliferated in the market, with vendors offering a wide range of functionalities that support multiple operations to automate the firm's customer-facing processes. As new communication and digital technologies emerge, the capabilities of CRM solutions have grown correspondingly to match the new possibilities that these advances throw up. For example, whereas older generations of CRM solutions provided limited interactivity using only Hypertext Markup Language (HTML), Active Server Pages (ASP), ASP Network Enabled Technologies (ASP.NET) and Common Gateway Interface (CGI) as the standard, newer solutions use more interactive technologies such as HTML5, Java (Java Server Pages), Node.js and Apache, among others. Under such circumstances, it becomes very difficult to compare products from different vendors and evaluate them for purchase.

Gaur (2000) identified the following key functional and technical requirements for CRM solutions:

- Business intelligence (BI) and analytical abilities
- Unified channels for customer interaction
- Support for web-based functionality
- A centralised repository for customer and other enterprise information
- Integrated workflow for business rules and procedures
- Integration with enterprise resource planning (ERP) and other enterprise-wide applications.

Functionally, CRM applications can be categorised into three main modules:

1 Sales Applications – Sales Force Automation (SFA) solutions
2 Marketing Applications – Campaign Management (CMA)
3 Customer Service and Support (CSS) Applications.

Several applications have started offering additional functionalities, including *Commerce*, which makes it easy for customers to buy online, and *Community* to build branded communities and portals for customers, partners and employees.

Almost all leading CRM solutions provide the following capabilities:

- Category Management
- Promotion Management
- Demand Planning
- Interactive Selling
- A Sales and Service Contact Centre
- Analytics Capability
- Contract Management
- Account Management
- Campaign Management

TABLE 8.1 Global CRM Solutions Market

Main Target	Server-Centric (On Premise)	Web-Centric (Hosted)
Large Enterprises	Siebel, Oracle/Peoplesoft, My SAP	Siebel CRM on Demand, Salesforce.com
Small and Medium Enterprises	Talisma, SalesLogix, Microsoft, Onyx, SalesNote	Salesnet CRM, NetCRM

- Automatic Routing Capability
- Workflow Management
- Mobile Sales and Services Support.

Some of the leading CRM solutions include Salesforce, SAP, Oracle/Siebel and Microsoft Dynamics. The global CRM solutions market used to be divided into on-premise and cloud/hosted solutions, with offerings focusing on large or small and medium enterprises (SMEs). However, the rapid adoption of hosted solutions has led to a hybrid approach by leading players such as Oracle and Microsoft, which offer clients both options.

The global CRM solutions market can be represented as in Table 8.1.

COMPARISON OF LEADING CRM SOLUTIONS

In this section, we briefly describe a few leading CRM solutions focusing on offerings for large enterprises. The enterprise CRM market has consolidated after a wave of mergers and acquisitions, including Oracle's acquisition of Siebel and PeopleSoft, in the last decade and a half. At the same time, the entry of new players like HubSpot and Adobe and traditional players offering CRM solutions through the SaaS model have resulted in more options for hosted CRM solutions. We have used each solution provider's websites and analyst reports as the primary source of information.

Salesforce

This company, headquartered in San Francisco, deserves much credit for building the on-demand segment of the CRM market. On-demand computing gives companies the option to plug in and subscribe to services built on world-class infrastructure via the internet, thus avoiding investment in proprietary software that require very high licensing fees. The 'pay for use' model is ideal for CRM initiatives in the trial stage or when adopted in a phased manner. The cloud solutions offered by Salesforce include:

- Sales Cloud to automate the sales processes and improve sales productivity
- Marketing Cloud to learn about customers and their needs and create personalised customer decision journeys
- Service Cloud to provide multi-channel support to customers, including social networks and communities

- Commerce Cloud to create an end-to-end online shopping experience
- Analytics and business intelligence, which leverage artificial intelligence (AI) and data for insights through a suite of products, including Tableau and Einstein.

Salesforce's cloud solutions allow users easy access to all CRM functionalities without the need to installing any application locally on their devices. This feature is especially beneficial for the field sales force as they just need to sign up to access all functionalities from anywhere in the world without logging into an on-premise system.

Salesforce has emerged as the leading enterprise software platform for CRM, with over 150,000 customers worldwide, ranging from Fortune 500 companies to small businesses. Its secure, scalable cloud platform has been adopted by charities and not-for-profits such as DonorsChoose and the World Economic Forum (WEF) to achieve their goals while serving their communities. Salesforce's 'Power of Us' program grants up to ten free licences to educational institutions and non-profits. Many government departments and agencies (such as Aylesbury Vale District Council in England) began using Salesforce to save costs, manage interactions with stakeholders and support community engagement programs (Macaulay, 2017; Preece, 2017).

Microsoft

Microsoft (MS) entered the CRM market through its MS Dynamics suite of products designed to help SMEs streamline their business processes and optimise their operations. Many of these firms already used MS applications for word processing, spreadsheets, presentations and emails. Integrating with other Microsoft products such as Office, SharePoint, and SQL Server allows for seamless data flow and collaboration across different departments within the firm. Modules on human resources management (HRM), financial management (FM), supply chain management (SCM) and project management (PM) enable SMEs to manage their finances, streamline operations and optimise productivity. Customisation options and scalability made this a popular choice for firms in the manufacturing, distribution and retailing sectors.

MS Dynamics 365 is a comprehensive, cloud-based suite with CRM, SCM, FM and PM functionalities. Advanced technologies including AI and machine learning (ML) enable leaders to gain deeper insights by identifying patterns and predicting trends to enhance decision making and drive innovation.

The company offers cloud and on-premise options for clients to run its CRM applications. The suite helps create more profitable customer relationships, boost sales effectiveness and provide consistent customer service through quick deployment, ease of use and interaction with back-office solutions, thereby enhancing information reliability, employee usage and productivity.

The 'Sales' module assists sales teams throughout the cycle, from lead and opportunity management to fulfilment and invoicing. The 'Customer Service' module helps customer service employees provide more robust, consistent and efficient support through Case Management, Activity Management, Routing and Queuing, Searchable Knowledge Base, Contracts Management and Automated Responses to Customer Requests, among others.

This integrated solution aims to maximise growth opportunities by enhancing revenue. It focuses on customer experience by centralising all customer-related information, automating all marketing-related activities, delivering business intelligence, facilitating internal collaboration, tracking sales processes and teams, analysing data and maximising customer services. In sum, Microsoft's CRM platform combines marketing, sales, customer service, field service and project services departments simultaneously to meet business needs and requirements.

Oracle CX

Oracle is a leading provider of CRM solutions for large enterprises and a prominent provider of business analytics and customer data integration software that connects all business data across marketing, sales and service. Oracle's Customer Experience (CX) applications are used to create, manage, serve and nurture relationships by building a complete view of customer interactions. The company's 'CRM for Everyone' philosophy empowers businesses to deliver exceptional customer experiences with solutions for various organisations, users and budgets. The industry-specific features, enhanced capabilities and usability improve the total cost of ownership (TCO). With almost two dozen industry-specific applications covering all aspects of CRM – including sales, marketing, service, interactive selling, partner relationship management, employee relationship management and analytics – Oracle offers a complete spectrum of solutions that can be bought as standalone packages or one full suite.

The company's industry-specific vertical solutions cover financial institutions, healthcare, insurance, communications, energy, consumer, life sciences, public, automotive, travel and transportation. These pre-built, topical and industry-specific analytic applications give it an edge in terms of offerings and functionalities.

Oracle also provides a configurable data warehousing solution that transforms data for actionable intelligence, a highly scalable and open analytic platform that delivers high levels of insight from data that spans sources across the enterprise, and extensive support for global deployment.

Oracle's 'CRM on Demand' is an online hosted solution accessible via internet browser for a fixed monthly fee per user. It enables customers to deploy CRM modules quickly, conveniently and affordably with no upfront additional investments in hardware, software or implementation. These myriad benefits are making it attractive for many enterprises to choose the hosted CRM option. The ability to integrate in ERP and customised solutions for specific industry segments makes Oracle a preferred choice, particularly for large enterprises.

Oracle CRM extends beyond simply automating operations by focusing on enhancing profitable relationships. Its 'Partner Relationship Management' tool allows firms to collaborate with distribution channel partners to maximise revenues and improve customer satisfaction. Some of the key functionalities include:

- Multi-channel access and support through the web, phone and email
- Business analytics and intelligence to better understand the marketplace
- Field service with mobile connectivity
- Scheduling, dispatch, assignment and routing support
- Account management and contact management
- Inventory and depot service management

- Contract tracking and management for prompt billing
- Integration with enterprise database.

Oracle provides an end-to-end solution to customers with a one-stop shop for all their needs by combining back-office and front-office e-business applications in a fully compatible package. Many clients are drawn to the end-to-end solution's ease of deployment.

SAP

As the CRM market witnessed rapid growth in the late 1990s, leading ERP players like SAP started coming up with CRM offerings. SAP counted many Fortune 500 companies as its customers for its ERP solutions. It was a natural move for the company to get into automating the customer-facing functions of marketing, sales and service. Traditionally an on-premises software solution, the company has gradually realigned its CRM offerings by shifting to cloud-based applications, now offered under the 'CRM and Customer Experience (CX)' suite. The CRM and CX solutions offer a strong business case for firms that have already implemented SAP's ERP solutions due to the ease of integration. In addition, embedding AI into SAP's CX solutions for marketing, sales, e-commerce and service helps firms predict, manage and understand their customers better. SAP highlights the following features to help firms planning to deploy its solutions:

- Consistent information across all touchpoints, enabling firms to interact with their customers across multiple channels, including mobile, email, chats, SMS, etc. Employees get role-based access to market data, analysis, applications and other aspects of the enterprise database needed to interact with customers and strengthen relationships.
- Automate communication campaigns and execute them on a global scale.
- Streamline sales processes and deliver engaging e-commerce experiences.
- Solutions cover the entire customer lifecycle to meet customer needs through all phases, from customer acquisition and multi-channel sales and digital commerce to order processing and customer service that accelerates issue resolution and improves customer satisfaction.

SAP's applications support the following functions, with options for cloud-based as well as on-premise deployment:

- Customer profile management through the Customer Data Cloud and Customer Data Platform
- Marketing through the SAP Marketing Cloud and SAP CRM Marketing (On Premises)
- Commerce through SAP Commerce Cloud
- Sales through SAP Sales Cloud and SAP CRM Sales (On Premises)
- Service through SAP Service Cloud, SAP Customer Engagement Center, SAP CRM Service (On Premises) and SAP CRM Interaction Center (On Premises)
- Billing through SAP Subscription Billing (Cloud) and SAP Billing and Revenue Management (On Premises).

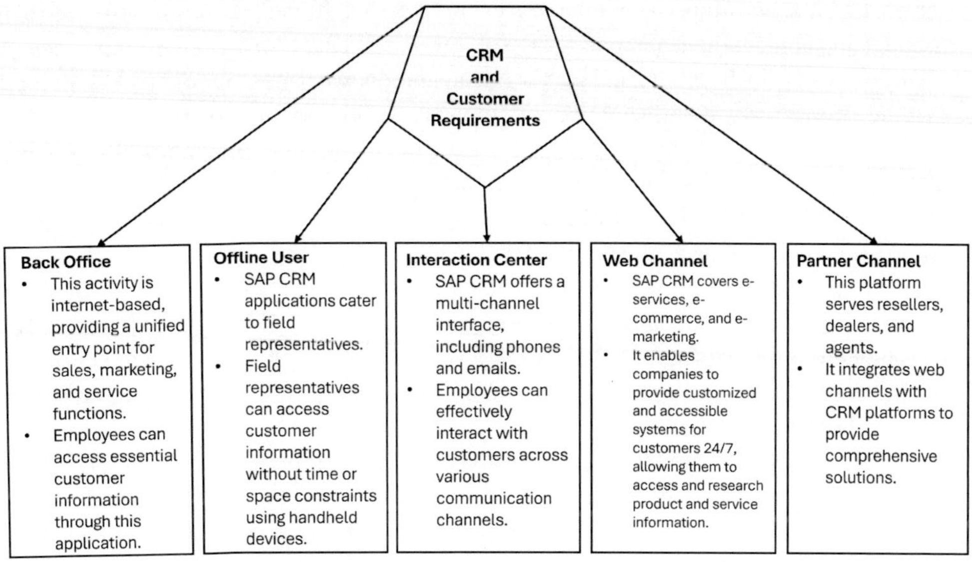

FIGURE 8.1 CRM and Customer Requirements

SAP's tailored industry-specific functions and workflow meet specific business needs for firms in the automotive, utilities, engineering, consumer products, banking, insurance, retail, telecom, travel, transportation, high tech and wholesale distribution sectors, among others. Figure 8.1 outlines CRM and customer needs in relation to SAP.

Adobe Experience Cloud

Adobe is a leading player known for its specialised software products such as Photoshop, Illustrator and Acrobat for creating and publishing content including graphics, photography, animation and multimedia, among others. The company has since moved to providing a suite of software for digital marketing and customer experience management.

Adobe's Experience Cloud combines advertising and intelligence, using generative AI and real-time insights, with digital marketing tools for content management to deliver personalised experiences across digital channels. It leverages customer data, AI and ML frameworks and content management capabilities to streamline processes. It automates data-driven decisions to deliver personalised experiences to customers across channels, thereby enhancing customer engagement and loyalty.

The vendor landscape also includes several specialised players focusing on solutions for one or two customer-facing functionalities. These include:

- Talisma, whose CX solutions focus on omnichannel customer service for firms in banking, financial services, retail and IT. Its unified inbox helps manage all customer interactions over multiple channels, including chat and social media, from a single platform.
- Infor CRM (formerly SalesLogix) focuses on streamlining sales processes for the mid-market segment covering SMEs by helping the sales team achieve its target by managing,

forecasting and reporting the entire sales cycle. The user-friendly solution offers tools for account and contact management, real-time interactive dashboards, opportunity management, a calendar with activity and advanced integration with MS Outlook. Its key strengths include affordability and ease of use and implementation. Its functionalities can easily be extended with various add-ons provided by partners. Partnerships with industry leaders allow users to learn about and use the solution quickly.

- HubSpot, a leading inbound marketing company renowned for its content management solutions and digital marketing hub, offers an AI-powered Smart CRM suite to help businesses (mainly SMEs) grow. Its free CRM solution for contact management can connect to various paid product offerings, including the Sales Hub, which has features such as deal pipelines, forecasting and dashboards. Many of its 220,000+ worldwide customers begin with the free version before signing up for the paid solutions spanning marketing, sales and service.
- Zoho, an online software suite, offers CRM as a SaaS application focused on marketing segmentation, sales cycle management and customer engagement. Popular with SMEs, Zoho automates daily activities, tracks sales and engages customers via multiple channels and platforms. The solution integrates widely used applications (e.g. MS Outlook, Mailchimp, Google apps, etc.) and cloud-based applications such as OneSaas and Cloudworks. The benefits of this suite include:
    - *Sales Automation:* Zoho CRM automates the daily activities of sales teams by managing the sales pipeline. Sharing, managing and monitoring customer accounts helps firms understand products, services, locations and purchase history and identify cross-selling and up-selling opportunities. Revenue forecast, sales productivity, personalised reports and dashboards are a few other commonly used features.
    - *Real-Time Data:* An opportunity-tracking tool helps firms understand the sales cycle, potential deal size, contact history, competitive profile and synchronised messages. It is coordinated with the notes section that delivers the time and content of interactions, which leads to seamlessly working on developing more profitable business-oriented decisions and processes.
    - *Social Media Usage:* Extensive use of social media platforms like Facebook and X (formerly Twitter) helps associate customers with products and services by following them on these platforms to categorise them as leads or contacts. Connecting with these leads enables these prospects to be invited to preview relevant offerings.
    - *Integration with Google apps* including Docs, Gmail, Calendar, Contacts and Tasks to combine customer accounts enables seamless access to Zoho's products and services.

Industry Best Practices

Comprehensive Evaluation

It is essential to use an established framework for CRM evaluation. This entails evaluating ERP integration compatibility, web functionality, centralised data management and business intelligence capabilities, and integration with various customer interaction channels. These standards guarantee that the CRM system precisely matches the business's operational requirements.

Future-Proofing Company Expansion

It is crucial for firms to select CRM systems that are scalable and expandable with the business as this strategy will help prevent performance bottlenecks in the future.

Smooth System Integration

Long-term success depends on selecting CRM solutions that provide strong integration with current systems and adaptability for upcoming upgrades. This guarantees that, without requiring a significant increase in investment, the CRM system can adjust to changing business needs. Businesses with highly integrated CRM systems report better service continuity and personalisation, which translates to higher rates of customer retention.

Value vs. Cost Analysis

In-depth reference checks are a useful tool for assessing CRM solutions because they reveal information about the effectiveness of the system and user experience. It is critical to weigh potential return on investment (ROI) against cost considerations. Businesses should steer clear of low-cost solutions that do not support their strategic objectives as these can lead to inefficiencies and functional limitations that increase long-term operating costs by 30%.

Selecting the best CRM system requires a well-rounded strategy that considers both short-term usability and long-term strategic alignment. Organisations can greatly improve their customer relationship capabilities and overall business performance by setting clear evaluation criteria, prioritising scalability, guaranteeing system compatibility and making careful selections based on thorough references and cost-effectiveness.

DISCUSSION QUESTIONS

1 Discuss the criteria for selecting an optimum CRM solution.
2 Compare the key offerings and functionalities of a couple of CRM platforms.
3 What are the benefits of implementing a CRM solution?
4 Contextualise the challenges of instituting a comprehensive CRM platform for small, medium and large businesses.
5 Discuss the importance and relevance of CRM architecture in customer engagement and business development.

REFERENCES

Gaur, S.S. (2000). Review and comparative assessment of CRM solutions for key verticals. In J. Sheth, A. Parvatiyar, & G. Shainesh (Eds.), *Customer relationship management: Emerging concepts, tools and application*. New Delhi: Tata McGraw-Hill.

Kresch, M. (2016). Customer driven: Catching up with Rolls-Royce and Blendtec. Retrieved March 16, 2017, from https://community.dynamics.com/b/msftdynamicsblog/archive/2016/06/16/customerdriven-catching-up-with-rolls-royce-and-blendtec.

Macaulay, T. (2017). Salesforce self-service platform helps Aylesbury Vale District Council save millions. Retrieved April 22, 2017, from https://www.itpro.com/cloud/362425/aylesbury-vale-district-council-transforms-service-with-salesforce-community-cloud.

Preece, C. (2017). Aylesbury Vale District Council transforms service with Salesforce community cloud. Retrieved November 20, 2021, from https://www.cloudpro.co.uk/sales-crm/6641/aylesbury-vale-district-council-transforms-service-with-salesforce-community-cloud.

CHAPTER 9

Contact Centres for CRM

CHAPTER OVERVIEW

After reading this chapter you should be able to understand:

1. The role of contact centres, such as call and interaction centres, by discussing the three key customer benefits of convenience, consistency and cordiality
2. Components of effective contact centres and interactions between elements of contact centres
3. The financial aspects of contact centres
4. The spectrum of services offered by contact centres

Vignette

AXA Seguros e Inversiones, a Spanish insurer, needed a deeper understanding of its customers to make more customised offers to boost loyalty. It therefore developed a predictive insurance policy cancellation model using SAS's data mining solution. The solution uses customer data to develop profiles and predictive models that more precisely tailor sales force automation, campaign management, call centre management and other customer relationship management activities. Before its implementation in Spain, the model was verified and tested on existing and cancelled policies in various offices. As a result, the cancellation rate of auto insurance policies was reduced by up to 9% in some targeted segments. AXA can now plan and implement custom actions and consumer engagement programmes that are developed and customised based on the needs and desires of high-value consumers using the model's recommendations.

AXA has leveraged its customer understanding by integrating customer-level knowledge into its contact centre operations to improve convenience, consistency and friendliness. Such customised interactions are helping the company build long-term relationships with its customers. The ability to engage with customers more efficiently while providing them with superior value has been driving profitable growth.

DOI: 10.4324/9781003518174-12

OPENING CASE

SRL Diagnostics: Enhancing Customer Experience

SRL Diagnostics, a leading pathology lab chain, partnered with Wipro, a leading global technology player based in India, to automate its customer care operations and deliver compelling customer experiences across multiple media and communication channels. SRL chose Oracle's Service Cloud solution to integrate its nationwide network comprising 11 reference labs, 306 network labs and 4 Centres of Excellence (CoEs) to work effectively and manage the entire customer journey. Wipro was the implementation and systems integration partner to roll out Service Cloud to provide a seamless digital experience at all customer touch-points. Streamlining of SRL's contact centre operations was facilitated by implementing an incident-tracking mechanism and a custom-built toolbar to manage all interactions (including emails, web, social media and phone calls) by integrating them with the existing customer care infrastructure. SRL uses this integrated system, ranging from registration of customer details and samples collected to delivery of reports, as it provides a comprehensive and effective customer experience that is scalable and cost-effective. The company can now track each customer's history and the service personnel can access customer details before interacting with them. Standardised processes and systems effectively executed using Service Cloud solutions have created new opportunities to serve customers. As organisations grow rapidly, operational stability is key to sustainability in competitive environments. At the same time, customers demand a seamless digital and virtual experience. As customers engage with brands through various channels (including social media, mobile apps, physical outlets, websites, chat and call centres), they expect a unified experience.

While SRL implemented Service Cloud to scale up its customer service management operations, it also enhanced the user experience of customer care employees by automating and simplifying many of their daily activities. This automation facilitates the call management process very effectively. Providing consistent customer service across the various media channels has been a game changer for the firm. Effective customer management boosted customer commitment while improving SRL's competitiveness (Hindu Business Line, 2014; Wipro, 2016).

THE ROLE OF CONTACT CENTRES IN CUSTOMER ENGAGEMENT

Businesses have increasingly been using contact centres to engage with customers. They blend effective and empowered personnel with a service process that relies on cutting-edge communication, database and digital technology. Contact centres have evolved from call centres, which were telephone-based service centres dedicated to handling customer calls for various tasks, including marketing, sales, service and support.

Call Centres

The call centre served as an intermediary between a firm and its customers. The conventional call centre was viewed as a section managed by several skilled people who handled client enquiries about products and services. These were gradually expanded to address client complaints. The telephone was the primary mode of communication, and the call centre would house a bank of phones connected to dedicated lines. A prospect or existing customer would call a call centre with a request for information about a product. Depending on urgency, the amount of information required to satisfy the customer and the opportunity for the firm to turn the prospect into a customer, calls are either attended to entirely by call centre representatives or, after preliminary interaction, relevant information is passed to the sales department to complete the interaction.

For example, a bank running an advertising campaign for a new home loan product with a flexible repayment schedule would include multiple contact options in the ad, including a toll-free telephone number for further information. Prospects calling the number will reach a call centre handler who will be able to provide them with more information. If the caller is interested and, the hander will collect the customer's address and pass it to the sales department, which will then send a representative to the prospect's home to explain the benefits, documents and other requirements to apply for the loan.

Thus, call centres provide an easy interface between the firm and its customers – a single point of contact for customers to connect with the firm for various needs by dispensing the right information to resolve queries, address problems and handle claims. They can also channel queries to the relevant departments within the organisation.

[24]7.ai, a leading provider of customer experience solutions and services, has built customer acquisition cloud solutions to help brands reach and engage with customers. The complete spectrum of marketing is covered under the cloud, and the synergy between the acquisition and engagement channels works well when customers are satisfied with the interaction and engagement.

Contact Centres or Interaction Centres

The contact centre, also referred to as a customer interaction centre, is an enhanced version of the call centre that delivers significantly more complete services through integrations at two levels:

1 Channel by combining multiple avenues used by customers, such as social media, messaging, apps, email, mobile, etc.
2 Functional by linking to a central database and working in concert with other business areas such as sales, service, marketing and so on.

The integrated contact centre connects all touchpoints (including phone, email, touch-screen kiosk, fax, chats, social media handles, etc.) in combination with customer-facing Customer

Relationship Management (CRM) modules including sales force automation, campaign management, customer service and community.

Two Conflicting Views about Contact Centres

There are two opposing perspectives about contact centres (Saberi et al., 2017): some academics believe that they were a cynical move by businesses to control costs and disempower the workforce, while others believe they are attempts by businesses to respond to customer demands for better service and access. The reality is that businesses need to respond to customer demand for more information about the firm's products and services. The fact that an arrangement such as a call centre also helps reduce costs by integrating information and utilising information technologies (IT) is also important and significant.

The Three Cs

Customers seek three critical benefits from any organisation they contact. The Henley Centre for Customer Management (part of the University of Reading, UK) reported three benefits sought by customers (Amin, 2015):

- *Convenience* – to be able to call at the customer's convenience
- *Consistency* – to let people do what they agree to do
- *Cordiality* – to be treated with the respect that any individual should expect and deserve.

Let us consider a typical customer–firm interaction. A customer consults the firm's self-service portal at 1 pm, places an online order via mobile app at 2 pm and messages the service representative at 3 pm about modifying the order. At 4 pm, she might use the app to check the status of the order. In each interaction, the customer refers to her previous interaction(s) and expects the firm to remember what transpired previously, even as the channel and medium of interaction change. Thus, the customer desires a single point of contact with memory. A contact centre is the modern-day organisation's response to this challenge as it helps integrate these interactions across multiple channels.

Channel Integration

The contact centre can provide a unified face to the firm only by integrating its various channels and touchpoints. Customer service representatives need to enter a single key into the system (e.g. customer identity or ticket number) to seamlessly access and update the relevant information while interacting using various communication channels. This repository serves as a knowledge base to offer consistent and accurate responses to end users and customer service representatives. Contact centre frameworks and technologies are moving towards integrating technologies such that customer service agents can see all channels from the same console to monitor multiple media.

Synchronous vs Asynchronous Channel Calls

Consider two distinct scenarios that can arise in a contact centre: (1) the customer views the firm's website and emails it requesting additional information about a particular product in the first instance; (2) a consumer calls customer services with specific product-related questions. The former is an 'asynchronous' contact, whereas the latter is a 'synchronous' contact (Bocklund, 2003). When consumers send an email, they receive an automated response; and, in most circumstances, this will suffice as they do not expect an immediate response. The service agent has time to respond, usually within a few hours. As a result, agents can handle additional responsibilities to support customers. Contrast this with a telephone call, requiring the agent to be physically present and answer the phone when it rings. However automated voice response systems can handle simple queries.

The organisation still needs adequate staff to handle the worst-case scenarios, such as peak demand. Synchronous channels are substantially more expensive than asynchronous channels as they require much higher numbers of service personnel (Figure 9.1). Therefore, firms are increasingly adopting self-service technologies (such as chatbots) and leveraging customer communities to support customers.

Agent Competencies

A customer sales and service representative (often an agent) in a contact centre is a multi-talented individual whose skill set is typically divided into three categories: sales, service and technical support. While several of these skills overlap, the fact is that a contact centre agent is not a passive intermediary who just routes queries. These agents play a very active role using a bank of telephones supplemented by computer terminals and high-end CRM

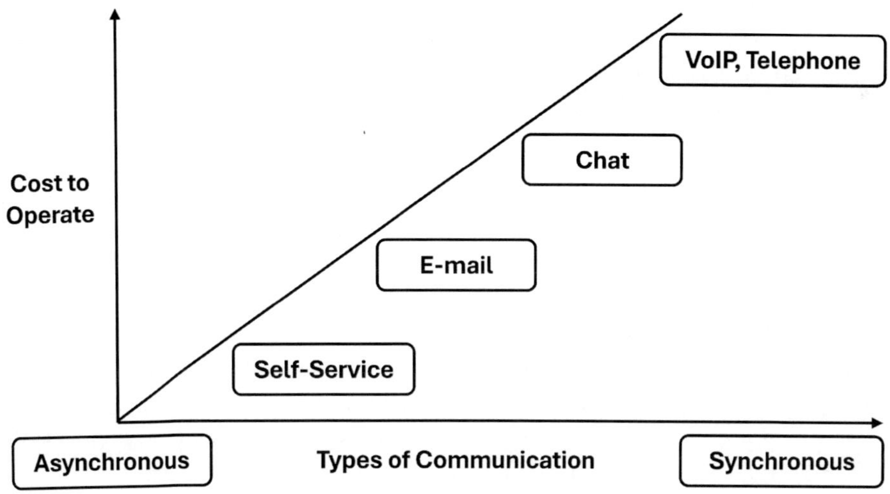

FIGURE 9.1 Types of Communication vs. Operational Costs

software. As the most basic customer interactions (such as queries) are increasingly being automated, contact centre agents get more time for sales or customer services that require greater personalisation. Typical contact centre software would link the telecom system to databases at the back end and communicate automated information to callers using interactive voice response (IVR) and pop-up screen layers through the agent. New systems incorporate internet technologies and are web-enabled, allowing more interactivity for callers while keeping the basic model for customer interaction unchanged (Dumblekar, 2000). Agents must therefore be tech-savvy while handling multiple requests patiently and politely. The job can be monotonous and dull, but also challenging.

Customers expect multiple channels to connect with firms so that they have various options. Companies can accommodate customers' wishes by using modern, digital contact centres to offer customers a diverse range of communication methods. As the costs of communicating over different channels differ substantially, firms use channels based on customer profiles or task characteristics. For instance, a firm can adopt a more synchronous means of communication with highly profitable and valuable customers, such as dedicated numbers served by highly qualified reps. The channel selected may also be determined by the nature of the communication. For instance, a business might classify interactions based on the task – viz. routine vs. specialised or complex transactions. Actual contact with a service rep over the phone will be reserved for more complex tasks, while others may be managed by IVR systems or mobile apps – e.g. booking an appointment with a doctor or reserving a table at a restaurant.

Contact centres provide the platform for firms to excel in customer service, especially those in banking, financial services, e-commerce, retailing, hospitality, etc. with a large customer base. Service requests, queries, bookings, product returns, subscription renewals and problem resolution can be handled through inbound calls, outbound calls, SMS, chat or other interactions and communications over social and digital media platforms. These activities are supported by digital technologies designed to fulfil the needs of both firms and their customers.

COMPONENTS OF A CONTACT CENTRE

Contact centre technologies are rapidly evolving, and most firms now adopt cloud-based solutions to manage their interactions with customers. This section outlines some of the key components and functionalities of the contact centre (adapted from PTP, 2016).

Omnichannel Integration

Omnichannel integration enables digitally enabled telecom and online touchpoints to function together. Contact centres leverage it to manage their customer interactions effectively. The integration supports the reps in handling customer calls while their computer screens display customer-related information (such as relevant account details) in pop-ups to help reps save time while having meaningful conversations with customers. It therefore speeds up and makes issue resolution more efficient as agents can provide better support when they have a complete picture of the customer and the issue.

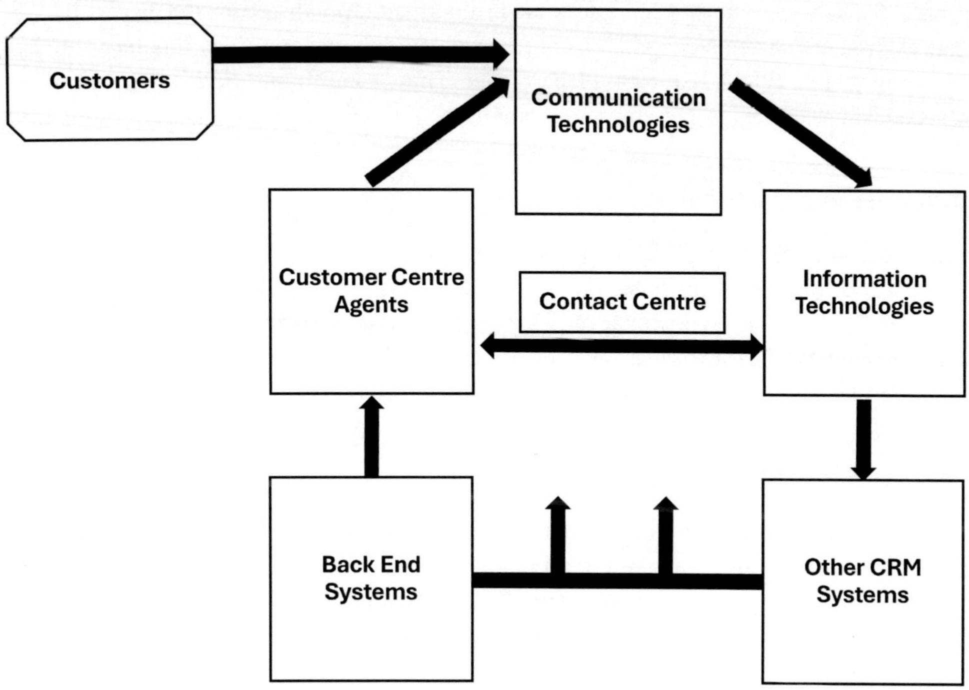

FIGURE 9.2 Interactions between Components of a Contact Centre

Omnichannel contact centres consolidate customer information gathered via chatbots, forms and representatives into one place. For example, a customer may begin by engaging with a chatbot. Based on the responses to a series of automated questions, a live agent may then get involved to support the customer, who will not want to repeat those answers to the rep. The omnichannel system picks up all the interactions between the customer and the chatbot (Figure 9.2). Hence the agent has complete information, including the customer and service request context, thus streamlining the rest of the interaction.

Automatic Call Distribution

Automatic call distribution (ACD) is a system based on telephony integration that can identify the answers and routes of incoming calls. This identification of solutions helps agents resolve customers' problems promptly as they utilise customer identification to access the most relevant data. Customers prefer this approach as it syncs with their specific needs and requirements, so the CRM experience is enhanced and strengthened. ACD is also helpful to agents as they can manage a high volume of regular calls, which helps companies function more effectively.

Intelligent Call Back

This lets incoming callers connect quickly to a contact centre agent. These quick connections are made when customers overlook some information or issue. When callers select the call-back feature, they do not have to wait in the queue to call again. Further, callers can update their status. Agents can also instantly connect with customers on this basis, and can track entire conversations that took place earlier. Thus, a call might be extended only for a few seconds. Customers might add more data based on their requirements during this time.

Interactive Voice Response

Interactive voice response (IVR) is an automated phone system that helps callers retrieve relevant service- and support-related information by interacting with the system – e.g. by entering keywords via a touchpad. Advanced IVR systems now operate through natural language speech recognition. These software platforms can also detect grammar and identify multiple dialects and languages for responses based on caller preferences.

Universal Queuing

This is used to pool and maintain all callers simultaneously in a single queue for a waiting list (e.g. for concert tickets) by integrating all the media channels used by different customers to contact the company, including phone, email, social media and other digital platforms. This single queue enhances consistency and responsiveness for customers.

Interactive Video

Interactive video (IV) is primarily used by companies for customer promotions, ad campaigns and entertainment. This method provides an excellent opportunity to showcase products and services on kiosk displays, bank ATMs and at information desks (e.g. in airports or in shopping malls).

Predictive Dialler

Predictive dialler or dialling (PD) automatically dials a list of customers from a database. This automation saves time and identifies busy (engaged) signals, voice mail messages, no answers and disconnected phone numbers. This detailed identification of all numbers helps agents as it works across all media platforms (mobile, text, email, chat, social media and other digital platforms) after identifying each customer's preferred media channel(s). Subsequently, the system directly connects the agent with that individual to address the issue or problem. PD can also be proactive by reaching out to customers in case of emergencies. Lastly, it can inform customers, especially when waiting in the queue to connect to an agent.

Call Recording Systems

These are used by contact centres to retrieve comprehensive information about interactions. Analysis of these recorded interactions also helps efforts to improve quality and identify training needs. Besides recording calls, these systems can undertake other types of interaction and communication (e.g. emails and chats). Calls can be recorded in two formats – historical and actual. Thus, agents can interact with this data and provide off-script guidance or advice to customers. Customers appreciate this approach when agents go beyond the companies' written script and help resolve their issues. Further, call recording and analytics are conducted simultaneously when agents require particular data for problem resolution.

Voice Biometrics

This software is used to validate the authenticity of an individual's identity based on their exclusivity and distinctiveness – primarily to prevent identity theft and fraud. This facility allows agents to redirect their time to help customers resolve service issues.

Workforce Management Software

Workforce management software (WMS) predicts the quantity and quality of customer interactions and communications across all media channels. These predictions help call centre agents meet pre-set standards in terms of quality established by the firm as part of service-level agreements (SLAs). WMS integrates with other workforce optimisation solutions to enable agents to interact with customers effectively.

Quality Management

Quality management (QM) applications provide managers with critical insights into the performance of agents and employees in real time. Subsequently, managers can also identify employee weaknesses to address them through training and development initiatives.

As satisfied customers are the key to success in competitive markets, contact centres play a vital role in managing interactions across multiple touchpoints. Digitally enabled technologies are helping businesses improve opportunities to engage with customers and prospects through their contact centres.

A contact centre is a front-end infrastructure that directly interfaces with customers. However, it requires integration with back-end systems like data warehouses and other CRM solutions such as sales force automation or campaign management. Thus, the pillars of a contact centre superstructure are service representatives, communication technologies and digital technologies, including software applications (Hegglin, 2011).

Contact centres have evolved to support business needs and requirements, and could be single-site or multi-site. While multi-site centres are more expensive than single-site centres to establish and operate, they are preferred by large corporations to support their business units worldwide. Multi-site contact centres need to leverage cloud applications and distributed data centres to pool resources to function effectively, save costs and reduce risks. Many multinationals operate contact centres across continents to provide 24/7 multilingual support to their global customer base.

British Airways (BA) operates in 74 countries, connects 194 destinations and serves over 36 million customers annually. In 2003, BA rolled out a global customer relations programme with relevant technology infrastructure, service processes and a comprehensive system for information gathering and reporting to improve customer touchpoints. The company focused on service quality as the critical differentiator to offer a world-class customer experience (Faull, 2015).

While it had a network of customer service offices that would respond to queries via email, phone, mail or fax, BA soon realised that its processes were complex and time-consuming. Multiple standalone databases created service failures, so the company started integrating all customer interactions and communications to improve service quality and enhance productivity and performance (Smith, 2014).

BA rolled out its new e-power centre solutions across all destinations. This online app provided a unified and consistent solution using a single application on a globally integrated customer database. This centre replaced 11 non-integrated systems used across 25 countries, and over 230 agents could process multiple cases across different countries simultaneously. Facilitating customer interactions by syncing with the reservations system, baggage and customer databases in real time improved customer experience.

BA also developed a unified passenger compensation solution across all airports and destinations for lost baggage or missed flights. Integrating the compensation solution with its contact centres allowed BA to address service failures quickly. The company managed over 1 billion customer interactions in a year through this new unified, simplified and efficient process to quickly resolve service issues. Service quality improved as workflows were automated, and increased visibility and real-time data provided in-depth understanding of the overall customer experience (Astute Solutions, 2016).

Indeed, as we have seen, customer contact centres are growing increasingly intense, with capabilities spanning multiple functional areas, including sales, marketing, customer service and support. Design aspects and other product and service issues can be communicated directly to production and other departments. For instance, if a client contacts a firm frequently about a particular problem with a product, it is highly likely that the issue results from a design error, so this information should be communicated to the design and production divisions for follow-up.

Organisations communicate with their customers via various channels, including phone, email, live chat, chatbot-enabled websites and face to face. Each channel introduces a new level of complexity to the contact centre and necessitates specific technical support solutions to manage these interactions. Successful firms with large customer bases continually invest in new digital technologies and channels to enhance their customers' engagement experiences. Contact centres have emerged as the key to providing positive experiences to customers throughout their decision journey with firms (Sealey, 2014; Osborne, 2014).

CONTACT CENTRE SERVICES AND ADDED VALUE

The contact centre's primary role is to ensure that all services (from a wide range) are seamlessly available to all customers, perhaps millions in a large firm. A company may operate its own contact centre or outsource it to a third-party provider. In any case, the contact centre adds value to the CRM process based on the service it delivers to the customer.

Contact centres provide two basic sorts of service – back office and front office. Back-office services do not involve direct, one-on-one contact with consumers and typically, require little by way of skill set from staff. Additionally, these services bring little value, implying minimal revenue potential. On the other hand, front-office services are those in which a consumer directly interacts with a firm's representative, and hence require greater capabilities to deliver high-quality services. As a result, the payoffs for contact centres for frontline services are significant. We will briefly highlight a few services provided by customer contact centres and how they fit into our fundamental structure of three components: client interaction, value addition and payoff.

Data Entry

Data entry is a low-value added activity required for transferring data from one medium (e.g. a form) to computers for processing and reconciliation, and so requires basic skills. Medical transcription, for example, is a data entry process that requires accurate transcription of voice records, dictated by doctors and other healthcare professionals. Doctors record their diagnosis and audio files are then transmitted to contact centres. Medical transcriptionists listen to these recordings, transcribe them into reports and mail them back. This is a very low payoff activity requiring low skill sets, the ability to understand English and the ability to type what is heard. It is also being replaced by virtual digital assistants and AI-based transcription services.

Revenue Accounting

Revenue and other accounting operations are services that, although still back end, require slightly higher skill sets. Accounting, data entry and other reconciliation operations are completed remotely, and data is uploaded to the enterprise system. The client's prime concern is 100% data availability and uptime of facilities. Many such contact centres are simply offshore extensions of shared back-office operations. Human resources (HR) operations involving payroll preparation, attendance and leave management are also being consolidated through contact centres.

Claims Processing

As we move up the spectrum of more value addition, we come across areas where domain knowledge and greater skills are required to perform the service. Insurance claims processing is one such service. With the help of well-laid rules on how they are to be processed – along with the availability of a large number of graduates literate in English, and a few doctors and accountants (to take care of trickier claims) – contact centres can offer such services. Many insurance companies outsource such services. Apart from the processing, a large amount of logistics is involved. However, the process guidelines are well established, and hence can easily be performed remotely.

Customer Interaction

Further up the spectrum are services that embody some element of customer interaction. Such services are similar to a help desk where the customer is provided with information about the firm's products and services. The interaction may be through multiple channels (phone, email, chatbots, social media, etc.). For an insurance company, the help desk could provide an annual appraisal service by maintaining an up-to-date database of all property records, creating property value estimates and providing for claims reporting centres around the clock. Basic query replies using chatbots and emails also fall into this category.

Outbound and Inbound Calls

Making outbound calls in a call centre activity can potentially deliver more value if the activity is customer-focused. The marketing department may select customers to be reached, and the contact centre agent engages with existing customers or prospects to promote the firm's service or product. Outbound call handling requires a higher level of expertise and experience than previous activities. These calls comprise the following:

- *Telemarketing*: Telemarketing is carried out by trained call centre professionals with excellent conversational skills who promote and sell products and services to existing and prospective customers and keep them updated. Recorded sales pitches are used to train these professionals, with companies also using automated sales pitches alongside human agents. Companies can quickly increase profits via telemarketing through excellent professionals, processes and technology.
- *Lead Generation*: Outbound calls work on lead generation, which, although not a new form of conducting business, is a novel approach. Lead generation involves collecting customer data and profiles (whether online or via phone or email) and guiding customers towards products and services. Although any business can adopt this process, it is usually used for education, insurance, office supplies, furniture, etc. Lead generation will become a more powerful tool in the future as businesses move towards service orientation because it helps marketing, sales and other business areas develop customer profiles and gather information that will be helpful for the entire organisation.
- *Surveys*: Data collected through customer surveys helps companies understand customer satisfaction levels with products and services, and so improve their offerings based on customers' suggestions. Recommendations/suggestions also help companies understand customer wants and needs, which are used to develop future products and services. Information gained also facilitates advertising.
- *Debt Collection*: Outbound calls are also used to collect payment from customers, primarily by financial companies, insurance companies and mortgage firms. This aspect is often outsourced to save time and money. However, this may be risky as it could potentially damage a company's reputation if such calls to persuade defaulters to pay monies due are not handled carefully.

Inbound calls are used for offering multiple services including:

- *Customer Service:* Inbound calls are undertaken to provide customer services in line with specific needs and requirements, e.g. after a product purchase to enhance customer satisfaction. Trained contact centre agents help customers improve their usage experience and satisfaction.

- *Help Desks* to provide assistance and guidance and resolve customers' issues and problems. Customer satisfaction is boosted when queries are handled efficiently and complaints addressed quickly.
- *Technical Troubleshooting* is related to product repairs, or advice or suggestions for customers. Technical support agents resolve problems and issues; undertake telesales, pre-sales and post-sales; offer support regarding technology, products, applications and networks; deliver onsite tech support, remote support and IT management services (among others), especially in terms of infrastructure. The main objective is to provide assistance 24/7.
- *Order-Taking:* This is helpful to customers placing orders via email, apps or phone as they may need to interact with agents, especially when queries need to be clarified. Order-taking adds significant value as it is directly related to improved sales. This service facilitates quick completion of sales processes and impacts revenue and profit (Gupta, 2022).

Expert Advisory Services

Finally, the greatest value is added through one-to-one expert advisory services, where experts with extensive knowledge of a particular domain are called on to advise customers. Such services are the most personalised that we can expect in the contact centre activity value chain. They require more expertise and time and are not easily available elsewhere. Consequently, they provide the highest payoffs. For example, in the case of insurance, a high-net-worth individual could ask for an expert to explore how to structure policies for property, family, health, etc. so that cover is maximised and premium payments minimised. In this case, an expert with extensive field knowledge is required.

The framework outlined above is depicted pictorially in Figure 9.3. As we move from left to right, knowledge, skill set required, added value, customer contact and personalisation increase. Consequently, a contact centre can make more profit if it focuses on the right-hand side of the services spectrum rather than the left.

With such a diverse set of available metrics, it is difficult to determine a contact centre's true income-generating potential and value to the organisation. However these centres serve

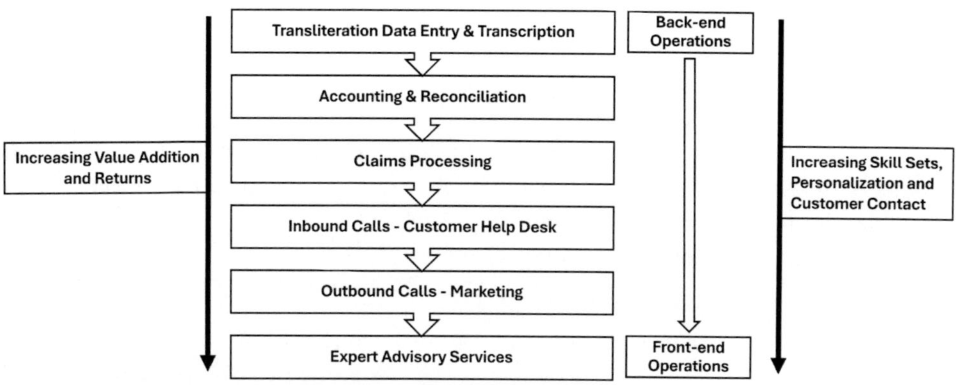

FIGURE 9.3 The Contact Centre Service Spectrum

as vital platforms for customer interaction. Initially designed to handle consumer complaints, contact centres now manage various functions, from sales and marketing to customer care and support.

SUMMARY

CRM practices are being enhanced through unified, cloud-based contact centre services. Incident tracking and improved responsiveness are positively impacting service provision. In addition, CRM practices and contact centre synchronisation enhance sales, flexibility, trust and credibility, which allows frontline contact centre personnel to access customers' history and engage with them through streamlined processes. CRM systems synchronised with contact centre systems function as seamless touchpoints for customers. They combine highly effective and empowered company representatives in a unified service framework. The enhanced ability to handle customer issues promptly boosts customer satisfaction.

Industry Best Practices

Digital Infrastructure and Capabilities

Contact centres with integrated digital and communication technologies require skilled and motivated employees to improve the customer experience.

Variability of Contact Centre Type and Use of Technology

Contact centres may run out of one location or several, customising technology at each to fit unique requirements and financial limitations. For example, multi-site centres may use more advanced technologies to handle more complex operations, improving coordination and cutting response times by about 15%. An illustration is British Airway's use of contact centres to improve customer service and streamline customer relations. It was demonstrated that this deliberate use of contact centres could raise the airline's customer satisfaction ratings by up to 25%, highlighting the importance of committed customer service procedures in the travel sector.

Technology Integration: Complex Instruments Employed

Automated call distributors (ACD), computer telephony integration (CTI), interactive voice responses (IVR) and other technologies are all integrated in modern contact centres. These technologies aid in the effective management of high call volumes, resulting in 40% better call resolution and 50% shorter wait times on average.

CRM and Social Media Integration: Boosting Customer Engagement

Domino's Pizza is one business that successfully leverages social media integration and CRM tools to improve customer interactions. The impact of combining these technologies in a cohesive customer service strategy is demonstrated by reported increases of 15% in sales and 20% in customer loyalty.

Contact Centre Service Offerings

Contact centres offer a wide range of services – from back-office services such as data entry and revenue accounting to front-office responsibilities like customer interactions and inbound/outbound call management. They can significantly increase a company's value by improving operational efficiencies and facilitating improved customer service management.

By way of summary, modern business strategies that aim to manage customer relationships and enhance service delivery rely heavily on contact centres. The use of cutting-edge technologies and the integration of flexible service capabilities help enhance both customer satisfaction and business performance.

DISCUSSION QUESTIONS

1 Review the characteristics of an effective customer contact centre.
2 Discuss the technical and support systems necessary to establish an effective customer care centre.
3 Contextualise the components of a customer care centre in terms of CRM and customer satisfaction.
4 Discuss the technical, economic and infrastructural challenges of establishing and maintaining an effective customer service centre.
5 Discuss the varied processes whose effectiveness can be maximised by establishing an effective customer service centre

REFERENCES

Astute Solutions. (2016). British Airways global consumer relations program takes off with Astute Solutions' ePowerCenter™. Retrieved November 21, 2021, from https://astutesolutions.com/customers/british-airways#:~:text=British%20Airways%20global%20consumer%20relations%20program%20takes%20off,airports%2C%20serving%20over%2040%20million%20p-eople%20a%20year.

Bocklund, L. (2003). Building the next-generation customer contact center. *Network World*. Retrieved November 21, 2021, from https://www.networkworld.com/article/2339322/building-the-next-generation-customer-contact-center.html.

Dumblekar, V. (2000). Building customer relationships through call centres in banking and financial services. In J.N. Sheth, A. Parvatiyar, & G. Shainesh (Eds.), *Customer relationship management: Emerging concepts, tools and applications*. New Delhi: McGraw-Hill.

Faull, J. (2015). Why British Airways believes marketing and commercial can work together for the customer. *The Drum*. Retrieved November 21, 2021, from https://www.thedrum.com/news/2015/01/26/why-british-airways-believes-marketing-and-commercial-can-work-together-customer.

Gupta, C. (2022). Inbound vs. outbound call centres: What is the difference? Retrieved January 13, 2025, from https://www.zendesk.com/in/blog/inbound-vs-outbound-call-centers-whats-difference/.

Hegglin, K. (2011). Components of a contact center. Retrieved November 21, 2021, from https://www.linkedin.com/company/compare-business-products/.

Hindu Business Line. (2014). Wipro implements CRM solutions for SRL diagnostics. Retrieved November 21, 2021, from https://www.thehindubusinessline.com/info-tech/Wipro-implements-CRM-solutions-for-SRL-Diagnostics/article20900341.ece.

Osborne, P. (2014). Case studies: How Domino's pizza increased customer interaction by 128%. Retrieved November 21, 2021, from https://www.contactcenterworld.com/view/contact-center-case-study/how-dominos-pizza-increased-customer-interaction-by-128.aspx.

PTP. (2016). Contact center technology 101: 16 contact center technologies you should know about. Retrieved November 24, 2021, from https://www.ptpinc.com/glossary/call-center-technology-101/.

Saberi, M., Khadeer Hussain, O., & Chang, E. (2017). Past, present and future of contact centers: A literature review. *Business Process Management Journal*, *23*(3), 574–597.

Sealey, D. (2014). Omnichannel: How Domino's delivers a highly integrated customer experience. Retrieved November 21, 2021, from https://www.mycustomer.com/service/channels/omnichannel-how-dominos-delivers-a-highly-integrated-customer-experience.

Smith, N. (2014). Customer relationship management (CRM) is gaining momentum. Retrieved November 21, 2021, from https://www.marketingweek.com/customer-relationship-management-crm-is-gaining-momentum/.

Wipro (2016). Wipro transforms customer experience at SRL Diagnostics with Oracle Service Cloud. Retrieved March 21, 2017, from https://www.wipro.com/newsroom/press-releases/archives/wipro-transforms-customer-experience-at-srl-diagnostics-with-ora/.

PART IV
Implementing CRM

CHAPTER **10**

The CRM Roadmap

CHAPTER OVERVIEW

After reading this chapter you should be able to understand:

1. The impact of Customer Relationship Management (CRM) on different functional areas of an enterprise and the stages of the CRM roadmap
2. Developing a relationship orientation for long-term and mutually beneficial relationships with core customers
3. Factors driving firms to adopt customer-centric marketing and processes
4. The development of organisational capabilities through internal marketing
5. Technology-, organisational- and people-related aspects of implementing technology solutions for CRM

Vignette

Jaguar Land Rover (JLR), one of the UK's largest automotive companies, is a designer and manufacturer that markets luxury cars worldwide. Its two iconic brands are Jaguar, which offers luxury saloons, sports cars and sports utility vehicle (SUVs), and Land Rover, with a range of premium all-terrain vehicles. Tata Motors acquired the loss-making Jaguar Land Rover from Ford for $2.3 billion in 2008. It invested over $14 billion in the following six years in design, new products, upgrading assembly plants, improving the quality of existing products and diversifying geographically by setting up manufacturing facilities in China and Brazil. As part of the turnaround strategy, the leadership adopted a customer-centric view to enhance the customer experience and deal effectively with the discontinuity and market disruptions from new technologies, competition and evolving customer behaviour.

JLR adopted customer-centricity as a core value, which meant considering what is relevant and timely for its customers. The customer experience rather than products is at the top of the vision pyramid, which drives a 'customers-first'

DOI: 10.4324/9781003518174-14

innovation to fulfil customer needs. Every decision that JLR makes, whether in the executive suite or on the shop floor, starts with customer needs and desires (Niessing et al., 2018). JLR experienced sustained growth by putting the customer at the centre of its strategy. JLR sharpened its focus on the premium segment by offering British design, market-leading engineering and digital technologies, and bespoke customer service and quality.

The new customer-focused strategy led to the rejuvenation of the company portfolio through outstanding new products and products that link the two brands to their respective heritage. By 2015, JLR had a 250-member team of CRM specialists and business analysts headed by the Director of Global CRM and Customer Insights. This was one of the largest CRM projects of its kind in the automotive industry. The team aimed to improve the systems and processes driving customer-centricity. JLR rolled out a global CRM solution to transform how its brands interact with customers throughout their journey. This involved developing an enterprise management platform that connected the entire organisation and processes covering research, design, manufacturing, marketing, sales, service and spares, and external dealers and service centres.

Market feedback and customer knowledge were critical inputs to be assessed through analytical techniques and intelligence methodologies. Bringing the 'voice of the customer' into the product launch cycle through concept clinics and pricing clinics helped JLR incorporate evolving customer preferences into the product development process. Observing the 'customer journey' from awareness, consideration, exploration, selection, purchase, ownership, use, maintenance and renewal decisions involved a continuous cycle of engagement with marketing, sales, after-sales service and support departments.

Digital tools such as a car configurator with a 360° camera within a 3D zone allow prospects to experience the interiors of cars virtually. Interaction with customers via online forums and on social media during the consideration and exploration stages speeds up calls to dealers for test drives. Customer feedback and insights form a key consideration for all decisions, be they budget-related decisions by top managers or engineers on the shop floor making operational decisions. Customer support functions combine insights and analytics to share research findings that help JLR's leaders and engineers understand their customers as complex human beings and their experiences with the company's brands.

This holistic approach, connecting people, processes and digital systems, transforms customer-centricity from an abstract corporate notion into a concrete, actionable project for everyone in the organisation. The strategy paid off as JLR's combined sales grew from 196,000 units in 2009 to over 583,000 in 2016. Creating a connected organisation to deliver a bespoke customer experience was the most significant learning.

OPENING CASE

Starbucks

Starbucks is an iconic, world-famous coffeehouse chain with over 32,000 outlets in 80 countries. As the premier roaster and retailer of speciality coffee, Starbucks is one of the world's most recognised brands for its innovation and impact. It was driven by the vision of long-serving Chairman and CEO Howard Schultz to bring the Italian coffeehouse tradition to America and create a place for human connection and conversation by fostering a sense of community. The brand positioned its cafes as the 'third place', outside home and work, for discerning customers to gather, relax and talk. A razor-sharp focus on enabling its baristas to craft the world's best coffee and connect with customers helped the company build a reputation for outstanding customer experience and high-quality products and services. The cafe experience is the cornerstone of the brand's differentiation in a competitive market. Instituting the Italian coffee bar experience that provides a welcoming ambience ensured customer satisfaction and enhanced loyalty.

Starbucks offered Wi-Fi in its outlets in 2002 and partnered with Apple in 2007 to provide free access to iTunes Music. Sales followed, so the company continued to expand its technology focus to include more content, loyalty rewards and, eventually, payments. Its mobile order and pay feature enables customers to order and pay for a drink via an app even before arriving at the cafe. Starbucks extensively uses communications programmes to connect with customers and retain its leading position. The brand logo was redesigned to highlight its sustainability policies and provide value to customers by strengthening CRM practices (Smith, 2015).

The Starbucks Rewards loyalty scheme started as a swipe-able points system on what looked like a store card. As mobile applications started gaining popularity, Starbucks launched its Rewards app in 2011 to encourage customers to increase their purchase frequency and average order size. The company increasingly invested in mobile apps and wallets to enhance its customer experience. These apps, with payment options generated via bar codes and quick-response (QR) codes, streamline the payment process. Customers preferred this new mobile app-based approach as it was fast, flexible and adaptable, and in 2015 more than 20% of payments for its US business came through the My Starbucks mobile app. The company had created a tool to generate loyalty and grow its customer base by using mobile technology to connect and help customers. Starbucks Rewards also helps customers earn freebies. By integrating this loyalty programme with others, members can earn 'stars' to redeem for free drinks when they use their phones, not just the Starbucks app. Digital deals with the *New York Times*, digital music service Spotify and ride-hailing service Lyft are value adds enjoyed by over 20 million members of the Starbucks loyalty scheme in 2015 (Alba, 2015). The process of building the capability to offer stars reward points (stars) through partnerships creates opportunities for customers to earn them at numerous different places and take them back to Starbucks.

Integrating CRM with smartphone apps enhanced service and brand experience as these apps were customised to meet customer needs and demands, leading to more productive offerings for Starbucks. Adopting mobile apps and personalised offers also helped create value while integrating online and offline experiences. App notifications, gaming and access to music through its partnership with iTunes from 2007 onward improved engagement with the brand through positive experiences.

In summary, Starbucks' focus on technology spans multiple areas (including payments, loyalty and rewards and content to drive sales), and it has leveraged innovations, creative ideas, competitive strategies and premium pricing. Critical differentiators, including new products, high-quality coffee beans, taste and pleasant cafe environments, all elevate the customer experience. Starbucks has adopted this integrated approach to enter new markets such as China and India through brand-centred relationships, and quickly developed these relationships through social media and digital channels such as Facebook, YouTube, Twitter/X, and so on (Panagiotaropoulou, 2015).

DEFINING CRM STRATEGY

CRM is an enterprise-wide initiative that aims to integrate the front-end customer-facing systems with back-end systems to drive the value delivery process. Developing a CRM strategy entails the active involvement of the top management to motivate the entire organisation and all functional departments. It involves taking a tough look at the business to identify needs and then searching for customer-oriented solutions. Implementation of CRM requires change management because almost all aspects of a business – viz. processes, goals, orientation, focus, technology, performance and effectiveness metrics – are subject to change. CRM implementation requires defining the programmes that are part and parcel of CRM, such as account management, retention marketing and others.

Usually, an implementation team or a steering committee with representatives from all the functional areas of the enterprise is set up. This team is responsible for the overall management, governance and implementation of the CRM strategy. The team must consider important aspects that concern team structure, role specifications, planning, alignment, communication, monitoring and communication. Last but not least, the team must reflect on employee motivation and training. Incentives are usually linked to customer-specific measures, while employees need to be trained to use the solutions.

CRM IMPLEMENTATION ROADMAP

A CRM implementation roadmap enables a business to foster cultural acceptance of CRM. It allows the business to adapt to organisational changes, new ventures, changing consumer needs and CRM technologies. The various stages of a CRM implementation roadmap (Figure 10.1.) are outlined below.

Scenario Analysis

Creating an enterprise CRM strategy requires a firm to look hard at its business and macro-environment. The leaders will typically have to address the following issues:

- What is the business of our firm?
- Who are our current customers? Who will be our customers in the future?
- What is the firm's competitive position?
- What is the present business scenario, and how is it likely to evolve in the short, medium and long term?

Scenario analysis helps leaders assess and understand the firm's position vis-à-vis its competitors. The firm can then define what it needs to do to improve its performance in its competitive market and strengthen customer relationships to improve its position.

Purpose and Objectives

After a comprehensive analysis of its macro-environment, the firm must define the purpose of strengthening customer relationships. Firms are usually driven by efficiency and effectiveness

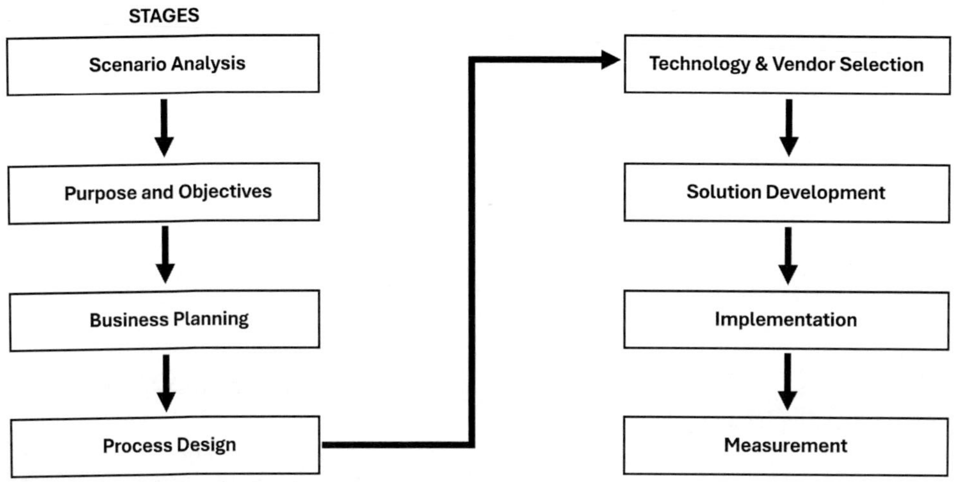

FIGURE 10.1 CRM Implementation Strategy Roadmap

criteria while aiming to build long-lasting relationships with customers. The firm should not embark upon a CRM exercise just to emulate its competitors or because it is the latest industry fad.

Business Planning

The planning stage is the next important step in the CRM implementation roadmap. The most critical operation here is to define the overall objectives at the department and enterprise level. The planning phase includes recording high-level CRM goals in a business document that becomes the focal point for strategy development. Planning also includes details of what needs to be done and assigning responsibility to individual managers and teams. Such an exercise will lead to several fundamental changes in the organisation, including among the following five interrelated areas:

- Business Focus
- Organisational Structure
- Business Metrics
- Marketing Focus
- Technology.

In the planning stage, the firm must therefore prepare for change, and teams need to be set up to handle various aspects of any changes. Regular, open and transparent communications and meetings are vital during this stage.

Process Design

CRM entails changing the entire focus of the organisation to a customer-centric one, with processes and operations designed around the customer. Process design is a crucial phase in which firms look at their current processes and redesign them to make them more customer-focused. Other factors, such as these processes' effectiveness and efficiency, are also considered.

Technology and Vendor Selection

In this stage, various technologies and vendors are evaluated. Factors such as the alignment of the technology with current systems and the capability of CRM solutions in terms of their functionalities (among others) are considered while evaluating digital solutions from different vendors.

Solution Development

The solution development stage consists of various activities, such as: the customisation of features; the development of new features that are not present in the product; process integration and testing by using the prototypes; and database design. The integration of different CRM solutions with each other and with back-end systems also sometimes occurs at this stage. The advent of subscription-based software-as-a-solution (SaaS) has simplified this stage significantly, especially for small and medium businesses.

Implementation

In this penultimate stage, the organisation deploys and documents the solution. End users need to be trained for faster adoption, and change management initiatives must be undertaken to break habits and ease switching to the new solution.

Measurement

The final stage in the CRM implementation roadmap involves the development of metrics for measuring the performance of the CRM solution and comparing it with the desired performance. If the CRM solution falls short of expectations, the firm might go back and refine its CRM requirements. Developing metrics enables the firm to measure the success of CRM implementation in terms of how well it has solved the business problem. Sometimes, the improvement may be gradual as users become more familiar with the new technology and business processes. Measurement should also incorporate user feedback to improve CRM usability and business effectiveness.

Thus, developing a CRM strategy and implementing it as a road map involves many interrelated stages. All these stages follow a sequential process and require corrective feedback at each stage. For example, from the measurement stage, we may find that the processes were incorrectly designed, and so may wish to go back and correct them. CRM strategy development is an enterprise-wide exercise, and its success depends on the organisation's customer focus.

DEVELOPING A RELATIONSHIP ORIENTATION

Relationship marketing is crucial in current business scenarios. The central focus of relationship marketing is on developing long-term and mutually beneficial relationships with customers. Good service and value proposition are required to attract new customers, maintain existing relationships and transform them into loyal customers. The first step a firm needs to take in developing the relationship orientation is to try and distinguish customers as individuals rather than numbers. Customers are not just numbers and cannot be replaced with other customers when they churn out. Whenever a customer starts interacting with the firm, she has the potential to build a relationship. This relationship could be broad or narrow in scope, continuous or discrete, or short- or long-lasting. The firm has to take the lead in driving this relationship. However, customer relationships, founded on trust and commitment, must be earned by the firm. Marketing can also be viewed as a process that revolves around customer relationships and where the parties' objectives are met through various exchanges that are undertaken to establish and maintain customer relationships. If close and long-term relationships can be achieved with customers, it lowers the costs.

A firm initiates its relationship orientation by recognising and acknowledging the value of customer relationships. The value in terms of financial impact, competitive advantage and long-term benefits emanating from long and fruitful relationships is evident. Commercialising customer relationships means that the cost–benefit ratio of transactions of goods, services or systems of goods is positive, at least in the long run. Developing a strong customer-centred culture boosts the value of the firm's offerings. It also has a positive impact on the employees of the firm, who become more focused on and responsible for the customers. They can see their jobs as 'solving customer problems' rather than simply providing them with a product or a service for a price. This also means that employees can appreciate their roles as part of a well-oiled machine that contributes to delivering value to customers. As customer behaviour cannot be totally standardised and predetermined, a distinctive service- and relationship-oriented culture helps employees to respond to new, unforeseen and even awkward situations.

Berry (1995) considered five strategies in developing relationship management:

- Core offerings, with high-quality offerings providing the differentiation for success.
- Relationship customisation provides opportunities to understand customer requirements to create customised options for loyal customers.
- Service augmentation to enhance the customer experience and even boost service portfolios by creating different levels of service offering.
- Relationship pricing to leverage opportunities to retain customers.
- Internal marketing to strengthen capabilities and motivate employees.

These strategies are not independent and can be used in combinations. A firm may also use all the strategies simultaneously. The common element in these strategies is the incentive offered to customers to remain loyal to the firm. Relationship orientation thus starts by acknowledging that the firm has a problem, and develops by looking at the firm's customers as individuals, each having a special relationship with the firm that needs to be preserved and further developed.

CUSTOMER-CENTRIC MARKETING AND PROCESSES

Customer-Centric Marketing

Initial approaches to marketing focused more on products and less on markets. The result was a product-centric firm that looked at reducing the cost of production. The main marketing activities of such a firm involved promoting, pricing and distributing products for mass markets. Subsequently, many new firms started entering the market, and the resulting increase in product variety forced firms to seek attractive market segments. Firms then organised around these segments, creating market segment-centric firms. Developments in the marketplace, shifts in the population, technology-led disruptions, dissatisfaction with marketing productivity, etc. have driven firms to adopt customer-centric marketing and processes in place of product- and market segment-centric marketing.

The InterContinental Hotels Group (IHG) uses data-driven marketing to enhance its interactions and communication with customers and prospects. It invested in technology and created a centralised customer organisation. The group developed a new data warehouse and real-time data mart to combine data from proprietary and third-party sources, allowing immediate access to data analysis and campaign creation. Outbound campaigns aligned internal processes, localised capabilities and integrated contact centres. Managed by a global agency, they coordinated multiple channels and tracks to optimise the content to engage with visitors and guests (VanBoskirk, 2010). The group started a new 'think beyond the booking' initiative through interactive marketing programmes to maximise revenue, growth and loyalty (Fletcher, 2013). Some of these programmes included the following:

- Right-time messaging that ensured outbound communication to customers at the right time – e.g. congratulatory messages sent when customers attain Gold status in the IHG One Rewards (formerly Priority Club) loyalty programme.
- Non-member marketing to track cookie data and online behaviour to make personalised offers and target relevant media to engage with non-members.
- A global approach that involved the use of global standards adapted for local messages to connect with prospects and customers.
- Interactive tools leveraged to run campaigns and other communication approaches to connect the customers.

Improving content relevance for customers by developing channel synergy and offering customised products/services on customers' preferred channels.

These initiatives helped the IHG group offer memorable experiences to its customers while attracting more prospects to sign up (VanBoskirk, 2010).

Customer-centric processes can be developed by following the following steps:

1. Understanding the value (products or services) currently being delivered to customers.
2. Scrutinising the current processes being employed to deliver the products and services.
3. Determining the wants, needs and convenience of customers.
4. Checking whether the current processes are centred on customer wants and needs or on convenience for the firm.
5. Estimating the gap between current customer-centricity and required customer-centricity.
6. Analysing whether the current processes can be designed around customers with everything focused on them.
7. Testing any new technology and delivery options that can be used to achieve these aims.

Customer-centricity is not always about perfectly aligning with all the needs of customers. It is often more concerned with customers genuinely being assured that the offerings are appropriate and 'right for them'. This association leads to long-term growth and revenue generation for companies. For example, US home improvement retailer The Home Depot increased its sales by diversifying its product range and customising its offerings based on the needs of the do-it-yourself (DIY) customers who were heavy users of its products and services. Similarly, Sephora, a global beauty retailer, enhanced its customer experience by developing interactive products, soft and emotional connections through digital channels and social media, and self-serve kiosks and counters. These initiatives led to a rapid growth in its number of stores to 1400 in 30 countries, boosting revenues and profits.

In another example, Aries Agro, an agri-nutrient company in India, launched a loyalty programme 'Khazana' (treasure) for farmers using its high-quality micronutrients and fertilisers. This programme allowed customers and retailers to earn points based on their purchase of Aries Agro products. These points could then be redeemed for gifts such as gold, household appliances and foreign trips. The company also introduced an insurance-based loyalty scheme that would cover risks for personal accidents, snake bites, electric shocks, falls from tractors, etc. The coverage was designed for farmers by grouping the risks collectively, so individual farmers and retailers derived insurance benefits for minimum levels of purchase. In addition, collaborations with leading brands of packaged goods firms improved the value of the loyalty programme for the farmers. The company's initiatives for dealers revolved around business development through collaterals including banners and contests with prizes such as merchandise and other goods. Training programmes including sessions on marketing and promotions by lecturers from local universities conducted during the festive seasons of Diwali and Dussehra were very popular. Localising these programmes – e.g. as *Mee Kosam*, which means 'for you' in Andhra Pradesh, and *Kondattam*, a festival with local flavours in Tamil Nadu – also helped connect with the community (Shainesh, 2018a).

In sum aligning strategies, operations and activities around customer needs drives business success. Understanding customer behaviour, attitudes and product usage will help orchestrate business operations (Kroner, 2016).

Customer-Centric Processes

As customer-centricity emphasises placing the customer at the core of operations and planning/designing all processes and activities around the customer, the most crucial step here is understanding and satisfying customer requirements. In customer-centric marketing, marketers assess target customers on an individual basis. They then decide whether to serve the customer directly or through a third party (something unthinkable a few years ago) and finally choose how the offering should be customised or standardised. The objective is to simultaneously maximise both efficiency (doing things right) and effectiveness (doing the right things) at a customer level.

Let us try to understand the concept of customer-centric processes by taking the simple example of a bank. Banks initially operated through branches. Customers had to go to the bank's branch to manage their accounts. The working hours of the bank were fixed. The layout of the bank and its internal processes of carrying out transactions were primarily driven by convenience for the bank – with no consideration of convenience for customers. Such internal focus resulted in gross neglect of customers' preferences, likes and dislikes. Customer service suffered immensely. The root cause of all this was the bank's view – viz., looking at transactions more from its point of view (efficiency, ease, etc.) and designing the system around that. No wonder customers suffered!

Customer-centric processes tried to change this outlook. When banks decided to adopt a more customer-centric approach, they looked to technology to help them out. The result was the setting up of automated teller machines (ATMs) and call centres at various locations in towns and cities, covering not just business areas but also residential areas. ATMs and call centres have brought banking to customers' fingertips. They offer easier access because of the location advantage, and customers can use them at any time of the day or night at their convenience. Transactions are also carried out much faster. Home banking and internet banking are further developments in customer-centricity, and have made processes even more convenient for customers.

The development of customer-centric processes is iterative, and new learning can be incorporated to positively influence the customer experience. This has the potential to snowball as it starts encompassing other stakeholders, ranging from employees, suppliers and partners to end users. Employees, especially those at the front line, learn from customers during their interactions while delivering services.

A leading global telecom firm adopted a multi-step and iterative approach to improve its customer experience throughout the buying and usage cycle. It involved the following considerations:

1 Clear definition of around ten feasible and manageable steps.
2 The development of metrics for customer insights and perspectives
3 Measuring performance regularly and frequently to assess customer experience. Metrics included customer satisfaction, net promoter score, retention rate, customer profitability and lifetime value.
4 Process analysis to stabilise performance.
5 The determination of goals based on current performance and emerging opportunities.
6 Analysis for continual improvements to identify bottlenecks and push the milestones.
7 Showcasing improvements and wins internally to motivate teams.

In this case the customer-centric process significantly improved the customer experience, boosted positive word of mouth and, finally, led to an enhancement of the positive buzz by 300%.

Customer-Centric Organisations

Organisations are fundamentally transforming as they navigate complex and challenging environments. As their focus shifts towards customers and the adoption of customer-centric marketing, it presents many opportunities for organisations to integrate their structure and processes around customers. The emphasis is on fully integrating all the customer-facing activities by aligning a firm's actions with customer value-adding activities. Customer-centric organisations integrate sales, marketing, customer service and non-marketing functions through digital solutions. For example, current CRM solutions allow sales to be tightly integrated with operations, production and logistics. Marketing metrics and performance incentives are oriented towards the share of customers, customer processes, customer equity and customer relationship management – e.g. customer retention and net incremental revenues from retained customers. The aim is to present a single face to customers from all touchpoints and resolve their problems instead of just trying to sell products.

Customer-centricity is equated with a proactive business strategy as firms experience a fundamental shift from a previous focus on products to a spotlight on consumers. Therefore, customers of customer-centric firms in business as well as consumer markets have a much stronger voice. Customer-centricity fits into an organisation in three ways (Deshpandé & Farley, 2004):

- Understanding customers as part of the firm's knowledge management system.
- Developing a customer-centric culture as part of the development of capabilities as a learning organisation.
- Serving the customer as the basis of corporate strategy development and implementation.

As leaders develop strategies and action plans for improving customer-centricity, they will have to focus on enabling organisations through training, incentives and systems for engaging with customers and anticipating their needs.

INTERNAL MARKETING FOR BOOSTING ORGANISATIONAL CAPABILITIES

To develop good relationship capabilities an organisation must analyse its internal processes and shape its abilities. 'Internal marketing' is key to the relationship strategy of many service firms. An organisation can consider its employees, especially the frontline personnel, as an internal customer and their role as the service offering. The idea is to resell to each customer (employee) the various roles within the firm while emphasising the need for high-quality standards to deliver results.

The concept of internal marketing first emerged in the services marketing literature and was adopted by practitioners in services firms. They found it useful because in people-intensive firms, the service providers, their skills and work attitude determine the quality of service and the final product delivered to the end customer. If the management of these firms uses internal marketing techniques to attract, retain and keep employees motivated, then the firm can further improve the ability to offer high-quality services to customers. Offering quality services, in turn, helps firms meet the quality requirements of the target markets. This is an important factor in developing strong customer relationships with the end-user customer. Service quality is a key driver of customer satisfaction. Unless the service offered to a customer meets the requirements of the customer, a firm cannot dream of even starting to build a relationship with that customer. Internal marketing has therefore emerged as a prerequisite for successful external marketing in today's business environment.

Internal marketing is a management philosophy. It stresses the need for the management of various firms to continually encourage employees and enhance their understanding of the roles they perform in the organisation. Employees should have a holistic view of their jobs. This means that the employee should consider himself or herself as an important part of the team that delivers services to customers and not just as doing a certain job or task. For example, it is important for a carpenter who is in a group building a house to see himself as a member of the 'house-building team' rather than as a person whose job is to saw various planks of wood. Similarly, unless an employee identifies herself as playing a part of a larger purpose and knows the importance of her job, an organisation will not be able to get the best out of her. There will also be no commitment or motivation to learn, improve and deliver better value to customers.

Thus, the focus of internal marketing is on how to attract and retain customer-conscious employees. The firm also needs to develop and maintain a service culture. Services as well as specific external marketing campaigns, new technology and new systems of functioning must first be marketed internally to employees before they can be effectively marketed externally. Leaders must enable the internal market of employees. This will ensure that motivated and capable employees look after the ultimate external markets. Effective services require people who understand what services are all about and where they fit in the delivery chain of the services.

Processes such as market research, market segmentation, product modification and communications are as relevant in internal marketing as they are in external marketing. Market research procedures can be used to identify the needs, wants and attitudes of the people in the internal marketplace. Leading service firms such as Marriott International regularly conduct surveys to assess employee satisfaction with their roles, work environment and various organisational aspects. Some firms have used town halls, open houses and small group meetings for interactions between senior management and associates to encourage dialogue and feedback. If a firm wishes to satisfy its employees, it must first identify their wants and needs. Here the tools and techniques of market research can help a great deal.

Secondly, employees should have opportunities to enhance their roles and stature while growing with the firm. Opportunities for development and personal growth will require regular development and training programmes that help employees acquire new skills and knowledge to move up the ladder within the organisation. Internal job rotations create opportunities for employees to take up different roles, additional assignments and greater responsibilities. When employees see progress, they will be motivated to learn, upgrade their skills and serve their ultimate customers better. Many service firms (including banks and software firms) have regular internal assessments and development centres to identify personnel with high potential for accelerated growth with more responsibility. Another way is to segment the internal market, recognise the heterogeneity within the work force and then modify the role descriptions to match the organisational requirements with diverse segments of the personnel. This can create opportunities for more employee-friendly policies like flexible hours, work from home (WFH), etc.

Finally, formal communication programmes that are designed to shape work attitudes and behaviour are often used as an important element of internal marketing strategy. For example, a firm's advertising that is created for or directed at external customers can often be designed in such a way as to motivate and/or educate employees as well. For instance, advertisements for leading firms such as IBM that showcase their employees are more like statements of what the firm represents, and are meant for customers as well as employees.

"In essence, internal marketing involves creating an organisational climate in general, and job products in particular, that lead to the right personnel performing services in the right way" (Berry, 1995, p. 73). In services, the task of marketing is not only to encourage customers to buy a product from a firm; it is also to encourage employees, the firm's internal customers, to perform. It is important to note that only satisfied employees can keep the customers of a firm satisfied. Internal marketing is an important strategy that aims to win the external market by extracting superior performance from satisfied and motivated internal customers – i.e. employees. Therefore, it can be stated that marketers can use internal marketing to drive the functions of organisations and maximise customer satisfaction. Marketing concepts, exchange processes and customer satisfaction must be integrated. Employees are internal customers who deliver value to the end users or final customers. This means that all corporate departments – such as research, operations, HR, IT and marketing – work towards these customer satisfaction and experience goals.

Apple's stores provide customers with an excellent experience when interacting with skilled and knowledgeable employees. Their communication with prospects and customers reflects their enthusiasm, passion and knowledge about the products. These positive experiences play a key role in helping customers make their buying decisions.

Nextiva, a cloud-based communications platform company with 100,000 customers and 1500 employees spread across the US, boosted employee engagement through several employee-led initiatives. The leadership found that employees were often unaware of their colleagues and teams, even though it was a relatively small organisation. Their internal newsletter did not resolve this lack of awareness (Tenfold, n.d.), yet they had a philosophy of growing their team by leveraging technology. They therefore undertook extensive internal marketing efforts to increase employee morale and align everyone with the corporate culture (Nucleus Research, 2016). One of the initiatives involved creating videos featuring colleagues from various departments announcing the latest developments in the company. Employees had to gather information from other departments and work with colleagues to complete this task. The communications team would then upload these videos as two-minute clips and share them internally. In addition to appreciating and connecting with colleagues in other departments, employees learned to collaborate and work with a larger cohort of co-workers. This enhanced togetherness among employees and led to the development of a video series, *NexTV*. These approaches worked very well for the company as engagement rate increased by 96%. Bonding through information and entertainment was strengthened among employees, resulting in transforming employees' attitudes towards the company and boosting morale (Banko, 2014).

These factors were also seen in the Indian company Titan's 'Tanishq' jewellery brand when it implemented the 'Tanishq way of life' in stores. The company realised that employees have a crucial role in customer engagement. The employees understood the moment of truth, which delivered pleasant customer experiences. This conviction was given and observed in the employees' effective interactions with the customers, which the company accomplished through training and motivating the employees. The idea behind this was that 'my store delivers the best customer experience'.

Consequently, the employees delivered this through the promise of the last smile of the customers. The company realised that favourable interactions are essential for customer engagement, which was reflected in the employees' gentility and politeness towards customers. For example, they addressed customers by name, which personalised the communication. Thus, the customers became fans of the brand, the company and the staff they interacted with pleasantly (Shainesh, 2018b).

ISSUES IN IMPLEMENTING A DIGITAL CRM SOLUTION

Although technology is just an enabler of CRM, many issues need to be kept in mind by a firm before it ventures into a digital solution. The issues are not just technical but also involve many organisational and human aspects. The most important and prominent aspect that needs to be considered is the technology itself. An organisation needs to test its product with regard to its features, its ability to perform the required functions as desired by the organisation and, finally, the degree of fit with the existing technological solutions in the organisation. Most organisations usually adopt a requirements-driven approach to identifying the most relevant solution.

- The first step is to define the business problem that needs to be solved and determine what needs to be done to solve the problem. This may mean identifying relevant processes that can be revamped before adopting digital solutions.
- The second step is to list the functionalities that meet the requirements. Each function should map to the business requirements. It requires identifying different aspects of the customer-focused processes that need to be supported with technology.
- The final step is to define the solution that supports the identified functionality.

Make or Buy

Many firms offer CRM solutions in the marketplace, but they might also look at developing their CRM systems under the following circumstances:

- They require core CRM capabilities that products cannot provide in the market.
- Off-the-shelf solutions might be perceived as too expensive. However, this situation is changing with many firms offering SaaS with significant savings in upfront investments for hardware and software.
- A single CRM solution cannot provide the core functionalities required by the firm.
- The firm wants a unique solution that the competitors cannot use, and vendors cannot develop other such products.

Although all such issues are pertinent, most firms are now signing up for SaaS solutions as even large firms consider custom software development as one of their core capabilities. Other relevant issues that must be tackled at this stage are the decisions that need to be made concerning the product's technical specifications and criteria, which include the following.

- Functionality
- Flexibility
- Customisation
- Scalability
- Fit with the existing architecture
- Fit with global best practices

- Upgradability
- Commercial impact
- Compatibility with other CRM solutions
- Degree of integration.

As companies deploy multiple digital channels to interact with customers, the rapidly evolving technology landscape is driving the adoption of cloud-based services. The cloud enables the full spectrum of marketing to create synergies between the company and its customers, leading to more effective customer acquisition and retention across channels (Inc.com, 2021).

Vendor Issues

Once the above issues are resolved and a decision made to purchase the product, the firm must identify the vendor and the system integrator. Some factors that should be considered when shortlisting prospective vendors include:

- CRM expertise, including industry vertical
- Implementation experience worldwide
- A focus on CRM – critical in the context of many extensive enterprise resource planning (ERP) providers that have moved into the CRM space
- Credentials, including financials and clientele
- Understanding of the firm's business opportunities and challenges
- Preferred implementation partners if the vendor is not able to provide the service.

Further evaluation may be based on factors such as:

- CRM solution implementation experience
- Clientele, scope and scale of implementation
- Technical hand-holding expected
- Upgradation.

A similar process can be followed to shortlist the system's integrators. Some of the criteria that might be considered include:

- CRM expertise and relevant industry expertise
- Focus on CRM
- Project team specifics, including indicative CVs of the team
- Product preferences.

After shortlisting product vendors and system integrators, firms usually make reference calls to several past clients. The reference calls are crucial because they bring out the actual implementation problems. The experiences of these reference clients help firms understand the user perspective and implementation experiences. Some of the parameters that may be judged at this stage include:

- Cost and time overruns
- Any surprises that may come up during the implementation
- Promised features as against actual features
- Vendor involvement during the implementation process
- Quality of the end-user training
- Quality of customisation
- Post-implementation support
- Experience with the product.

All the above issues need to be considered in selecting the product.

Implementation Issues

After choosing the CRM solution, a different set of issues arise during the implementation stage. As CRM impacts all customer-facing functions, it requires involvement and buy-in from the teams in those departments. Therefore, a cross-functional implementation team with representatives from different departments is preferred, with roles specified clearly and deadlines set. This team will be responsible for regular, periodic reviews during project implementation. As the implementation results in a significant change in how individuals and teams approach the processes, it is essential to manage this change by regularly communicating and sharing the progress and relevant details regarding the project to enlist their support. Also, all frontline employees and other users must be trained to smooth the transition and ease adoption.

The challenges in implementing the digital CRM solutions can be classified as people-related and other factors.

People-Related Challenges

These are usually driven by a lack of senior management support and commitment beyond allocating the budget. If these personnel are unwilling to champion the project, it becomes difficult to drive the change management required by CRM.

- *Potential solution:* Have an internal CRM champion from top management.

A second issue concerns high expectations within a short time period. The main problem is that returns cannot be expected when the CRM initiative is launched because customers and employees need to adjust to the new system.

- *Potential solution:* Aim for quick wins with low-hanging fruit – e.g. sales process efficiency improvements or lowering turnaround time for service issues.

Change management leads to resisting a new process, way of working or habit change.

- *Solution:* All the stakeholders should be aware of the benefits and advantages of the CRM system and the incentives to use this process. More importantly, CRM should be easily implemented and quickly adoptable in the various business departments with proper planning and relevant training.

Other Challenges

These include deploying one CRM solution across different geographical locations without localisation. This lack of localisation affects the adoption rates and overall functioning of the solution. Additionally, unnecessary pressure to execute CRM quickly leads to unrealistic deadlines and significantly affects the implementation of CRM. There could also be changes in the business's priorities after implementing CRM. These changes can be related to mergers, acquisitions, regulations or the external environment. Lastly, there could be issues regarding data privacy and information security in terms of standards, governance, regulations and access, among others.

Addressing these various issues and implementation challenges will lead to adaption by users to create long-term success by enhancing the customer experience to drive satisfaction and loyalty. Enabling consistent engagement and communication between the firm and its customers by aligning them with customers' preferences will provide a 360° view of their relationship.

CLOSING CASE

Virgin Airlines: A Customer-Centric Approach

Richard Branson, founder of the Virgin Group, entered the airline business after acquiring Belgian Airlines and renaming it Virgin Atlantic. The brand differentiated itself by going against the established and accepted way of running a traditional airline. There was a strong focus on the 'Virgin' brand and customer orientation. Training the cabin crew to provide outstanding service and cordially engage with customers helped add to customers' happiness and satisfaction. Customers were treated as friends instead of 'mere customers'. This orientation helped the brand strengthen its relationship with the customers. Further, this approach was complemented by a comprehensive range of high-quality in-flight entertainment, and an in-flight bar and masseuse for business and first-class passengers. Virgin aimed to get all customers to love the brand and strengthen the brand relationship. Listening to customers and employees systematically through research helped it fine-tune the service. The company also believed in a 'let us do it' approach to minimise risk and evaluate its processes. Close engagement with customers was effectively channelled through social media platforms, which provide excellent forums to communicate with customers and strengthen relationships (Regan, 2017).

SUMMARY

CRM has become integral to create sustainable brand differentiation by optimal use of digital technologies that sync with customers' desire for convenience, flexibility and speed. Despite the manifest advantages, implementing CRM solutions has proved to be challenging. The CRM roadmap provides guidelines based on best practices and experiences of firms that have implemented CRM solutions. Developing a relationship orientation and a customer-centric organisation creates the foundations for success while implementing digital solutions that require change management.

DISCUSSION QUESTIONS

1 Discuss the key aspects of relationship orientation.
2 Illustrate the application of 'customer-centric' marketing for a service firm.
3 How do you establish a foundation for customer satisfaction?
4 Discuss the role of employees and the organisation's internal culture in improving customer-centricity.

REFERENCES

Alba, D. (2015). Starbucks' grande plan: Selling coffee via apps. *Wired*, 3 November. Retrieved 24 January, 2024, from https://www.wired.com/2015/11/no-one-is-killing-it-with-retail-store-apps-like-starbucks/.

Banko, A. (2014). Internal marketing: B2B's employee-exclusive video series fosters team morale. *MarketingSherpa*. Retrieved November 19, 2021, from https://www.marketingsherpa.com/article/case-study/internal-marketing-b2b-video.

Berry, L.L. (1995). Relationship marketing. In A. Payne, M. Christopher, M. Clark, & H. Peck, H. (Eds.), *Relationship marketing for competitive advantage: Winning and keeping customers* (pp. 65–74). Oxford: Butterworth-Heinemann.

Deshpandé, R., & Farley, J.U. (2004). Organizational culture, market orientation, innovativeness, and firm performance: An international research odyssey. *International Journal of Research in Marketing*, *21*(1), 3–22.

Fletcher, H. (2013). Data-backed CRM helps IHG Create real-time marketing program, emails. *Target Marketing*. Retrieved April 22, 2017, from http://www.targetmarketingmag.com/article/data-backed-crm-helps-ihg-create-real-time-marketing-program-emails/all/.

Inc.com. (2021). How to use technology to improve customer service. Retrieved November 21, 2021, from https://www.inc.com/guides/cust_tech/20909.html.

Kroner, E. (2016). The 7 pillars of customer centricity. Retrieved March 28, 2017, from https://www.ama.org/publications/eNewsletters/MarketingInsightsNewsletter/Pages/7-pillars-of-customer-centricity.aspx.

Niessing, J., Henry, B., & Peters, K. (2018). Jaguar Land Rover: Towards a customer-centric organisation – leveraging customer intelligence and data analytics for sustainable growth. INSEAD Case study. Retrieved December 20, 2023, from https://shorturl.at/thcfm.

Nucleus Research. (2016). Salesforce Pardot benefit case study: Nextiva. Retrieved November 20, 2021, from https://nucleusresearch.com/research/single/salesforce-pardot-benefit-case-study-nextiva/.

Panagiotaropoulou, S. (2015). Starbucks case study: Innovation in CRM strategies, means of enabling e-commerce, Oxford University Press. Retrieved November 21, 2021, from https://www.academia.edu/27195284/Starbucks_Case_Study_Innovation_in_CRM_strategies_means_of_enabling_E_Commerce_Oxford_University_Press.

Regan, H. (2017). How to empower your customer service reps. Retrieved November 21, 2021, from https://www.softwareadvice.com/resources/empower-customer-service-reps-richard-branson-style/.

Shainesh, G. (2018a). Loyalty programs in the agri sector: Interview with Rahul Mirchandani, chairman – Aries Agro. MOOCs on CRM edX. https://bit.ly/40iS2WO. Accessed on January 14, 2025.

Shainesh, G. (2018b). Loyalty programs in Titan: Interview with heads of CRM and retail. MOOCs on CRM edX. https://bit.ly/40iS2WO. Accessed on January 14, 2025.

Smith, A. (2015). Why Starbucks wins at CRM. Retrieved November 21, 2021, from https://marketingdiscussions.wordpress.com/2015/11/09/why-starbucks-wins-at-crm/.

Tenfold. (n.d.). Integrate Nextiva CTI with your CRM now: Tenfold dialer. Retrieved November 21, 2021, from https://www.tenfold.com/integrations/nextiva.

VanBoskirk, S. (2010). Intercontinental hotels: A case study in customer-centric marketing. Retrieved November 21, 2021, from https://www.forrester.com/blogs/10-05-19-intercontinental_hotels_a_case_study_in_customer_centric_marketing.

CHAPTER 11

Operational Issues in Implementing CRM

CHAPTER OVERVIEW

After reading this chapter you should be able to understand:

1. The process view of Customer Relationship Management (CRM)
2. Resource allocation through budgeting for attracting and retaining customers
3. Learning from customer defections
4. Customer retention programmes

Vignette

Harmoney is a New Zealand-based peer-to-peer (P2P) lending network that links retail lenders with creditworthy borrowers seeking personal loans. It had paired borrowers and lenders with loans totalling more than $960 million in nine years, from inception in 2014 to 2020. Its nearly 10,000 individual lenders had generated an average annual return of 11.6% (Listcorp, 2023).

The company adopted Salesforce's suite of products to support a seamless, 100% online user experience – from loan origination to risk management to repayments (Heroku, n.d.). It chose a robust, secure and scalable CRM engine to deliver excellent service and manage customer relationships. It built a comprehensive cloud-based platform in eight months by integrating the Sales Cloud CRM engine to manage customer interactions, apps from the Salesforce AppExchange, such as FinancialForce for end-to-end accounting services, and the Heroku platform.

Harmoney implemented the SAS Visual Analytics platform to classify and identify creditworthy applicants (SAS, 2016), whereby potential borrowers complete a detailed online registration process when applying for a loan. Visual Analytics combs through this data, including the applicants' demographics and financial details, to identify those most eligible for loans. About 25–30% of applications are accepted by the platform to minimise repayment default and ensure that the lenders' interests are protected.

DOI: 10.4324/9781003518174-15

Being first to the P2P market meant that the unknown Harmoney brand had to create awareness about P2P lending while building its own brand equity, especially among lenders, so that they would trust Harmoney enough to lend their money. Salesforce's marketing automation platform, Pardot, allowed Harmoney to track prospects – from Google AdWords or banner ads – to lead conversion. More personalised communications and campaigns helped nurture leads and reduce drop-off rates.

Harmoney's marketing team leveraged digital channels to reach potential lenders and borrowers. Real-time data analysis helped improve creative decisions, e.g. removing search keywords that drive unsuccessful applications. The analysis helped the team identify the keywords attracting visitors leading to higher approvals, and then bid higher amounts for these select keywords to attract the right kind of applicants with a higher probability of approvals.

Integration of the Heroku platform with their CRM platform provided easy access to third-party credit agencies, document verification systems and other finance-related apps, thereby helping the company speed up the loan application and approval process. In addition, providing every minute detail regarding repayment, interest rates and fixed costs in a detailed and upfront manner helped build trust and boost long-term relationships with clients (Harmoney, 2015). In March 2020, the company discontinued its P2P loan funding and switched to a more profitable way of operating through a warehouse funding model by borrowing from banks instead of retail lenders (Listcorp, 2023).

OPENING CASE

Diageo: Leveraging Digital for CRM

In 2012, multinational drinks company Diageo developed a campaign in Brazil by bringing three premium Whisky brands from its extensive portfolio – Johnnie Walker, Buchanan's and Old Parr – into the digital environment (Allchin, 2013). The company partnered with software firm Evrythng to convert the physical bottles into 'smart' bottles by connecting them online through +More, a proprietary platform (O'Hear, 2017). The bottles were transformed into an interactive, digital medium offering personalised information and experiences to consumers. For example, on Father's Day, consumers could create personalised film tributes to their dads on the bottle they were gifting. The platform allowed giver and receiver to socially share the digital content and sign up for ongoing CRM programmes. The ability to create a bespoke message to an individual consumer via an interactive bottle created unique and personalised gifts.

This software connected the information from the bottle and customer experience through digital interactions while capturing details on customer choice, and finally extended digital interactions with retailers and suppliers. Analyses of these interactions were used to understand product distribution, sales and consumption patterns. By turning its bottles into digital channels, Diageo could connect with its customers on social media while they engaged with the brand and provide effective services, entertainment and information.

Based on the encouraging results from the pilot in Brazil, the company rolled out similar campaigns in its other markets. The key learning was that digital technologies can be used to strengthen relationships by leveraging their potential to connect with customers (Allchin, 2013).

INTRODUCTION

In this chapter, we focus on the operational issues in implementing CRM. We start with a process view of CRM which will help us focus comprehensively on the key elements of CRM. We will then cover operational issues related to budget allocation for customer attraction and retention programmes. While CRM aims to attract and retain profitable customers, in competitive markets, customers have choices and do defect to competing offerings. Firms planning to minimise, if not completely eliminate, customer defections can learn from those who choose to defect. This learning can then be used to develop retention plans. Therefore, we will also focus on learning from customer defections, developing customer retention plans and evaluating those programmes.

A PROCESS VIEW OF CRM

Parvatiyar and Sheth (2001) proposed a four-stage CRM process framework comprising the following four sub-processes: (1) customer relationship formation: (2) relationship management and governance; (3) relational performance evaluation: and (4) CRM evolution or enhancement.

Customer Relationship Formation

As seen in Figure 11.1, relationship formation consists of three decision areas. These activities include defining the goals (or objectives) of CRM, identifying appropriate customer partners for CRM programmes and establishing programmes or relational activity schemes for engaging with selected customer partners. CRM's overarching goal is to boost marketing productivity for the benefit of all parties involved in the relationship. Marketing efficiency can be increased by pursuing and attaining operational objectives such as reducing marketing,

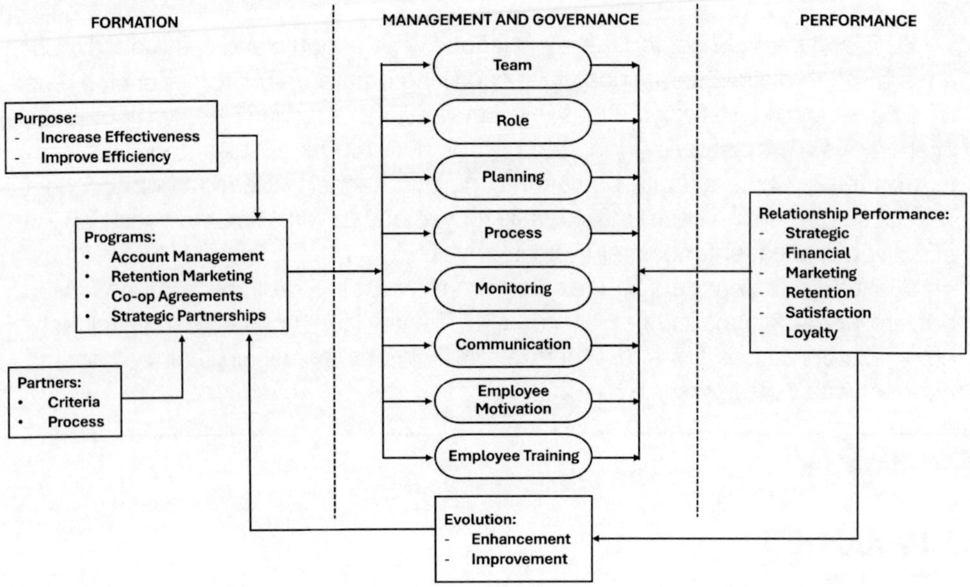

FIGURE 11.1 A Process View of CRM

Adapted from Parvatiyar and Sheth (2001).

communication and distribution costs, improving order processing and inventory management, lowering customer acquisition expenses and optimising client retention economics. Similarly, businesses can improve their marketing effectiveness by carefully selecting customers for various programmes: individualising and personalising market offerings to anticipate and meet the emerging needs of each customer; cultivating customer loyalty and commitment; partnering to enter new markets and develop new products; and redefining their competitiveness.

Before implementing CRM in any organisation, it is essential to identify the objectives and purpose of CRM to help clarify the type of CRM programmes and activities the organisation and its partners should undertake. Additionally, defining the purpose assists in choosing appropriate relationship partners who have the requisite expectations and capabilities to accomplish joint goals. Finally, it aids in evaluating CRM performance by comparing achieved results to goals established before embarking on the CRM journey.

Relationship Management and Governance

The management and governance sub-process ensures the smooth functioning of the CRM programmes. Managers must make decisions related to *role specification*, *communication*, *common bonds*, *planning process*, *process alignment*, *employee motivation* and *monitoring procedures*. Role specification concerns the role of partners in fulfilling the CRM tasks as well as the role of specific individuals or teams in managing the relationships and related activities. It helps in clarifying the nature of resources and empowerment needed by individuals or teams responsible for managing relationships with customers. Regular communication with customers and partners is necessary to strengthen relationships and foster trust by providing information and sharing knowledge required to undertake cooperative and collaborative activities. In many ways, it is the lifeblood of CRM. A firm can enhance relationships by establishing proper communication channels to engage and connect with customers. In addition to communicating with customers, it is essential to establish intra-company communication, particularly among all relevant individuals and corporate functions that play a direct role in managing relationships with specific customers or customer groups.

Social bonds, built through interactions and communications, help sustain relationships. In business markets, social bonds are developed through regular interactions with customers. However, in-person interactions are not feasible for large firms with millions of customers in mass markets. Therefore, marketers aim to create social bonds through symbolic relationships, endorsements, affinity groups, membership schemes or online communities. Irrespective of the mode, social, reputational and structural bonding is useful in institutionalising customer relationships.

Another important aspect of relationship governance is planning and the degree to which customers are involved in the planning process. Lead users and consumer panels are involved in idea generation during the product development process of many firms in packaged goods and technology businesses. However, the involvement of key accounts in business markets in the planning process is desirable for managing cooperative and collaborative relationships.

Several aspects of the operating process need to be aligned, depending on the nature and scope of the relationship, to avoid problems in CRM implementation, such as order processing, accounting and budgeting, information systems, merchandising, etc.

Similarly, human resources (HR) decisions are also important in creating the right working environment for managing customer relationships. Training employees to interact with customers, work in teams and manage customer expectations is important. So is providing the right motivation through incentives, rewards and compensation systems to strengthen customer relationships. Although institutionalising relationships is desirable for the long-term benefit of the company, personal relationships are nevertheless formed and impact institutional relationships, so proper training and motivation of employees to professionally handle customer relationships are needed.

Finally, proper monitoring processes are needed to prevent failure and manage conflicts in relationships. These include: periodic evaluation of goals and results; initiating changes in relationship structure, design or governance process if needed; and creating a system for discussing opportunities as well as problems and for resolving any conflicts. Robust monitoring helps avoid relationship destabilisation and the creation of power asymmetries, and helps keep the CRM programme on track by aligning goals, resources and results.

Performance Evaluation

This helps firms review programmes, take corrective measures regarding relationship governance or adjust relationship marketing objectives and features. The performance measures help assess CRM activities and aid decision making regarding their continuation, modification or cancellation. Performance metrics are a challenging part of any CRM project as many current marketing indicators, such as market share and total sales volume, may not be applicable in the context of CRM. The performance evaluation measures for the CRM programme should mirror the established objectives. A multi-dimensional measure is advised so that customer loyalty does not end up as a pursuit without simultaneously addressing the vital issue of client account profitability (Reinartz & Kumar, 2002). In their analysis of longitudinal data in four firms in retail, financial services, catalogue and information technology (IT) services, Reinartz and Kumar contended that managing clients for loyalty is not the same as managing them for profitability. Their findings underscored the need for measures that capture all facets of the relationship. CRM performance can be conceptualised as a multi-dimensional metric comprising strategic, financial and marketing measures.

Strategic measures include process improvements, new product development and access to new markets. Strides Arcolab, a leading export-oriented pharma company based in Bengaluru (Bangalore), India, entered into a collaborative agreement to supply medicines to a global firm for eventual sale in Africa. As part of the preparation process, the London-based audit teams of the client firm travelled over to audit the operations at Strides' factories. The learning from the audit and process improvements was subsequently implemented in all the company's 14 factories. This relationship proved to be beneficial to Strides in two strategic ways: (1) it helped establish its reputation as a supplier to attract new potential customer accounts while deepening its relationship with its partner; and (2) it could improve its organisational processes at low cost.

Financial measures include relationship profitability and returns on CRM investments. Relationship profitability is usually measured at the level of the individual customer in business markets and the segment level in consumer markets. The concepts of customer share and lifetime value are extremely useful in operationalising financial measures.

The marketing measures of the impact of CRM include relationship satisfaction, customer loyalty and customer retention as companies derive multiple benefits from customer retention. They derive customer lifetime value. If customers are retained for longer periods, this becomes an essential point of return for the business. It is therefore not unusual to find firms displaying an obsession with retaining their customers by delivering excellent experiences to enhance the customers' lifetime value.

CRM Evolution or Enhancement

CRM programmes evolve and alter over time due to the dynamic nature of competitive markets and changing customer requirements. Regular decisions about the continuation, termination, enhancement and adjustment of relationship programmes are made. The performance and satisfaction of relationships affect the progress of CRM programmes. When partners achieve satisfactory performance, they are driven to continue or develop their CRM systems. However, when a partner's performance falls short of expectations, they may contemplate ending or changing the relationship. Numerous collaborative relationships, particularly in business markets, cease due to predetermined termination dates. CRM strategies would be more systematic for firms if they planned and charted the relationship evolution cycle while accounting for contingencies. After analysing the CRM process framework, the following section discusses the operational issue of budgeting.

BUDGETING FOR ATTRACTION VS. RETENTION

Traditional marketing emphasised attracting a stream of new customers rather than retaining existing customers. As a result, the front-end function of attracting a customer was allocated more resources and the top management paid more attention to growing the customer base, while the back-end processes related to customer retention and development were neglected. However, of late, customer retention has generated considerable interest, supported by research findings and new developments in 'relationship marketing'. This approaches marketing from the relationship point of view, and looks at building long-term, mutually beneficial relationships with customers that maximise the firm's share of the customer wallet. Customer retention has received much attention as it costs up to eight times more to recruit a new customer than to generate similar business from an existing customer. Further, long-standing customers tend to spend more with a firm because of their familiarity and comfort with its services, products and personnel. Finally, the firm also benefits because existing customers can be served more effectively and efficiently as firms improve their capabilities over multiple transactions and interactions over time.

On the other hand, it is just as important for firms to attract new customers because these customers will counteract the defections that are bound to happen despite all efforts by a firm to prevent them. Second, in a growing industry, a firm must look at retention and expansion through new customer acquisitions. Mere customer retention coupled with the addition of defectors will not allow a firm to grow. This implies that a firm in a high-growth industry should look at customer acquisition as a possible strategy for growth. If retained, these new customers, who might not be very profitable today, may become highly profitable tomorrow.

Firms work with fixed annual budgets for marketing. One of the decisions that managers make is how much of this budget is to be allocated for customer retention as opposed to customer acquisition. This is not a trivial decision as the development of each customer segment requires resources from a fixed pool, so a balance is required. The risk reward structure across the two segments also differs substantially. On the one hand, while budgeting for customer retention, the firm will be serving those customers with whom they are familiar with, and hence much easier and cheaper to serve. On the other hand, first-time customers are a difficult proposition as the firm knows nothing or very little about their likes, dislikes, tastes and preferences. The firm might just look at providing them with its basic offering rather than a personalised service as might be the case with existing customers. For customer acquisition, the focus might be more on front-end activities (such as advertising, marketing research, branding, etc.), while for customer retention activities such as after-sales services, customer support and the like are more important.

Raman and Angur (2001) considered the problem of allocating a firm's resources over two segments:

1. The current segment, which is predictable and growing at a fixed rate; the customer retention strategy is more applicable here.
2. Prospects, where the focus is on customer acquisition.

A firm's objective is to maximise the utility of expected return from the allocated resources between the new and the existing segments. As the firm's resources are essentially limited and the activities in the two segments are different, more allocation to one is usually at the cost of performance in the other. Such a problem cannot be said to be exclusive to the finance or marketing domain as elements of decision making cuts across both marketing and finance.

Below are some of the issues that firms need to consider before allocating resources either to activities focused on customer retention or on customer acquisition.

Nature of the Industry

The industry in which the firm is operating (e.g. consumer durables/non-durables, services) plays an important role in deciding whether to focus predominantly on customer retention or acquisition. In commodity-like businesses (including groceries and packaged goods) – where customers do not perceive much difference between brands, and switching from one brand to another is easy and routine – it is better to opt for a customer attraction strategy. On the other hand, a firm in consumer durables and services needs to seriously consider customer retention as an important strategy because building long-term relationships with the customers may prove to be the key to long-term success.

Industry Growth Rate

In high-growth sectors, acquisition is important, especially when the firm aims to grow rapidly and aim for a leadership position. When the industry is not growing at a high rate and the market is saturated with many players, customers may switch easily, lured by better promotional offers. In such a situation, a firm needs to dedicate more resources to retain its customers, such as loyalty or reward programmes.

Position in the Industry

Customer acquisition is important for a firm entering a competitive market with several players. As a new entrant, the firm may create a new product or service and is set to introduce it into the market. During market entry, all resources must be dedicated to new customer acquisition. As the firm starts establishing itself by developing a customer base and its offerings gain acceptance, the attention will shift to retaining existing customers and attracting new customers.

Uniqueness of Offerings

In many cases, a firm might be in an industry such as banking and travel where the core service can easily be copied. Customer retention can help the firm in such situations if it invests in building emotional and social bonds to create switching barriers.

Readiness

A firm's readiness with respect to its customer orientation also has an important bearing on its strategy of acquisition versus retention, which calls into play the firm's internal capabilities. This is an intra-firm factor that influences, among other areas, the firm's orientation regarding acquisition or retention. Effective customer retention calls for more customer-oriented readiness on the part of a firm opting for it. Both front-end and back-end processes need to be fully attuned, and the firm also must be in greater touch with customers in order to cater to their personal needs. On the other hand, in the case of customer acquisition, the firm is taking a broader view. It looks at the characteristics of the customer segment to target and not at the individual customer.

Resource allocation should also account for expenses beyond the costs of promotions targeted at attracting new customers. Acquisition costs should incorporate other expenses related to elements of the marketing mix.

LEARNING FROM CUSTOMER DEFECTIONS

When a customer switches to a competitive offering, we classify the customer as having defected or churned out. Customer defections reveal a lot about a firm, its products, services and the customer's experiences from an external perspective. Customer defections also have a surprisingly powerful effect on a firm's bottom line. In fact, in the case of a service business, defections can have higher negative impact on profits than scale, market share, unit costs and many other factors usually associated with competitive advantage. Defection rates are therefore an accurate indicator of what the future holds for a firm. When defection rates soar, a firm's bottom line often takes a beating.

Companies must invest in acquiring customers to replace those who have defected. However, as the cost of acquisition is significantly higher than the cost of retention, preventing defection is imperative for companies to enhance customer lifetime value and reduce acquisition costs (Capraro et al., 2003).

Surprisingly, customer defections, which lead to losses and business failures, are also a source of great learning. Customers usually defects because they are dissatisfied with a firm's services/products and has discovered an alternative that can provide better services/products. Customers see a deteriorating stream of value from the firm. Customers who have defected to a rival can help the firm identify all aspects of its business that need to improve. Firms that have the will and desire to learn search for root causes of customer defections. They systematically solicit feedback from former customers, group the causes and identify any underlying systemic causes before fixing or improving them. Sometimes, they can win the customers back and re-establish the relationship on firmer ground.

Although, customer defections are a great source of learning, many businesses do not learn or even try to learn from them. Reichheld (1996) identified the following reasons for customer defection:

- Many firms are not alarmed by customer defections or are alarmed too late. This is because they do not understand or perceive the direct causal relationships between customer loyalty on one hand and cash flows and profits on the other.
- Trying to analyse failures is not a pleasant activity for business managers, and it may even have a detrimental effect on their performance appraisal and career. In other words, the top management does not encourage such exercises because it might show them in a poor light.
- In industries such as retail banking defections are often hard to define if the customer retains some balance in her savings account or continues to use the service minimally.
- Dividing customers into those who are and are not worth keeping is often difficult.
- It is extremely hard to uncover the real root cause of customer defections and learn appropriate lessons.
- It is sometimes a challenge getting the right people in the organisation to learn about customer defections and then commit to acting on them.
- It is difficult to set up mechanisms to continuously monitor ongoing customer defections and enable senior management to respond quickly to them.

It is well known that the longer a customer stays with a firm, the more value he/she brings to the firm because of higher spending, lower service costs, word-of-mouth referrals, less sensitivity to price changes and no acquisition or startup costs. Most chief executive officers (CEOs) understand the value of loyalty. However, unless a CEO is shown using hard figures related to a customer's worth to the firm over the course of a customer's lifecycle or the net present value of the customer base, CEOs will still gauge the firm's performance on the basis of cash flows and profits rather than on the one statistic that reflects how much real value the firm is creating – customer retention. Managers often lack the tools that would enable them to see the value of their customer base and then communicate it throughout the organisation. Customer satisfaction surveys and other standard market research tools are not up to the task of measuring and analysing customer defections. Defecting customers are the first to know when a firm's value proposition is being beaten in the face of competition.

Most people are preoccupied with success. Therefore, they see failure as something that needs to be forgotten. However, failure analysis can provide a wealth of information to firms that really want to understand why they did not do well.

Analysing Customer Defections

The first step in analysing customer defections is to define a 'defection' because people are unaware of customer defection in many situations. Sometimes, a customer might defect fully by completely closing their subscription or account with the firm. This type defection is easy to spot. On the other hand, they might shift a significant portion of their business to a competitor but continue to their account with the first firm, in which case the definition of customer defection is somewhat trickier. The firm should not ignore that some defections can be partial but are defections, nevertheless. Sometimes, however, apparent defections may not be defections at all. For example, if a bank customer has closed an account (e.g. a student loan account), she cannot be classified as a defection if she continues to use the bank's other services.

The next step is to identify the 'core' customers of the firm. Defining core customers is certainly not easy, and often might lead to a deep discussion of the firm's primary mission and ultimate goals. Core customers are the most profitable and loyal, and prefer stable, long-term relationships. They find the firm's products, services and strengths best fit their needs. Finally, they are worth more to a firm than to its competitors. These attributes will often identify a firm's core customers. While defining and separating a firm's customers into core and non-core categories, the firm should have some statistics, which might include; lifecycle profit patterns; the net present value of each customer segment; the share of the customer's wallet; and average customer retention by segment, age and source. Not all customers are equal, and firms that have achieved extraordinary levels of customer loyalty usually deliver superior value to their core customers.

The next step is to get to the root of the problem – i.e. customer defections. Root cause analysis is not easy, and one can get lost in the maze of reasons, neglecting the actual root cause of customer failure. A good place to start is by reviewing the history of customer interactions. A single event leading to defections ('a bank clerk swearing at a customer') is the exception rather than the rule. A series of events slowly leads to a decision to seek better value elsewhere. An interviewer can assess the root cause of a defection by typically identifying three or four disappointing events and then weighing them appropriately. It is important to hear from at least a sample of former customers to understand their experiences and reasons for switching to a competitor.

It is vital to involve senior management in such tasks, along with frontline employees. First, it will open the eyes of senior management to the actual reasons and causes of customer defections if they are directly involved in the exercise. Secondly, it is often easier to get former customers share their experiences when senior management is directly involved. In many firms (such as Lexus), the CEO and senior managers directly call customers who switch to a competitor's car. A firm needs to identify the customers who are worth calling based on their analysis of customer data or through market research.

The defection analysis team needs to develop an action plan based on its research findings from surveys, reviews on social media and review sites as well as interviews with former customers. Sometimes, they might come up with some remedies that require little preparation or spending and can therefore be tested at once. Others might require further research or analysis to make investments, such as a digital solution for social media listing.

Finally, a firm should communicate the learning to the right personnel and give them a good reason to want to use it. This can be done by linking their incentives, career paths and other measures to fixing defections and customer retention. Often, the most important barrier to learning from defections is that employees cannot see how the learning relates to their success. Employees might need constant reminding of the need for customer retention and the dramatic effect it has on the firm's bottom line. This removes the complacency that tends to creep in sometimes.

In the next stage, a firm might want to make the defection analysis system permanent. To do so, the first step would be to build a measurement system to monitor whether and how effectively the solutions arrived at are reducing the defection rate. Senior managers also need to be continually informed about frontline customer feedback.

The key to customer loyalty is the creation of value through organisational learning enabled by grasping the value of failure. As Reichheld (1996) stated, "Customer defection is a unit of error containing nearly all the information a firm needs to compete, profit and grow." Companies can reduce customer defection by following some of the following best practices:

- *Monitoring and tracking:* Companies must monitor and keep track of customer interactions.
- *Analysing the root cause:* This could be poor fit between customer needs and product attributes. It might be related to the customer being oversold on a product or service. There could be issues related to the product or service attributes; employees may also fail to customise their services and products based on their requirements and needs and customer expectations regarding service experience.
- *Fixing the root cause:* Companies work on existing customers to remedy the root cause. Conversely, prospective customers also become attracted by how a company has dealt with the problem (Reichheld, 1996).

CUSTOMER RETENTION PLANS

Customer retention is becoming increasingly important as firms understand the value of loyal customers (Smith, 2019). Most firms now reward such customers as it has been seen that rewards can and do build customer loyalty. However, in practice, many rewards schemes are misunderstood and often wrongly applied. Unless they are properly designed, they will, at best, return only a fraction of their potential value. Firms can profit from their current customers through customer portfolio analysis; reorganising for customer retention; and a customer retaining marketing mix.

Customer Portfolio Analysis

Before developing customer plans or reward programmes, a firm needs to know the purchasing history of a product or firm's customers. A customer portfolio is a combination of customer types for each product that generates sales and resulting profit. An optimal customer portfolio consists of a balance of new and repeat customers, yielding target sales and profits. Depending on the competencies of the firm and the state of the market, this optimal mix can be altered. The design of a portfolio begins by seeking meaningful customer classifications based on market research of actual purchase patterns. The portfolio segments can be measured in terms of number of customers, number of purchases, demographic and psychographic profiles, and contributions to sales and profits. For example, a firm can analyse how the customer portfolio contributed to sales in terms of contributions from each segment, and this can be used to set the following year's sales targets.

TABLE 11.1 Sample Customer Portfolio

Customer Category	Actual Sales (2024), %	Target Sales (2025), %
First-Time	28	25
Repeat	40	60
Switched Away Then Returned	10	5
Last Time (Defectors)	22	10
Total	100	100

Thus, in the sample in Table 11.1, the firm hopes to reduce the share of defectors to 10% (from 22%) while increasing the share of repeat customers to 60% (from 40%). Three factors must be addressed when attempting to achieve optimal balance in the customer portfolio:

1 Products vary according to how readily product differences can be perceived by consumers. When product attributes are perceived to be superior to the competition, it is relatively easy to retain most customers.
2 Product category volume growth impacts the balance of a customer's portfolio. If a firm has too many repeat purchasers in the rapid-growth stage of the market, it might mean that insufficient attention is being paid to the 'attracting' function.
3 Finally, the relative costs and benefits of attracting and retaining customers must be compared. The customer portfolio must be based on sound customer feedback research by periodically monitoring marketing performance and measuring customer dis/satisfaction.

Reorganising for Customer Retention

An important factor that frequently contributes to the loss of customers is the lack of organisational control and coordination, which takes two basic forms: (1) lack of concern about customer churn rates: and (2) insufficient links between marketing and operations teams.

Realistic customer retention rates should be set for evaluating market performance. Otherwise, organisations would find it very easy to rely on promotions to recruit new cohorts of customers rather than retain existing ones. Another approach that would emphasise customer retention is executive accountability for customer retention. This would send clear signals all over the organisation about the importance the firm is attaching to customer retention. In many types of firms and industries, coordination between marketing and operations teams is suboptimal. This frequently results in problems such as over-selling, where the marketing function sees its task solely as attracting customers by promising virtually anything. Customer expectations are raised to such an extent that invariably they are left disappointed, despite the product or service being as good as the best in the industry. One way of improving the coordination between the two functions is by specifying the interdependency of both functions. This means targeting some promotional strategies towards repeat usage while others pursue new purchases. The customer is the final arbiter of service and product quality. The firm can also look at jointly setting up and periodically reviewing quality and service standards.

Customer Retaining Marketing Mix

The customer retaining marketing mix is a set of programmes and strategies aimed at improving customer retention. Ideally, a firm should have two mixes – one for customer retention and the other for customer acquisition. Such a mix usually includes several elements, such as product extras, reinforcing promotions, sales force connections, and specialised distribution and post-purchase communications, among others.

Product Extras

This entails giving customers more than the basic product that initially attracted them. The main approach is to create a total product/service system that contains not only the items the customer purchased initially but also related benefits by offering other items from the product line. For example, McDonald's no longer just sells hamburgers, but complete meals at all times of the day. Customers get involved with the system and might remain with the firm as opposed to when just provided with the basic product that might be subject to aggressive competition. When a product breaks down or a service is not provided, the situation can be retrieved by anticipating such problems and offering customers easy-repair features and self-service technologies for diagnosis, and having preventive maintenance schedules and adhering to them carefully.

Reinforcing Promotions

Product promotions work better when aimed at existing customers because they already knows about the firm's products, so the firm can look to advancing their knowledge of those products. Such promotions can also introduce customers to the firm's other products. A firm can reinforce customers by promoting customer-only publications targeted at buyers who have exhibited some degree of commitment to the product or firm through one or more purchases. Post-purchase dissonance can be reduced considerably by after-sales communication by direct mail, telephone calls or other means. This also helps clear up any consumer doubts or confusion regarding the purchase.

Sales Force Connections

A sales force must be oriented to maintaining long-term relationships with customers. In many industries it is the salesperson who is in direct contact with the customer. Sales personnel who are inadequately trained and/or lack preparation and knowledge about the product line and try to sell a product rather than resolve customer problems usually do not keep customers for long. Some retail banks, for example, seek to enhance relationships with customers through the concept of 'personal bankers', whereby an employee is allocated a few customer accounts and those customers' interactions with the bank take place only through this employee. Over time, customer relations are strengthened through such an arrangement, ultimately resulting in more personalised services. CRM solutions and other supportive expertise and specialists enhance the sales force's ability to help customers.

Specialised Distribution

Firms can try to retain customers by having separate distribution channels for the attracting and retaining functions. This depends on how the distribution strategy is formulated. For example, in retail markets, the layout of facilities can be designed so that attracting and retaining customers are handled separately. Numerous businesses (e.g. airlines, credit card firms and e-commerce firms) typically have different levels of access for customers based on their value, preference for speed and willingness to use digital channels for self-service. Support from intermediaries is also important to foster repeat purchases of a firm's brands. In many situations involving high-involvement purchases, intermediaries such as dealers play a critical role in the final stages of the purchase funnel, so a customer's commitment to a brand can aid selling and cross-selling if they get adequate attention from the brand's marketing and sales teams.

Post-Purchase Communication

A firm must anticipate that some of its customers might experience problems with their purchase (whether major or minor). Post-purchase activities can be helpful in preventing customers from defecting. Customer complaints should be investigated promptly, and this function can be assigned to personnel already dealing with those customers. The firm should encourage customers to initiate contact, whenever the need arises, to clarify instructions, request further information, point out a problem or seek a remedy. Omnichannel service options – including digital channels, online communities, social media handles, toll-free help lines and service desks – can facilitate this process.

Loyalty and Reward Programmes

Customer loyalty and reward programmes are other popular approaches used by firms to retain customers by rewarding them for their loyalty. They have been around for several decades, and more and more companies in different industries are rolling out such programmes. Examples include: airline frequent-flier deals; mobile service firms offering attractive rate plans for heavy users; and banks and credit card firms offering financial incentives and cash-back schemes. In practice, however, customer loyalty programmes are widely misunderstood and often misapplied. If treated as short-term giveaways or specials they might create some value by motivating new or existing customers to try a product or service. However, unless they are designed to build loyalty, they will return at best a small fraction of their potential value. A rewards programme can accelerate the loyalty lifecycle by encouraging relatively new customers to behave like the firm's most profitable customers. The aim of all the schemes is educating customers about the rewards for loyalty and encouraging them to earn it. A customer's loyalty creates value for the firm. The firm must find ways and means to share this value with its customers, and so tries to achieve this through loyalty programmes.

As companies increase in size and complexity, their ability to identify valuable customers falls steeply. Personalised customer relationships and accompanying keen judgement on value sharing disappear. Most firms try to deliver increased value to profitable customers to turn them into loyal customers. Loyal customers become even more profitable over time.

O'Brien and Jones (1995) highlighted the following principles for customer value sharing via reward programmes:

- Not all customers are equal for a firm.
- Value created must exceed the cost of value delivered.
- Customer behaviour should drive the value sharing and rewards should be given to customers displaying desirable behaviour.
- Full potential is realised when customers change their habits to become loyal.
- The offers must only target the attentive target segments.

A reward programme is a competitive strategy and, as such, must meet certain criteria (O'Brien & Jones, 1995). First, it should align with the firm's capabilities as there is no point promising something the firm cannot deliver. The firm should not continue providing something just because a competitor is doing so. The right question to ask is what customer needs can profitably and differentially be met. Second, customers should value the programme. From a customer's perspective, five elements determine a reward programme's overall value – cash value, choice of redemption options, aspirational value, relevance and convenience. The cash value of a reward can be thought of as what the customer would have to pay in cash to acquire it as a percentage rebate on what the customer spent to earn the reward.

Sometimes, the redemption choice for a customer is limited. For example, an airline will probably only allow customers to redeem frequent flyer points as free tickets on its flights. However it would be more attractive to the customer if customers could also redeem them for holiday packages at a resort. This would naturally call for the airlines to tie up with resorts but would make the programme more attractive and valuable to the customer.

Firms use the 'aspirational value' element by trying to appeal to customer psychology. A discount on a telephone bill does not have the same aspirational value as dinner with a famous sportsperson or celebrity. The key is offering the right choice of aspirational redemption options.

The final two factors that determine the value of a rewards scheme are its relevance and convenience. It lacks relevance if customers are not rewarded with something in the short run for their loyalty. If they must wait years before becoming eligible for some reward, most customers will probably not join such a programme. If it is not convenient to redeem rewards as and when desired, the attractiveness of a scheme will also take a beating. Rewards linked to a charge card or credit card have a clear convenience advantage because neither the customer nor the merchant needs to exert incremental effort. Customers can also accumulate rewards in a single programme based on all their card spending.

If a firm cannot offer everything its customers deem attractive, partnering with other firms would help to make reward schemes more attractive and alluring for the customers. However, the principles of value sharing and rewarding should be followed.

Finally, a rewards programme cannot continue indefinitely. A firm should have thought out an exit strategy in advance to avoid facing the embarrassing situation whereby it is not able to fulfil its promises because of changed circumstances. The firm should set limits on the programme's lifespan, the number of points earnable or on activity and reactivation thresholds. The firm should announce its intentions clearly with enough lead time to allow customers to earn and redeem their rewards. Finally, the firm should display targeted generosity by recognising the best customers.

Getting an organisation to focus on customer loyalty and to design and implement an effective rewards programme is a challenging task. Each functional department views loyalty differently and consequently promotes its own set of solutions. Managers might also use familiar but inappropriate measurement systems and incentives in their new programmes. As growth is a top management priority at almost all firms, this can lead to an emphasis on acquiring new customers rather than retaining current ones and building loyalty. These are but a few of the roadblocks to developing and implementing effective loyalty programmes. A firm will succeed if it directs its resources and marketing programmes to develop a loyal customer base.

EVALUATING RETENTION PROGRAMMES

A firm needs to review its customer retention, rewards and loyalty programmes at regular intervals to ensure they are having the desired effect and are valued by customers. A firm launches a rewards scheme to increase its following by rewarding those customers who are loyal to the firm, for example with lots of freebies and other rewards. However, it should also get equivalent value from its customers. Below are some factors that need to be taken into consideration when evaluating retention programmes (O'Brien & Jones, 1995).

Targeting the Right Customers

A firm should periodically review the customer retention plans to monitor whether they are targeting the right customers – customers who are loyal and who belong to the segment the firm was considering targeting. If the firm designed the programme with the intention of attracting a particular customer segment and ultimately found it was being used by another segment, it would do well to review the continuation of the programme. The most valuable customers should be targeted and rewarded.

Value Provided

The firm should also periodically review whether customers value the programme and what perceptions they have about it. If it is seen that customers are not valuing the rewards the firm provides then it is appropriate to change the reward structure. The firm should also not provide more value than the programme can generate so as to avoid standing at a loss. For example, an airline might start a frequent flyer scheme to reward its customers. However, in some cases, it might find that it does not have the capacity to serve its customers and that many of its future flights consist of travellers redeeming their free mileage. In such circumstances, it is better to exit a programme rather than face losses because of an inappropriately designed programme.

A rewards scheme generates a lot of customers through purchases, transactions and interactions with the firm. Data captured automatically by operational systems such as point of sales (PoS) help firms understand usage patterns, redemptions, volume and value of purchases, changing trends, etc. Analysing customer data, tracking their behaviour and generating insights can be used profitably to engage with customers and create mutual value.

Measuring Increase in Loyalty

Finally, a rewards programme should generate an increase in loyalty, which should be seen in a rise in the number of purchases and repurchases made by customers. If a rewards programme does not improve sales or profits, its continuation should be reviewed. If the firm does not derive any benefit from the programme, then it is better to discontinue it.

It is very common to find competitors matching the key features of a successful rewards programme. If customers switch, this obviously means rival companies are providing better value.

Finally, we can say that the main yardstick by which retention programmes should be evaluated is the value they provide to the firm and their effectiveness in generating a growing base of loyal customers.

CONCLUSION

In this concluding chapter, we have addressed several important issues related to operational aspects faced by firms when they embark on the CRM journey. The process framework gives an overview of the areas that tend to be overlooked by managers due to their enthusiasm for riding the CRM bandwagon – especially management and governance. Budgeting is pivotal to ensuring that the firm pays attention to retaining customers compared to the traditional marketing focus on attracting customers. The goal of 'zero customer defections' (Reichheld & Sasser, 1990) is challenging to achieve, and lessons from defections will prove invaluable in reducing customer churn. Retention programmes play a significant role in ensuring valuable customers have enough reasons to continue patronage.

The following sections follow the path of ICICI on its CRM journey, as summarised in Figure 11.2.

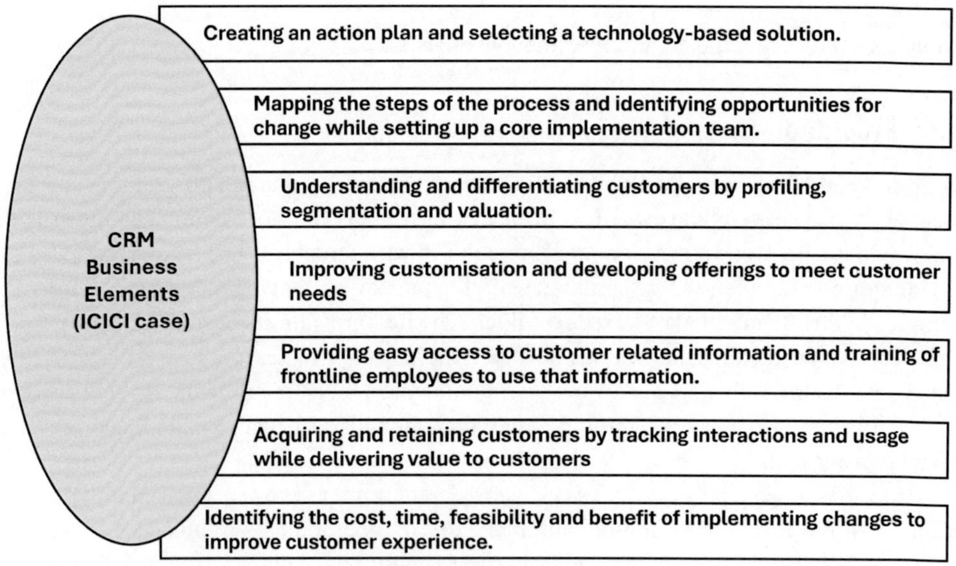

FIGURE 11.2 CRM Business Elements: The Case of ICICI

CLOSING CASE

A Technology-Based CRM Solution: The ICICI Experience

Indian company ICICI, set up as a development financial institution, diversified into retail financial services in the early 1990s and transformed itself into a technology-intensive financial services group. ICICI had raised debt from the retail market and had increased its reach by mobilising resources and offering quality investor service through a subsidiary, ICICI Infotech Services. In 1994, it established ICICI Bank as a commercial bank that was flexible, innovative and quick to meet customer requirements. It also created retail initiatives such as personal services, capital services, online trading and life insurance, among other services (Choudhuri & Shainesh, 2001).

THE RETAIL STRATEGY

ICICI's retail strategy centred on the intensive deployment of technology to help reduce service costs, increase customer retention and help in cross-selling and up-selling while improving process efficiencies. The bank looked to allow customers to use multiple electronic channels, including the internet, ATMs, call centres, contact centres, laptops, kiosks, mobiles and other hand-held devices for conducting financial transactions. The group adopted a 'click and brick' strategy to leverage the power of electronic channels and physical presence to ensure rapid product delivery, financial deals and documentation.

As part of the plans, it implemented several projects to establish world-class CRM practice, which would provide an integrated view of its customers to everyone in the organisation. CRM at ICICI involves increased communication between the virtual universal bank, its customers, prospects and the group itself. The underlying idea is to enhance every instance of contact with the customer. ICICI believes that a genuine customer-centric relationship can only be accomplished by considering the unique perspectives of every one of its customers. Hence, there was a pressing need to put in place a technology-enabled CRM solution.

THE CRM ROADMAP

At ICICI, CRM was viewed as a discipline and a set of discrete software technologies focused on automating and improving the business processes associated with managing customer relationships in sales, marketing, customer service and support. The organisation aims to achieve the end goal of one-to-one marketing. The CRM software applications will facilitate the coordination of multiple business functions. It coordinates numerous communication channels with customers (face-to-face, call centres, ATMs, web, telephone, kiosk, bank, branch, sales associates, etc.) to enable ICICI to carry out cradle-to-grave customer management more efficiently. It should allow ICICI to engage in one-to-one marketing by tracking the complete customer history. It will automate process-flow tracking in the product sales process, generate customised reports and promote cross-selling. It will also enable efficient campaign management by providing a software interface for defining, tracking, executing and analysing campaigns. From an architecture perspective, the enterprise-wide CRM solution should seamlessly integrate non-transactional customer information in the front office with the transactional information in the back office.

ICICI then looked at implementing the enterprise CRM strategies, which included:

- Business Focus
- Organisational Structure
- Business Metrics
- Marketing Focus
- Technology.

The key to developing the CRM action plan was comprehending where the organisation stood concerning the five change components. Interviews with key employees assisted in identifying various CRM-related projects that were implemented.

The next step in the planning process was a 'gap analysis', which was compared to the optimal setting for the five aspects of business to identify and precisely explain the gaps. Along with the more obvious gaps, this analysis helped identify the following CRM organisational holes:

- Marketing, sales, and service practices.
- Collection, capture, processing and deployment of customer information.
- Distribution and operation effectiveness at customer touchpoints.

Another critical component in finding gaps is having a firm grasp of the organisational functions related to the CRM business cycle. A standard, underlying activity cycle should guide all CRM initiatives and infrastructure development. All initiatives and infrastructure development should somehow be tied to this core cycle of activity. Careful evaluation of the organisation's ability to execute this cycle will pinpoint and qualify additional organisational gaps.

THE CRM BUSINESS CYCLE

All businesses begin and grow with customer acquisition. However, every effective CRM endeavour depends greatly on a thorough understanding of customers. The business cycle outlined below is a useful process to understand the concept (Nykamp, 2001).

Understand and Differentiate

Organisations can strengthen their relationship with customers only if they understand them – what they value, what types of service are important to them, how and when they like to interact and what they want to buy. True understanding is based on a combination of detailed analysis and interaction. Several activities are important, including:

- Profiling to understand demographics, purchase patterns and channel preference.
- Segmentation to identify logical unique groups of customers that tend to look alike and behave in similar fashion. While the promise of 'one-to-one' marketing sounds good, organisations still struggle to treat each customer uniquely.
- Customer valuation to understand profitability as well as lifetime value or long-term potential. Value may also be based on the customer's ability or inclination to refer to other profitable customers.

Analysis and research alone, however, are insufficient. To create and foster a relationship, organisations have to act on what they learn about customers. Customers need to experience how the company is differentiating service and communications based both on what they have learned independently and on what the customer has told them. At the same time, differentiation should be based on the value customers are expected to deliver.

Develop and Customise

In the product-oriented world of yesterday, companies developed products and services and expected customers to buy them. In a customer-focused world, product and channel development has to follow the customer's lead. Organisations are increasingly developing products and services, and even new channels, based on customer needs and service expectations. Products, services, channels and media can be customised based on the needs of customers. The extent of customisation should be based on the potential value delivered by the customer segment.

Interact and Deliver

Interaction is another critical component of a successful CRM initiative. It is important to remember that interaction does not just occur through marketing and sales channels and media; customers interact in many ways with many different areas of the organisation, including distribution and shipping, customer service and online. To foster good relationships, organisations must do the following:

- Ensure that all departments, especially frontline employees, have easy access to relevant, actionable customer information.
- Use customer information to tailor interactions based on both customer needs and potential customer value.

With access to information and appropriate training, organisations will be prepared to steadily increase the value they deliver to customers. Delivering value is a cornerstone of the relationship. Customer perceptions of value are based on a number of factors, including the quality of products and services, convenience, speed, ease of use, responsiveness and service excellence.

Acquire and Retain

The more a firm learns about its customers, the easier it is to identify the most valuable. The company will want to 'clone' similar customers in its prospecting and acquisition efforts. As firms continue to learn about what is valuable to each segment, they will be much more likely to score a 'win' with the right channel, right media, right product, right offer, right timing and the most relevant message.

Successful customer retention basically involves 'getting it right' on an ongoing basis, which is exactly what the firm aims to achieve from its CRM initiatives. Successful customer retention will be based on the organisation's ability to constantly deliver on three principles:

- Maintain interaction; never stop listening.
- Continue to deliver on the customer's definition of value.
- Remember that customers change as they move through differing life stages; be alert to the changes and be prepared to modify the service and value proposition as they change.

And so the cycle continues … As a cycle, the stages are interdependent and continuous. As one moves from one stage to the next, the company hopes to gains insight and understanding that enhance subsequent efforts. The organisation will become increasingly sophisticated in the implementation of CRM processes and, over time, will become increasingly profitable by doing so.

Implementation

Implementation was divided into the following stages:

1. *Analysis:* A 'business requirements study' or analysis provides requirements for each product group identified for phased implementation. Business heads offer suggestions/seek modifications incorporated in the study before signing it off. Gap analysis helps identify gaps between package functionalities and business requirements.
2. *Mapping Design:* In mapping the design to the package, user interaction and business interaction components, gaps are addressed by prototyping.
   - *High-level design:* (*a*) Work around the package; (*b*) Take a call and say it is not possible.
   - *Low-level design:* Screen-level details are taken care of to meet the specific information needs of the users.
3. *Customisation:* Gaps and design customisation and logical development grouping – sequential vs. parallel:
   - Testing – white box testing (flow testing)
   - Independent testing (someone else within the organisation does the testing)
   - Quality testing of all projects/plans.

4 *Integration* – Data setup, testing plans, releasing criteria.
5 *User Acceptance Testing*:
- Two types
- Snags
- New requirements.

Data migration is done at this stage. Sometimes the steps may be iterative, with each giving feedback; consequently, the team might have to revisit some issues.

Lessons from ICICI's Experience

If CRM involves optimising product, price, place of distribution, promotion, sales and service, why are so many firms struggling? Has no one mastered the art and science of CRM? And, if not, why is it so difficult?

- CRM is complex because it is an enterprise-wide initiative. CRM is not a technology initiative. Many firms wrongly identify CRM as a technology initiative and assign the CRM implementation project to their information system or IT group. Technology is needed to implement CRM, particularly the customisation part; however, technology is not the driver of CRM. It is just an enabler.
- CRM is not exclusively a marketing, sales, service or technology initiative. It involves all of those, along with other inner workings of an organisation. Probably the most important requirement is acknowledgement that the organisation becomes customer-focused and conducts its operations from the point of view of its customers.

CRM requires all areas of the organisation to exist in harmony and work toward the common goal of stronger customer relationships. At ICICI, the CRM initiative highlighted the importance of having such a holistic philosophy about customers rather than looking at them from narrow departmental windows.

SUMMARY

CRM implementation involves a series of operational issues. The first key issue revolves around customer attraction vs. retention decisions as it impacts apportioning budgets between existing and prospective customers. Avenues where financial resources need to be dedicated include individualisation and market offerings to develop customer loyalty and commitment. These goals can be achieved by effectively monitoring relationship-building processes and programmes.

Traditionally, marketing departments emphasised attracting new customers rather than retaining existing customers. Therefore, the front-end function of attracting customers gained attention while the back-end processes required for customer retention and development were neglected. In recent years, managers have realised that relationship maintenance involves building long-term, mutually beneficial relationships with customers that maximise the firm's share of the customer's wallet. Managers must therefore balance thc budget allocation between customer retention and acquisition.

Companies track metrics, including customer loyalty, profitability and lifetime value, to bring renewed attention to customer retention. Analysis of customer defections help identify reasons and develop action plans to improve retention of desirable customers. In competitive markets, customer satisfaction, quality and value delivered by offerings help retain competitive advantage.

DISCUSSION QUESTIONS

1 Discuss the process view of CRM for improving customer loyalty and profitability.
2 Discuss the most important issues affecting the allocation of financial resources between customer retention and acquisition.
3 Discuss the role of metrics to assess a CRM programme.
4 What lessons can managers learn from customer defections?

REFERENCES

Allchin, J. (2013). Case study: Diageo's connected whiskies. *Marketing Week*. Retrieved November 19, 2021, from https://www.marketingweek.com/case-study-diageos-connected-whiskies/.

Capraro, A.J., Broniarczyk, S., & Srivastava, R.K. (2003). Factors influencing the likelihood of customer defection: The role of consumer knowledge. *Journal of the Academy of Marketing Science*, *31*(2), 164–175. doi:10.1177/0092070302250900.

Choudhuri, A., & Shainesh. G. (2001). Implementing a technology based CRM solution: The ICICI experience. In J.N. Sheth, A. Parvatiyar, & G. Shainesh (Eds.), *Customer relationship management: Emerging concepts, tools and applications* (pp. 174–184). New Delhi: Tata McGraw-Hill.

Harmoney. (2015). The rise of peer to peer lending. Retrieved November 25, 2021, from https://www.harmoney.co.nz/making-it-happen/rise-of-p2p-lending.

Heroku. (n.d.). Heroku and Salesforce power New Zealand's first licensed peer-to-peer lending platform. Retrieved December 20, 2023 from https://www.heroku.com/customers/harmoney.

Listcorp. (2023). HMY completes the closure of its legacy P2P platform. Retrieved December 20, 2023 from https://www.listcorp.com/asx/hmy/harmoney-corp-limited/news/hmy-completes-the-closure-of-its-legacy-p2p-platform-2941380.html.

Nykamp, M. (2001). *The customer differential: The complete guide to implementing customer relationship management*. New York: AMACOM.

O'Brien, L., & Jones, C. (1995). Do rewards really create loyalty? *Harvard Business Review*, May–June. Retrieved November 20, 2021, from https://hbr.org/1995/05/do-rewards-really-create-loyalty.

O'Hear, S. (2017). Evrythng, the Internet of Things platform for 'smart products,' scores $24.8M Series B. *TechCrunch*, 14 March. Retrieved November 20, 2021, from https://techcrunch.com/2017/03/14/evrythng-series-b/.

Parvatiyar, A., & Sheth, J.N. (2001). Conceptual framework of customer relationship management. In J.N. Sheth, A. Parvatiyar, & G. Shainesh (Eds.), *Customer relationship management: Emerging concepts, tools, and applications*. New Delhi: Tata McGraw-Hill.

Raman, K., & Angur, M.G (2001). Optimal allocation rules for customer relationship management. In J.N. Sheth, A. Parvatiyar, & G. Shainesh (Eds.), *Customer relationship management: Emerging concepts, tools and applications*. New Delhi: Tata McGraw-Hill.

Reichheld, F.F. (1996). Learning from customer defections. *Harvard Business Review*, *74*(2), 56–67.
Reichheld, F.F., & Sasser, W.E. (1990). Zero defections: Quality comes to services. *Harvard Business Review*, *68*(5), 105–111.
Reinartz, W., & Kumar, V. (2002). The mismanagement of customer loyalty. *Harvard Business Review*, *80*(7), 86–94.
SAS. (2016). SAS helps Harmoney approve the right customers. Retrieved November 20, 2021, from https://www.sas.com/content/dam/SAS/en_au/doc/customer-stories/harmoney.pdf.
Smith, G. (2019). Customer retention strategies: 4 phases for development. Retrieved November 24, 2021, from https://cxl.com/blog/customer-retention-strategy/.

Index

Note: page numbers in *italic* type refer to figures; those in **bold** type refer to tables.

FSC
www.fsc.org
MIX
Papier | Fördert gute Waldnutzung
FSC® C083411

Kolibri 360 GmbH
Ferdinand-Jühlke-Straße 7
99095 Erfurt, Deutschland
produktsicherheit@kolibri360.de